PRACTICAL ADVERTISING AND PUBLICITY

D0899152

PRACTICAL ADVERTISING AND PUBLICITY

Effective promotion of products and services to industry and commerce

Norman A. Hart
MSc, FCAM, FIPR, F Inst M

McGRAW-HILL BOOK COMPANY

London · New York · St Louis · San Francisco · Auckland
Bogotá · Guatemala · Hamburg · Lisbon · Madrid · Mexico
Montreal · New Delhi · Panama · Paris · San Juan · São Paulo
Singapore · Sydney · Tokyo · Toronto

Published by
McGRAW-HILL Book Company (UK) Limited
MAIDENHEAD · BERKSHIRE · ENGLAND

British Library Cataloguing in Publication Data
Hart, Norman A. (Norman Arthur), *1930–*
  Practical advertising and publicity. —
  4th ed.
  1. Industries. Publicity
  I. Title   II. Hart, Norman A. (Norman
  Arthur), *1930–* Business to business
  advertising
  659.2
  ISBN 0–07–707079–8

Library of Congress Cataloging-in-Publication Data
Hart, Norman A.
  Practical advertising and publicity : effective promotion of
  products and services to industry and commerce / Norman A. Hart.
    p. cm.
  Rev. ed. of: Business to business advertising / Norman A. Hart.
  c1983.
  Includes index.
  ISBN 0–07–707079–8
  1. Advertising.   2. Publicity.   3. Sales promotion.   I. Hart,
  Norman A. Business to business advertising.   II. Title.
  HF5823.H3245 1988
  659--dc19   88–129020

First published as *Business to Business Advertising*
Copyright © Norman Hart 1971, 1978, 1983

Copyright © 1988 McGraw-Hill Book Company (UK) Limited. All rights reserved.
No part of this publication may be reproduced, stored in a retrieval system, or
transmitted, in any form or by any means, electronic, mechanical, photocopying,
recording, or otherwise, without the prior permission of McGraw-Hill Book Company (UK) Limited.

123 898

Printed and bound in Great Britain by
Latimer Trend & Company Ltd, Plymouth

To M.D.H.

CONTENTS

FOREWORD

John Samuel FCAM, FIPA
Director of the Association of Business Advertising Agencies

In the last ten years, industrial marketing has been finally accepted as vital to national and individual company interests, where markets lie in the commercial or business area.

If the acknowledgement is finally there, performance is not universally good and recent audits show that companies attacking these markets are still not satisfied with the quality of their promotional planning and execution, nor with the skills of their people and the interest of their agencies. Improvement is slow and the need for the use of the highest skills and talent not yet wholly accepted. Promotion in all its forms is still seen in too many boardrooms as an *alternative* to profit and not a *cause* of it and investment in it treated with suspicion and prejudice.

The need is to raise standards 'on the job' and each marketing director has a unique problem in training and inspiring his present team. This new book is an effective starting point and should be mandatory reading for everyone concerned with industrial or business marketing.

For senior management, it gives an opportunity to understand the real nature of the task and of the contribution communications can make. It makes clear that this is an area of company investment that can be managed and controlled as effectively as any other. It removes the jargon and myth of which senior management (often from the more precise disciplines of accountancy or engineering) are rightly so suspicious but equally challenges them to understand more fully the workings of communications so that their judgement of proposals in this area will be more discerning and less subjective.

For middle managers—particularly those already expert in one aspect of the marketing mix (sales, PR, research)—the book yields an unprejudiced picture of the totality, making clear the overriding need for calm assessment of *all* media; for unbiased choice of the most effective mix; and, above all, for the full-blooded integration of the total program.

For the younger or less experienced, the book is a marvellous accelerator of their understanding of the total communications picture while they work, inevitably, in only one narrow area of it.

The book IS *practical* but don't be misled. After careful reading you will find that you have learned a great deal; will be readier to accept and demand better planning of communications; can argue your corner more coherently and assess more dispassionately the validity of the recommendations of your colleagues or agency.

PREFACE

The marketing concept is well on its way to being accepted by most companies in Britain and Europe even though they continue to lag behind the United States. Indeed, from the commercial area, the idea of 'customer orientation' has spilled over into institutions, government services, charities, social activities and even political parties.

Acceptance of marketing, however, has always been faster among consumer goods companies than in those concerned with industrial/business products and services. Every single function in consumer marketing has developed to a high degree of sophistication: research, product development, advertising, sales promotion, selling, distribution, planning and budgeting— all have become specialist activities with an increasing emphasis on productivity and effectiveness.

Business-to-business marketing has developed at a much slower rate and with some companies is still little more than the old selling function repackaged under a new name. And little wonder since in contrast with consumer marketing there are few opportunities to learn about business marketing: few courses and seminars, few textbooks, few periodicals and no institution or association dealing with the special needs and interests of executives in this particular sector. Similarly, in the academic world, the introduction of marketing to many business studies continues to concentrate on consumers and mass media, which is after all where public visibility is high and where massive million-pound budgets are commonplace.

When it comes to business-to-business advertising this is perhaps the most neglected area of all, a situation which existed when this book was first published under the title *Industrial Advertising and Publicity*. Since that time it has become the accepted work on the subject, both in the United Kingdom and elsewhere. Over a number of editions and reprints it has gathered together such meagre data as has emerged, relying heavily on American research, and it is now presented as a completely updated text, devoted simply to getting the best value for money out of budgets which are almost universally low compared with their consumer counterparts.

Practical Advertising and Publicity has been written with a belief that in putting together a promotional campaign there is a need to consider every channel of communication in order to arrive at a media mix which will target with accuracy the precise audience that has to be reached in order to secure action. The book is intended for those managers and executives who have a responsibility for planning and undertaking business-to-business marketing communications, i.e. advertising, public relations, sales promotion and all the related activities. Students will also find it of value: indeed it has been a recommended text from the outset for those studying for the CAM Diploma and the Diploma of Marketing.

ACKNOWLEDGEMENTS

Acknowledgements are due to the following organizations for the very considerable help they gave the author in producing this new edition:

Maclean Hunter
TVS Television
Mack-Brooks
McGraw-Hill
Cahners Publishing Co.

In particular, acknowledgement is given to Hugh Johnson, Controller of Marketing Services, TVS Television, for the extraordinary help he gave in writing the new chapter on television advertising, and for his expert knowledge in this rather specialized subject.

Part 1

STRATEGIC PLANNING

1.

PROLOGUE

Terminology in business-to-business marketing is particularly susceptible to ambiguity and confusion. For this reason, it is necessary at the outset to give some definitions to ensure a complete understanding of the terms used. Evidence of this need is to be found in the United States where 'publicity' is commonly understood to refer to 'free editorials', whereas in the United Kingdom the term is used in an all-embracing sense of publicizing anything for any purpose. It thus includes activities which contribute to selling and may be known as sales promotion, and those which set out to provide information to any of a number of publics and are therefore related more to public relations.

The terms 'publicity' and 'sales promotion' are both subsumed by 'marketing communications' under which heading are included all the various 'channels of persuasion' such as advertising, direct mail, exhibitions and so on. It is not, however, 'the medium' which qualifies an activity as *marketing communications* or *public relations*, but rather 'the purpose for which the medium is employed'.

Public relations is dealt with separately and briefly since its objectives are far broader than simply the promotion of sales, though it must be emphasized that almost without exception the channels of persuasion used for sales promotion purposes are applicable in some form to public relations.

A good deal of confusion exists about the meaning of advertising; whether this applies only to press and television, or whether direct mail, for instance, is included in the term. For the sake of clarity it will be used only when it relates to press and television; moreover it will be qualified, e.g. press advertising.

There is even more confusion on the meaning of marketing. For many people, particularly in the industrial sector, it is taken to be synonymous with selling. For others it means getting a product to market, or simply distribution. Since both these interpretations are incomplete, and since this book is based upon publicity within the marketing concept, it is essential to agree at the outset on the meaning of the term when it is used here.

Adam Smith was close to the mark when he wrote, in 1776, 'consumption is the sole end purpose of all production; and the interest of the producer ought to be attended to, only so far as it may be necessary for promoting that of the consumer'.

A more recent explanation has been by L. W. Rodger[1] who states that

marketing has come to be increasingly concerned not merely with the problem of how to dispose profitably of what is produced but also with the much more basic problem of what to produce that will be saleable and profitable, in other words, with nothing less than the profitable matching of a company's total resources, including manufacturing technique, to market opportunities.

The Institute of Marketing goes further by defining marketing as 'the management process responsible for identifying, anticipating and satisfying customer requirements profitably'.

Marketing starts then in the market-place, with the identification of the customer's needs and wants. It then moves on to determining a means of satisfying that want, and of promoting, selling and supplying a 'satisfaction'. The principal marketing functions might be defined as marketing information and research, product planning, pricing, advertising and promotion, sales and distribution.

It is sometimes argued that while the marketing concept is vital in relation to consumer goods, the situation is so different in the industrial sector that the same concept cannot be usefully employed. It is true that many managements have achieved great success in the past by intuition and brilliant guesswork, and it can also be argued that many areas of industrial marketing are quite different and sometimes a good deal more difficult than their equivalents in the consumer field, but a convincing argument against this is given in *Marketing in a Competitive Economy*.[2]

The differences between industrial and consumer goods and their respective markets in no way invalidates the applicability of the marketing concept to industrial goods. Indeed because of the high value of unit sales and unit purchases of many industrial goods, and because of the longer manufacturing cycle and high cost of building and maintaining stocks associated with a wide range of such goods, the importance of the marketing concept may be even greater than consumer goods to the extent that the consequences of being wrong—through bad business and sales forecasting, faulty product planning, inadequate or inaccurate information, failure to identify, contact and follow up sales prospects with well conceived sales promotional activity—can be a great deal more costly.

The differences between industrial, or business, and consumer marketing are not in their concept, nor indeed in their value or relevance. Rather they are to be found in the techniques to be employed, the nature and complexity of the purchasing decision-making, and the size of the budgets available for achieving the objectives. This latter factor if anything makes the task a great deal more difficult, especially in view of the continuing lack of data on which to make valid judgements.

References

1. L. W. Rodger, *Marketing in a Competitive Economy* (Associated Business Programmes, London, 1974), Preface.
2. *Ibid.* p. 65.

2.

It is vital to the efficiency of the operation that all publicity activities be conducted within the broad framework of a marketing plan. Moreover, such planning must be comprehensive and written down in a master document which relates all the functions to one another for maximum effect. This key document sets out to define:

1. *The market* Size, location, type, special features and characteristics, trends.
2. *The market needs and wants* Consumption patterns, buying motives, changes in demand.
3. *Competition* Market shares, product specifications, prices, locations, promotions and expenditure, company images, nature and magnitude of selling activities, capital investment, profit margins, strengths and weaknesses.
4. *The product* Specification, assessment of benefits in relation to customers' known needs and wants.
5. *Price* A pricing strategy in relation to competition, special incentives and discounts, special offers.
6. *Selling platform* Unique selling propositions (USP), outline of features to be stressed in all selling activities.
7. *Sales targets* Total long-term plan, territory analysis, short-term targets.
8. *Production plan* Build up of output, flexibility and relation to sales targets.
9. *Distribution channels.*
10. *Promotion strategy* Separate document interrelating all the promotional activities needed to back up the direct selling operation.
11. *Sales strategy* Plan of campaign for the sales force embodying timing, calling, presentation, sales aids, use of sales manual.
12. *Sales service.*
13. *Profit objectives* Both short- and long-term.
14. *Product development* Further developments and additions to product range.

Before coming to the promotional strategy in detail there is a sequence of events that must necessarily occur if a product or service is to be launched within the framework of a marketing operation.

Development of a marketing operation

MARKET ORIENTATION

The changes that have led to the acceptance of marketing as a management function can be traced to the situation in the United Kingdom directly after the Second World War when factories changing over from war work were oriented to and around their production capability. The plant and equipment existed: the management problem was how to fill it. This was production orientation and while there were shortages and a lack of sophisticated consumer demand, it was adequate.

With the re-emergence of branded products, and as supply began to overtake demand, managements were faced with an excess of products and the need to find markets for them. This then was a position of sales, or product, orientation. In the first instance the management universe revolved about a production nucleus; in the second case, selling and sales were the centre of the operation. Finally, and following the lead of consumer marketing, the industrial nucleus has changed to the market-place—to the buyer and his needs and wants.

It should not be assumed too readily that the marketing concept has become accepted fully or even widely in the United Kingdom. A study by the author of what practising marketing managers considered should comprise a marketing strategy showed that the majority of respondents associated this primarily with market research and advertising. This is shown clearly in Figure 2.1.

MARKET RESEARCH

A marketing operation starts then with an examination of markets and the needs which exist or can be demonstrably created. Clearly many needs can be discarded as outside the scope of an organizations's activities, but certain opportunities will be identified which can be translated into products that appear to meet basic criteria on manufacturing suitability, capital investment, management capability, profit margin and growth potential.

PRODUCT DESIGN

The identification of a potential product is a vital part of marketing development. This involves the services of research and development, design

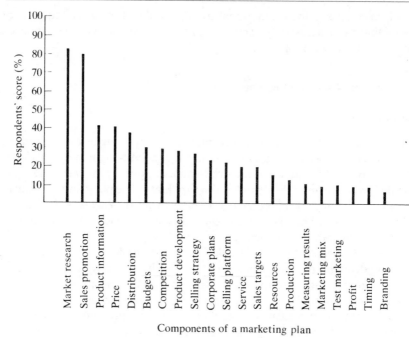

Components of a marketing plan

Figure 2.1　Contents of a marketing plan

engineering, production and buying departments, all of which coupled with a viability study contribute to the evolution of a prototype.

If at this stage the project appears to be sound and profitable, there follows a period in which the product is tested on the market to determine whether it provides the necessary benefits to satisfy the market needs. This may be termed compatibility evolution in which all the elements are subject to minor changes, product performance, appearance, price, shape, market segmentation ... until there is a match between product and market needs and enough profit to justify the investment.

TEST MARKETING

The proving of the product in the market-place, based upon a prototype or pilot batch, after the policy decision to continue the project, brings the operation to the stage where a full marketing strategy is written.

It is more than likely that such a strategy will call for further sounding out of the market before the final stage of decision is reached. This is the point of no return for management and the last opportunity to assess the chances of success or failure.

The product must now be test marketed, that is to say given a full scale launching but in a restricted area. This is sometimes more difficult with an industrial product or service than with a consumer product or service, but nevertheless it is possible. Marketing can be restricted to a specified region only, or to a relatively small overseas market. Alternatively, the product can be promoted and exploited exclusively in one industry or market segment. All these activities will provide feedback of essential information which will lessen the risk of failure.

DECISION

In the light of the assembled data, coupled with the best experience and judgement which can be brought to bear, the point of decision is reached.

The launch of a product within the framework of a marketing operation resembles a military exercise in which many armaments are brought to bear upon a target according to a carefully produced strategic plan. Furthermore, all the logistics of the operation are provided for, objectives are set, and contingency plans made for unforeseen events: in particular the reaction of the enemy forces.

The marketing strategy is such a plan and it outlines in detail the method of launching a product and the means for feedback and research in order to provide intelligence on how the campaign is progressing. Having set sales targets and campaign objectives against which to compare performance, it is vital to provide for flexibility in the organization so that rapid changes can be made in order to intensify or reduce the campaign as this becomes necessary.

ROUTINE MARKETING

Much of this chapter has dwelt on the marketing of a new product but clearly each of the disciplines involved can be applied to an existing product and its future development. Indeed each of the functions described above is essentially of a continuous nature.

The marketing mix

Just as in the recipe for a dish, the ingredients must be specified in quantity and quality, and the ways of mixing them together and cooking them made clear, so in marketing, the mixture must be blended to achieve maximum effect. The marketing mix has been defined as the 'planned mixture of the elements of marketing in a marketing plan. The aim is to combine them in such a way as to achieve the greatest effect at minimum cost'.[1]

A more academic approach to the marketing mix postulates that it comprises what is known as the 4 Ps and S:

1. Product
2. Price
3. Promotion
4. Place

The S stands for service. The balance of ingredients then is made under 4 or 5 heads and depends largely upon the nature of the product and the markets it serves. For instance with petrol, price and place may be the key factors to success. With a new scientific instrument it is the product that counts. For a computer it may be both pre- and post-sales service which secure the sale.

In this book the mix will be considered as it relates to marketing communications in which each component has a communications element. The 'product', for instance, in addition to ultimately providing satisfaction to the customer, also sends out pre-sales messages which contribute to the development of the overall perception upon which a purchasing decision will be made. Its size, shape, colour, weight, presentation and packaging may signal high or low quality, reliability or ruggedness. The 'price' of a product can also have a communications element. In many instances where performance is difficult to evaluate, the price is taken as a measure of quality—the lower the price, the lower the quality. The 'promotion' element of the marketing mix is obviously where the main thrust of marketing communications is to be found. As to 'place', with industrial and business products this usually relates to a combination of distribution outlet and delivery time and is less important as a message source than in consumer marketing where the outlet may be a key factor in the purchasing decision. For instance, who could ever doubt the reliability of a product which Harrods decided to put on display? Finally 'service', pre-sales, sales, and post-sales, sends out a continuous stream of messages which enhance a product, or undermine it. In other words, first-class service can only help to build up a perception of a first-class product.

CHANNELS OF PERSUASION

From the definition of the market, distinct groups of prospects will emerge whom it is desired to influence. To achieve this object, a number of methods of communication are available, such as personal selling, exhibitions and advertising. These are channels of persuasion, and the extent to which any of them is used must depend on the nature of the market and how far each communication channel fits in.

It is useful to consider each typical prospect in a given segment of a market and then to examine each channel of persuasion to determine if it is relevant. An 'impact diagram' (Fig. 2.2) can be developed in which the promotional mix can be demonstrated simply and visually. From this can be developed

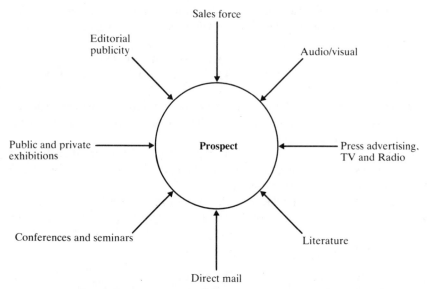

Figure 2.2   'Impact diagram'—channels of persuasion

the timing, intensity and interrelationship of each individual item (see Chapter 3, Fig. 3.3).

The appopriation as between one channel and another is changing rapidly as the cost of personal selling increases at a faster rate than any of the non-face-to-face media. Hard evidence for this comes from the United States where selling costs have risen by 222 per cent in 10 years, reaching $230 per call in 1985[2]. This compares with the consumer price index increase of 148 per cent over the same period. Looking at each of the media, costs have increased more in line with the price index.

In the United Kingdom the average cost per 'industrial' sales call is estimated to be around £100 and rising. The outcome of this fact must lead to a completely new approach to what may be termed the media mix. For instance, in comparison with a salesperson who can influence say three or four persons a day, a publication can reach thousands or indeed millions of people in the same time. The message in an advertisement must necessarily be shorter and the percentage of readers upon whom the message will have any impact may be of a low order but the impact can be increased by various devices such as the number of appearances, size of space and so on. To be effective, a salesperson must first find the prospect and then secure an interview. With an advertisement this is not necessary: prospects need only be defined in general terms and a publication by virtue of its blanket circulation will ensure a large coverage of a potential market. The cost of delivering a particular message is also relevant since for a salesperson it may amount to tens of pounds per contact whereas for an advertisement only a few pence.

Since the nature of relative media costs is vital, not only in examining press advertising, but in the chapters which follow, it is worth considering in a little more detail.

Recent research in the United States has shown that the cost per sales call is rising at a rate approximately double the rate of that of advertising space. Figure 2.3 shows the trend.

In order to make a comparison with press advertising, another piece of American research has been taken,[3] and here a sales call costs around 500 times that of an 'advertising contact'.

While the above data relates to the American market, it should not be difficult for any advertiser to produce his own figures in relation to his own company. These can be examined using the same criteria as in Chapter 3.

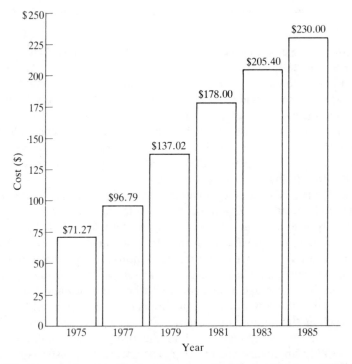

Figure 2.3   Increase in cost of industrial sales calls (*Source:* McGraw-Hill Research Report[2])

Setting targets

It is now time to examine in more detail the way in which the various promotional elements fit into the marketing strategy.

It cannot be over-emphasized that in progressing towards more efficient and effective management, it is necessary to set objectives and to quantify them: to identify targets that are attainable and can be measured. Only in this way can exact courses of action be planned and progress compared with objectives.

The marketing strategy, in addition to outlining the plan of action, must set targets for each component part of it to achieve. There must be sales targets, production targets and profit targets. Such targets do not only deal with the short term, but cover as many years ahead as the nature of the business requires, sometimes up to five years, and, for capital-intensive industries, even longer.

Targets and forecasts differ in their nature and their purpose. A forecast can be considered to be an estimate for the future, assuming a number of constants and given an adequate amount of historical data from which to make an extrapolation. It is based upon the assumption that the past pattern of development is likely to continue in the future, subject to the influence of current events and possible future occurrences. A target is a positive statement of intent backed up by whatever plan of action is judged to be necessary to achieve it. It may or may not have its basis in historical data or other guidelines.

To be effective a marketing strategy must include a quantitative and qualitative statement of objectives to be achieved by promotion. It is not enough for a campaign only to provide a general background of support for the selling operation.

As will be seen later, such campaign objectives may or may not include a direct relationship with sales targets. It is most important to discriminate between 'communications goals' and sales since the former can well be achieved, and the latter not, due to other factors such as price, service or product performance.

An authoritative statement on advertising objectives comes from *Managing Advertising Effectively*.[4]

- If advertising is to be effective and handled with the maximum efficiency it is necessary to know what it is intended to achieve. Hence the need for advertising objectives.
- Advertising objectives need to be expressed in clear, precise, appropriate, attainable and written terms.
- Advertising objectives must be distinguished from marketing objectives, but must be compatible with both these and the overall company goals.
- The process of setting precise advertising objectives is an invaluable management discipline which focuses thinking on the service or product.

- Objectives ensure that management are aware of the assumptions being made and consequently know the degrees of risk involved.
- Precise objectives assist in determining advertising budgets.
- Setting objectives aids the appraisal of advertising plans and control of ongoing situations by top management.
- Written objectives help the advertising and research agencies to prepare and evaluate relevant plans for advertising practice.
- Setting advertising objectives permits meaningful measurement.

The particular goals of a campaign will vary from time to time and company to company. A piece of research on this in the United States[5] identified six major goals of advertising programmes, and these are shown in Figure 2.4 below.

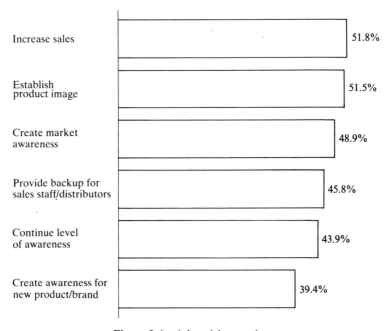

Increase sales — 51.8%

Establish product image — 51.5%

Create market awareness — 48.9%

Provide backup for sales staff/distributors — 45.8%

Continue level of awareness — 43.9%

Create awareness for new product/brand — 39.4%

Figure 2.4   Advertising goals

Marketing communications strategy

A prerequisite of a promotional strategy and a plan of action is a detailed set of targets upon which the success of the marketing operation depends just as much as the capability of the factory to produce the goods.

If sales leads are required, a marketing plan must state how many; if a product awareness is to be built up, this must be represented as the percentage of the potential market it is required to influence.

For example, a new branded range of electric switches is to be launched. It can be defined in advance whether they should become known as quality switches with built-in reliability, or whether as very cheap and easy to replace. Given the market share which it is required to achieve, a figure can be set for the number of buyers who must recall the brand name and be able to associate the product with the company name after a given period of time.

A further example might be the requirement in a large potential market, say for internal telephones, to identify the proportion of potential buyers who have an active interest at that particular moment; in other words to build up a live sales-call list. This may demand a campaign which will bring in large numbers of enquiries: the number can be quantified in advance. Given an existing conversion rate and knowing the sales objectives, the quantity of enquiries can be calculated. A further calculation as a double check will be the number of calls per salesperson, multiplied by the number of salespersons, minus the number of calls on existing accounts, which will equal the number of new sales leads.

If such targets are calculated for, say, a year, then split up into weekly figures based upon the build-up of the campaign and perhaps seasonal factors, it is possible within a very short time to determine whether the promotional mix is right and whether the campaign is producing the desired results.

Just as in the marketing plan there needs to be an optimum mix of the 4 Ps and S, so in marketing communications the media mix must be carefully formulated to ensure optimum performance. The appropriateness of each medium must be assessed methodically in relation to such factors as the potential market—its size, nature and location; the degree of competition and thus demand; the nature and availability of the media themselves.

The strength of each medium, therefore, must be considered and then each element brought to bear on the target in relation to the campaign as a whole. It is only at this stage that the cost of achieving the results can reasonably be considered. Matching costs to desired results is commonly known as the 'task method' of budgeting (see Chapter 3).

Running parallel with the selection of media and budgeting will be the interpretation of the selling message in terms that fit the various media to be employed. The two inevitably interact. A complex message may not be suited to posters or even sometimes to press advertising. Alternatively such a message may require large space advertisements to cover all the points adequately: or a series of small advertisements taking one point at a time may be more suitable. The number and form of direct mail shots will be influenced by the sales message and vice versa.

Finally an essential feature in any properly planned campaign is a predetermined scheme for measuring results and feeding them back quickly for corrective action (see Fig. 2.5.)

Given the setting of written and specific goals the planning of a campaign has been summarized by L. W. Rodger[6] as involving six basic elements:

1. Identifying the audience to be reached.
2. Determining and creating the specific advertising messages to be directed at this audience.
3. Selecting the most effective and most economical media to reach ·this audience.
4. Scheduling the chosen media to provide the best timing, frequency and impact.
5. Determining the advertising budget.
6. Measuring advertising results.

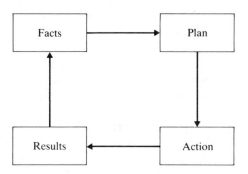

Figure 2.5 Feedback of results

Creative strategy

It is not the intention of this book to examine the creative aspects of industrial publicity in any detail since this is a specialized subject worthy of a book in its own right, but it would be wrong in this chapter on strategies to ignore the essential planning element which can be applied to the creative function.

It is in fact rare to come across the application of a disciplined approach to creativity. One agency[7] has developed what is known as the 4D approach which, while devised largely in consumer terms, has equal relevance to business-to-business advertising. 4D is an abbreviation for four dimensions, which break down as follows:

FIRST DIMENSION

Pinpoint the single selling idea—the particular consumer need that the brand satisfies

1. Understand the consumer needs and attitudes in relevant product fields.
2. Appreciate what competitive brands are offering in each field and all that our particular brand can offer.
3. Select and define what our brand will offer and to whom.

SECOND DIMENSION

Create the most effective and appealing expression of the idea

1. Recognize the real problems of gaining consumer attention and what is already competing for it.
2. Make sure the selling message is clear, distinctive, believable and convincing in consumer terms.
3. Create in all material an equally clear, distinctive total identity and underline the brand name.

THIRD DIMENSION

Find the most efficient media to communicate the idea

1. Select the media that reach the right people.
2. Choose the media best capable of carrying the message.
3. Use the media with the greatest impact, economically; with understanding of competitive strategies.

FOURTH DIMENSION

Eliminate uncertainty as far as possible before and after the advertising appears

1. See whether research can help, and understand just what is to be measured.
2. Be creative and forward-looking in the use of research.
3. Present results clearly, to help decision-making.

A methodical approach such as this does not set out to replace creativity, but merely to channel the creative process through each stage of development in a minimum of time and with maximum effect.

Checklist

1. Has a marketing strategy been prepared?
2. Does the marketing strategy set specific goals to be achieved by marketing communications?
3. In formulating a promotional strategy, has consideration been given to
   (a) Identifying the potential market?
   (b) The selling platform and the advertising message?
   (c) The most effective media?
   (d) Timing in relation to other sales activities?
   (e) The budget to achieve the objective?
   (f) Feedback, and measurement of results?
4. Has the usefulness of each of the following media been evaluated in order to arrive at an optimum media mix?
   (a) Press advertising
   (b) Direct mail
   (c) Exhibitions
   (d) Literature
   (e) Audio-visual
   (f) Photography
   (g) Editorial publicity
   (h) Conferences and seminars
   (i) Sales aids
   (j) Posters and display
   (k) Point of sale and packaging
   (l) Gifts and novelties
   (m) Television and radio
   (n) Brand name
   (o) Special events
5. Has the marketing communication strategy been developed in conjunction with the advertising agency?
6. Is marketing/sales management fully aware of its contents and purposes?
7. Has the cost per sales call been calculated together with the average number of calls required to secure the first order?

References

1. N. A. Hart and J. Stapleton, *Glossary of Marketing Terms* (Heinemann, London, 1987).
2. McGraw–Hill Research Report 8013.8.
3. *US Steel/Harnisachteger Study* (American Business Press).
4. D. R. Corkindale and S. H. Kennedy, *Managing Advertising Effectively* (MBC Ltd, 1975).

5. Cahners Advertising Report No. 101.1.
6. L. W. Rodger, *Marketing in a Competitive Economy* (Associated Business Programmes, London, 1974), p. 198.
7. Lintas Ltd.

3.

PLANNING AND BUDGETING

The need for a marketing strategy, encompassing all the elements of marketing and their interrelationships, was emphasized at the beginning of the book. From this overall strategy stems a plan of action for marketing communications which uses and integrates the channels of persuasion which are applicable.

After assessing the advantages and limitations of each medium, and the extent to which it can be used, a quantified media mix emerges. Expenditure figures can be put against each of the media on the basis that the total deployment of these forces will result in the objective being achieved. Thus the budget is compiled. In practice it is not simple, and the difficulties likely to be encountered will be examined in some detail later.

Planning

One aspect of marketing communications that needs to be touched on now is the time-scale. There is clearly an interrelationship between the start of a campaign and the receipt of the first order. Hence production planning must be related to sales planning and in turn it will be evident that sales will influence the timing of raw materials purchasing, tooling, finance, labour, up to the end of the whole business operation.

The chart, Figure 3.1, shows how certain key functions may relate to each other on a time and quantity basis. Here an investment of £500 000 is shown at a certain point in time. This is intended to represent a piece of capital equipment for the production of a new product. Soon after the initial investment, a publicity campaign begins—way before the equipment becomes operational. Start-up of production is shown to coincide with the first order being received. This planning is essential if adequate funds are to be available at each stage of development. Moreover it follows that having laid down such a plan it is necessary to build in accurate feedback in order to identify deviations as soon as they occur so that corrective action can be taken.

The time-scale of some industrial developments can be of a very long-term nature. Obviously it takes time to build a factory and to install new plant,

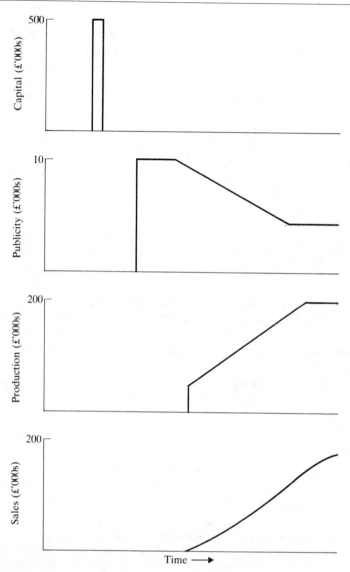

Figure 3.1 Timing of publicity in relation to capital, production and sales

often a year or two. It is equally important to remember that it can take fully as long to build up a demand for a product. The idea of beginning a campaign two years before the product becomes generally available may be rare for some managements but for certain products and services, this is the length of time involved. This is not only true of a new product launch. For existing products there is a good deal of evidence that the sales of today are largely the results of efforts made months or years before and this is a significant factor in determining the promotional budget.

The detailed scheduling of media on a time-scale is the next stage in planning. A typical plan is shown in Figure 3.2. It begins with a press conference and is followed by the campaign launch which reinforces the editorial publicity, with trade press advertising and an intensive direct mail operation backed by advertising in the national press. The sales force is held back in this plan in order to achieve sales leads which will enable it to operate more efficiently and with greater impact.

Trade press advertising, personal selling and editorial publicity are shown to be continuous with periodical sales review meetings. A second intensive phase is centred around a trade exhibition when direct mail and national press are introduced.

Campaign evaluation research is timed for the end of the first year, though there will be continuous feedback of results weekly or monthly against targets in respect of enquiries, quotations, visits and orders throughout the year.

Administratively all the activities will follow a budget broken down into monthly expenditure with strict control exercised. Thus the work which has gone into the preparation of the marketing strategy begins to manifest itself in a co-ordinated drive to achieve preset targets with maximum effect and at minimum cost.

Before reaching the stage of implementation, the final part of the plan has to be determined and agreed. This is the budget.

Budgeting

The basis upon which a marketing communication budget is established must clearly be the 'objective' in view or the 'task' to be done. This has been summed up well by the Institute of Practitioners in Advertising:

> Advertising expenditure must be related to the marketing objectives which the company aims to achieve. Therefore the company should start by forming a realistic marketing plan. Such a plan needs to be based on the knowledge of the overall size of the market, the company's share of the market, the economic trend of industry in general, and the trend of the company's own particular market. It should be shaped to take account of the weak as well as the strong points of the product and its probable life cycle, and the same competitive products. It should pin-point who buys the product and why, and the several influences on the buying decision that may exist at various levels from the factory floor to the board room.[1]

In view of the good sense contained in this statement, it is surprising to find that on the evidence of some researchers and in the experience of many experts, the 'task method' of budgeting is rarely used in industrial marketing.

	Jan.	Feb.	Mar.	Apr.	May	June	July	Aug.	Sept.	Oct.	Nov.	Dec.
Sales conference Sales review meetings	X	X			X			X			X	X
Press conference Press releases		X	X	X	X	X	X	X	X	X	X	X
Private exhibition			X									
National press advertising		▯	▯								▯	
Trade press advertising		▯▯▯▯▯▯▯▯▯▯▯ (Feb–Dec)										
Direct mail		X	XX	XX						XX	XX	
Sales literature Sales aids	X											
Trade show											X	
Personal selling			▯▯▯▯▯▯▯▯▯▯ (Mar–Dec)									
House magazine feature article		X										
Campaign evaluation research												X

Figure 3.2 Detailed scheduling of promotional media

The same IPA publication makes a statement which seems too far-fetched to be believable were it not supported by many similar views—'Think of a number. Halve it. Then decide what your advertising has to do. This is not the exaggeration that it may seem of some companies' way of deciding how much to allocate for industrial advertising.'

Another authority, Harry Henry, has written,

> Since British industry is currently spending upwards of £1,800 millions a year on advertising, it might be expected that the companies and organisations responsible for such expenditure would take reasonably seriously the problem of deciding just what ought to be the size of their advertising budgets. Whether or not this is invariably the case, examination of the variety of methods used for the purpose, and the wide divergence often found between what an advertiser thinks he is doing and what he actually does in practice, indicates that this is an area of managerial activity replete with confusion.[2]

Finally, from L. W. Rodger, 'Because of the difficulty in measuring, let alone forecasting, the results of advertising, manufacturers have tended in the past to use certain rule of thumb criteria in working out what to spend on advertising'.[3]

An enlightening piece of research work on this subject is to be found in McGraw-Hill's *Special Report on Buying and Selling Techniques used in the British Engineering Industry*. This analysed[4] the various methods of arriving at a promotional budget (see Table 3.1).

Table 3.1   Basis of advertising budgets (1)

	Percentage of respondents
(a) Percentage of last year's sales turnover	7
(b) Percentage of this year's expected turnover	17
(c) Percentage of last year's actual and this year's estimate	4
(d) A fixed target without specific reference to sales	39
(e) No known basis	29
(f) Other formulae	4

A later piece of research conducted by the author provided data which is given in Table 3.2. This brought to light the fact that many industrial companies are now using techniques which approximate to the task method. Since the data in Table 3.2 was derived from the larger industrial advertisers, it is probably not typical, but it can certainly be regarded as indicative of a more rational approach to the matter.

It is perhaps useful to examine briefly each of the bases upon which a budget is arrived at.

Table 3.2 Basis of advertising budgets (2)

	Percentage
% sales turnover	17
Cost related to objective	53
Arbitrary sum	30

PERCENTAGE OF LAST YEAR'S TURNOVER

This has the advantage of being simple to arrive at and indeed may be valid in circumstances in which a market is static both in terms of total demand and competitive activity. It makes no provision for a company to use promotional expenditure to improve its position, neither does it take into account any change in products, economic conditions, customer requirements or competition. It must therefore be regarded as a hazardous method of determining the level of promotion.

PERCENTAGE OF THIS OR NEXT YEAR'S ANTICIPATED SALES

At least this has the merit of being related to future events and at the same time being easy to calculate, but it does not face up to the reality of the marketing situation. If the demand for products has suddenly increased, a promotional budget based upon a fixed percentage of forecast sales may be higher than necessary, and indeed may result in orders being received which cannot be satisfied by the production capacity. Conversely if market demand enters a period of decline a higher percentage expenditure may be required to produce the required sales targets. Furthermore, to use next year's sales as a basis ignores the fact that for some capital goods, the gestation period for promotional activities is more than one year.

In any case to use a percentage of anything presupposes that one can obtain from some source the optimum percentage level for efficient expenditure. That this is not so is evidenced by the wide range of percentage expenditures in different industries. An example quoted in the appendix to the IPA publication mentioned above shows the range of expenditure in the United States (see Table 3.3).

FIXED FIGURE UNRELATED TO SALES

The kindest observation that can be made on this method of fixing the budget is that it may be supposed that over a period of years it has been found by trial and error that a given expenditure results in a level of sales and profit which is regarded as satisfactory. This method, however, can hardly claim to

Table 3.3 Advertising as a percentage of sales

Industry	% of industrial sales expended for industrial advertising	
	High	Low
Paper	4.0	0.2
Printing and publishing	1.65	0.1
Chemicals	9.3	0.003
Rubber and plastic products	8.0	0.1
Primary metal industries	3.0	0.0004
Fabricated metal products	16.2	0.003
Machinery	18.5	0.001

N.B. Even where specific product groups are examined, wide differences occur.

have any place in modern marketing, or, indeed, in modern business management.

COMPETITIVE ADVERTISING

Some companies are known to base their publicity on what their competitors are doing. While this has the advantage of at least countering competitive activity, it assumes that it is possible to measure competitors' expenditure with some degree of accuracy: it also assumes that the competitors know what they are doing and have arrived at their budgets on a sound basis. Both assumptions are unlikely.

THE 'TASK METHOD'

This involves defining the objective, or the task to be done, then determining the best media mix to achieve it. From this a budget can be drawn up which will represent the best estimate of the optimum promotional expenditure. (See Fig. 3.3.)

In a comprehensive review of budgeting methods Harry Henry[5] lists ten other possible lines of approach:

Intuitive, or rule of thumb This is someone's subjective assessment of 'what should do the job', and is an amalgam of hunch and experience (experience being what has been done before, not necessarily having regard to its outcome). It is very dependent upon the person making the decision: should he be replaced, a different view may be taken.

The affordable method This method, spending 'as much as can be afforded' (which means what is left over after all other cost and profit requirements have been met) is not one which many firms claim to follow. But the attitude

Figure 3.3   'Task method' of budgeting

towards advertising which this approach reflects does in practice often emerge as a constraint on a good many other methods of budget determination, including those which on the face of it are rather more logical.

Residue after last year's profits   Often regarded as being a ploughing-back of profit, or as re-investment in the future, this approach concentrates on the source of funds rather than on the purpose to which those funds are devoted.

Percentage of gross margin   This keeps advertising expenditure in proportion to turnover and profits, but begs the question of what advertising is for, or how its cost-efficiency may be improved.

Fixed expenditure per unit of sales   Although expressed in different terms— 'so much per case for advertising'—and born of standard costing procedures, this method is not all that different in its effect, in the short term, from the percentage of sales method.

Cost per capita   In this approach, which is used mainly by industrial advertisers, the advertiser calculates the advertising cost per head for his present customers and, when he wishes to gain more, increases his expenditure pro rata.

Matching advertising to brand share   This is an apparently sophisticated approach, based in fact on rather simplistic analysis. It is essentially a development of matching competitive advertising.

The marginal return approach   The cost of an extra unit of advertising activity is compared with the increased profit which is expected in consequence. A standard technique in direct response advertising, it becomes very complicated when there are other factors in the marketing mix, and has to be used in conjunction with marketing models.

Marketing models These are designed to describe the relationship between sales or profit and the main elements in the marketing mix—including advertising—and from these relationships it is theoretically possible to determine the optimum advertising budget. The technical problems involved in gathering and interpreting the necessary data are, however, formidable.

Media weight tests The theory behind this approach is that if, in a test situation, a given weight of advertising expenditure produces a particular level of sales, the level of advertising in the total market which will produce a required level of sales can be deduced. For a variety of reasons, the theory rarely works in this way.

Cost of advertising

As has been indicated, the cost of advertising in relation to the overall marketing expense and to turnover varies considerably, and particularly between one industry category and another. Tables 3.4 and 3.5[6] provide new evidence here.

BREAKDOWN OF EXPENDITURE

In drawing up budgets, it is important to make provision for every element of expenditure and to relate it as far as possible to each product group or profit centre.

Table 3.4 Marketing expenditure by British manufacturing industry

	£ million	Percentage
Wages and salaries of sales and marketing	1300	35.8
Media advertising	450	12.4
Publicity and point-of-sale material	100	2.8
Market research	20	0.6
Packaging	900	24.8
Transport and distribution	800	22.0
Miscellaneous charges (including postage, telephone and telex)	60	1.6
Total marketing	3630	100.0
% Sales revenue	9.5	
% Value added	24.0	

Table 3.5   Estimated marketing expenditure by industry sector

	Percentage sales revenue
Food, drink and tobacco	14.0
Chemicals and allied	13.0
metal manufacturing	5.0
Engineering and electrical goods	10.0
Shipbuilding and marine engineering	5.0
Vehicles	6.5
Metal goods n.e.s.	6.0
Textiles	5.0
Leather, leather goods and fur	5.0
Clothing and footwear	7.0
Bricks, pottery, glass, cement, etc.	14.0
Timber and furniture	8.0
Paper, printing and publishing	9.5
Other manufacturing industry	9.0
Total manufacturing industry	9.5

A good example of the various items which might be included in a typical publicity budget is given below

1. Advertising programme:
   (a) Space costs
   (b) Production
   (c) Service fee
   (d) Agency commission
   (e) Pulls for internal circulation
   (f) Research
2. Other media:
   (a) Direct mail
   (b) Exhibitions and trade shows
   (c) Postage
   (d) Sales literature
   (e) Customer publications
   (f) Films and AV
   (g) Photography
3. Public relations
4. Department's expenses:
   (a) Salaries (plus extras)
   (b) Travel and entertainment expenses
   (c) Office equipment and supplies
   (d) Telephone and cable costs

(e)   Rent, light and heat for department
(f)   Subscription to associations, news services, magazines
(g)   Press cutting services

To allocate each of these items to profit centres may be difficult and will certainly involve a degree of estimating, but the procedure is necessary if a true level of profit is to be calculated. Perhaps the biggest obstacle is attitude of mind which tends to allocate publicity expenditure as part of the general overhead rather than an intrinsic part of the cost of 'production and distribution'. A cost accountant, however, will find that the breakdown of publicity costs is no more involved or inaccurate than the breakdown of works supervision or even of machine time and expense on the shop floor.

ANALYSIS OF MEDIA EXPENDITURE

The allocation of expenditure to the various media varies a good deal as between consumer and industrial publicity (see Fig. 3.4).

The results in Table 3.6 based on the author's own research show press advertising at the head of the list, with sales literature featuring predominantly. On the whole, the breakdown between principal media groups has

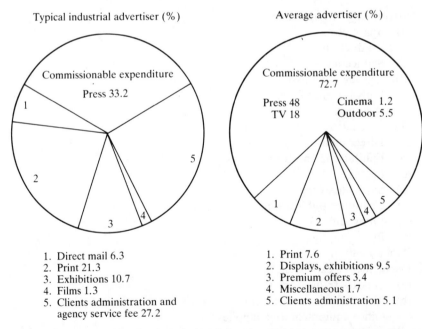

Typical industrial advertiser (%)

Commissionable expenditure
Press 33.2

1. Direct mail 6.3
2. Print 21.3
3. Exhibitions 10.7
4. Films 1.3
5. Clients administration and
   agency service fee 27.2

Average advertiser (%)

Commissionable expenditure
72.7

Press 48   Cinema 1.2
TV 18   Outdoor 5.5

1. Print 7.6
2. Displays, exhibitions 9.5
3. Premium offers 3.4
4. Miscellaneous 1.7
5. Clients administration 5.1

Figure 3.4   Comparison between industrial and consumer appropriations (*Source:* IPA Forum 19, Institute of Practitioners in Advertising, London)

Table 3.6 Analysis of media expenditure[7]

	Percentage
Press advertising	40
Sales literature	27
Exhibitions	15
Direct mail	9
Public relations	9

Table 3.7 Expenditure on business-to-business media, 1986

	Percentage
Business press	34.5
Brochures, catalogues	14.4
Exhibitions	14.1
Direct mail	8.1
PR	6.0
Directories	5.5
Regional newspapers	2.9
National newspapers	2.8
Videos/AV	2.8
Premiums	2.1
Point of sale	1.5
Posters	1.4
TV	1.2
Sponsorship	1.0
Radio	0.5
Others	1.2
(Base 807 advertisers)	100.0

shown very little change over time. Further confirmation is given in a study by MIL Research which is reproduced in Table 3.7

The promotional mix will of course vary considerably from one company to another and the above data are simply averages for industry as a whole.

Financial appraisal

The failure of the task method of budgeting to gain the widest usage in business can be explained in two ways. Firstly it involves a great deal more work, and a considerable measure of expertise. Given that this is available, the second reason may be the belief that, having arrived at a budget by 'scientific' means, it is now sacrosanct and regardless of any other considerations cannot be changed. It must be emphasized that the only element of science in the task method of budgeting is its methodology. The essential 'mixture' is still a matter of judgement, and can be accurate or inaccurate.

Most important of all is that a budget, arrived at in this way, must now be subjected to appraisal in terms of its relationship to the total sales expense, and in particular to the projected turnover and profit. It is more than likely that adjustments will have to be made, not only to the publicity budget, but to the sales expense and turnover before a profit margin is arrived at which is satisfactory in business terms.

An advertising campaign may be expanded or cut back providing the implications are known, and it is not done blindly. As with any investment, the returns are seldom linear, and it may be found that a reduction in advertising expenditure, say, of 40 per cent will result in a reduction in effectiveness of only 15 per cent or a reduction in sales turnover of only 2 per cent. A planned initial approach to the budget enables revisions to be made from a sound base which is likely to produce results closer to target than a blind guess.

Finally it is interesting to note how the budget breakdown compares with that in the United States (see Table 3.8).

Table 3.8   Media expenditure, United States (Source: McGraw-Hill Research Report 8009.4)

	Percentage
Press advertising	36
Sales literature	24
Exhibitions	20
Direct mail	8
PR	5
Other	7

Checklist

1. In timing a promotional campaign, is there a clear understanding throughout the company on the length of time between starting publicity and seeing results in terms of sales?
2. Is a master schedule produced, as a routine for each campaign, to show the relationship between all the various media and including sales force activities?
3. Is budgeting for promotion based upon the 'task method'? If not, is top management aware of the shortcomings of other methods?
4. Is the advertising agency committed to 'task method' budgeting, rather than accepting a sum of money and recommending the best way of spending it?
5. Has any attempt been made (a) to monitor competitors' expenditures: (b)

to obtain inter-firm comparisons—in particular the proportion of promotional expenditure in the marketing expense budget, and as a percentage of sales?

6. Has a strict system of budgetary control been established?
7. Is this broken down into shorter control periods than a year?
8. Has provision been made for each item of expenditure to be set against product groups, as in Table 3.9 (on p. 34)?

References

1. *How to Budget for Industrial Advertising* (Institute of Practitioners in Advertising).
2. H. Henry, Deciding how much to spend on Advertising, Cranfield Broadsheet No. 2 (1979).
3. L. W. Rodger, *Marketing in a Competitive Economy*, (Associated Business Programmes, London 1974), p. 214.
4. *Special Report on Buying and Selling Techniques used in the British Engineering Industry* (McGraw-Hill) p. 3.
5. H. Henry, *op. cit.*, pp. 3 and 4.
6. C. West, *Marketing on a Small Budget* (Associated Business Programmes, London, 1975).
7. *How British Business Advertises* (British Business Press, London, 1986).

Table 3.9   Budget outline

	Product 1	Product 2	Product 3	Total

Publicity department
  salaries
  overheads
  expenses
Advertising agency
PR agency
Press advertising
  space
  production
Direct mail
  lists
  production
  distribution
Exhibitions
  space
  design
  standfitting
  transport
  staff
  miscellaneous
Literature
  creative
  production
  distribution
Photography
Films and AV
  production
  distribution
Research
Editorial publicity
Posters
Point of sale
Packaging
Conferences and seminars
Sales aids and manuals
Gifts and Christmas cards
Miscellaneous (enumerate)
Contingency				

Total				
Sales forecast % Promotion to sales				
Other marketing expense *Total marketing expense*				
% Marketing expense to forecast sales				

Part 2

MARKETING COMMUNICATIONS

4.

PRESS ADVERTISING

Press advertising relates to any form of advertisement which appears in a publication and is paid for. It is viewed primarily from the point of view of selling a product or service, though clearly it can have other aims such as building goodwill, establishing confidence in an organization, or recruiting personnel.

Purpose

The purpose of press advertising, as of any other channel of persuasion, is primarily to communicate a selling message to a potential customer.

The starting point is what is known as a 'target group audience' or a defined market or public, i.e. a number of people whom it is wished to influence. A proportion of this public will be exposed to the advertising pages of various publications and, depending upon the impact of an advertisement, a proportion of these will take note of a message.

Press advertising in the industrial sector has come in for a good deal of criticism on the grounds of its ineffectiveness, relative to the money spent on it. Much of this has arisen from the inadequacy and inaccuracy of media selection and the incompetence of some advertisement design and copywriting. Often the failure, however, is traceable to different reasons, namely that the purpose of advertising has not been defined in advance or, if it has, it has been lost sight of.

For example, there is the sales manager's view when he or she sees some tens of thousands of pounds being spent on press advertising, and relates this to the number of additional salespeople that could put on the road for such an expenditure. If, however, the purposes of these two channels of persuasion have been pre-defined, the one to provide active sales leads, the other to clinch the sale, they become mutually dependent and not competing alternatives.

The position of press advertising within the broad communications framework must be established at the outset, and its strengths and weaknesses analysed. The following criteria examine press advertising in relation to other media.

1. *Market size*   The total size of a market segment and all of the people that go to comprise it must be the starting point of media choice. With a market size of 10 units there is clearly not much room for more than personal contact backed by whatever back-up might be required. Move to 100 units and the situation hardly changes. At 1000 the personal contact must become selective, and here one can add direct mail, specialized press, editorial publicity, literature, maybe sponsored films and AV, local demonstrations and perhaps telephone selling. At 10 000 personal selling falls away and press advertising and most other non-personal media take over. Exhibitions have a particular merit here, combining unit economy with the benefits of face-to-face contact. Direct mail sometimes starts to become difficult to handle. Editorial back-up is of course well worth full exploitation. At 100 000 one starts to move into mass media with television, radio, national newspapers and posters replacing or heavily supplementing the other media already listed.

2. *Intrinsic impact*   The extent to which an advertising message is transmitted, received, stored and able to be recalled with accuracy is vital. Each medium has its own intrinsic impact potential. Clearly a medium which facilitates two-way communication is top of the list, and so personal selling, exhibitions, demonstrations, telephone selling are all worthy of a high rating. Direct mail, properly conceived, can expect to perform well here, as can editorial publicity, sponsored films and literature. All the research evidence we have on page traffic and Starch measurements would indicate that press advertising performs least well in achieving impact.

3. *Message*   What is the nature of the selling message? Is it simple or is it a reminder? Is it complex, technical or innovative? In the former case, press advertising, point-of-sale, posters and radio will do well. For a complicated message, however, the need is for demonstrations, seminars, feature articles, literature, sponsored films, and the sales force.

4. *Coverage and penetration*   This is the breadth and depth of a medium's capability. In breadth the question is what proportion of the target audience (i.e. people within a market segment) is covered by readership as opposed to circulation? In other words, will they have an 'opportunity to see'? In direct mail the answer could be 100 per cent, with a national newspaper perhaps 60 per cent but with great wastage. Commonly one is looking for an in-depth coverage of around 80 per cent. Turning to penetration, certain media are known by long-standing practice to penetrate decision-making units even where the actual names of the people involved cannot be identified: a major trade fair, for instance, or a weekly trade magazine that has to be seen by anyone who is anyone in order to keep up to date.

5. *Negative characteristics*   Some people resent some advertising and it is

as well to check out in advance of using a particular media group whether your intention could be counter-productive. Most people in the United Kingdom dislike advertising messages on the telephone or at the front door or on the street corner. They also dislike loose inserts, direct mail that is too intensive or repetitive, and for many, radio and television commercials are intrusive. On the whole, however, press advertising does not suffer from 'intrusion'.

6. *Positive characteristics* We are looking for an added plus which comes over and above the basic medium itself. Examples are with an ad in a very prestigious publication where to be seen in good company lends an extra credibility to an advertising proposition. Similarly a strong editorial base helps. With an exhibition stand a comfortable lounge can be a welcome oasis after the formal business has been completed. An in-house exhibition or seminar may draw together people with common interests who have not met for some time and who welcome the chance of informal discussion almost as much as the event itself.

7. *Cost* There are two costs—and also the price—to be considered. The first cost is the total capital investment involved and whether this is compatible with the cash-flow position, and also the other major capital expenditures in marketing activities. Then the cost per contact must be evaluated, ranging as it does from the latest estimated call cost for an industrial salesperson of over £100 to just a few pence for press advertising. Media planning decisions are often made on the outcome of aggressive media buying, and this is where price comes in. All rate cards have their price, and 10 per cent or more off quoted rates can be a lot of money.

8. *Speed* Under pressure, television, radio, newspapers and direct mail can all be transmitting messages within 24 hours or less, and to very large audiences simultaneously. The sales force can respond even more quickly, but at a rate of just a few people a day. At the other extreme it may be two years before an appropriate trade fair takes place. Thus, if the time for activating consumer/customer behaviour is a critical factor then choice of media must be influenced by this.

9. *Complexity and convenience* Nothing could be simpler than taking half a million appropriation and allocating half of it to a single commercial network on television, and the other half to full pages in national newspapers. Such a media strategy may even be right. As against this can be compared the complexity of a multi-market multi-shot direct mail campaign, coupled with regional presentations tied in with local PR, back-up sales visits, regional press, supporting literature and posters with a culminating business gift. Media choice just might be influenced by ease of use (idleness), coupled with such other non-professional factors as good or bad agency commission. Is there any possible justification for some media paying commission and others not? Media

choice within an agency must therefore have some regard to the amount of effort required to service each medium (a cost) in relation to the income and aggravation it is likely to receive. Specialized trade press and small spaces may be very effective but they can be complicated to handle and with only 10 per cent media commission are expensive for an agency to handle.

10. *Feedback*   Examine any advertising medium and you will find that the greater majority of advertisements invite no explicit response in the way of a direct feedback, and thus they receive very little. Hence press advertising, and television, are essentially single-channel communication systems. Since impact is greater where a dialogue can be established, there must be an intrinsic advantage in all the face-to-face media, and even with direct mail and editorial publicity where there are some instances of feedback. It is worth noting that many of the popular sales promotion techniques draw heavily on the customers' participation.

11. *Creative scope*   Should a medium be chosen for its creative scope? Increasingly this is regarded as a major factor but within the rather strict limits of availability of colour or movement. What is meant here is the opportunity for some quite novel or extraordinary approach to be made entirely as a result of the medium being used. In press relations the creative opportunities to set up an extremely newsworthy event are limitless, and needless to say this would be done in such a way as to involve the product or company inextricably. With direct mail there is complete freedom on material, size, shape, colour, smell, timing, audience and frequency. Exhibitions also have an almost infinite variety of creative opportunities. Where the product itself is mundane, the choice of media where creativity can be exploited fully is especially relevant. Clearly creative opportunities are somewhat restricted in press advertising.

12. *Data availability*   There is a somewhat old-fashioned idea in industrial advertising that since the amounts of money to be spent are relatively small the need for information about what one is buying is not therefore very great. This is a quite extraordinary and quite illogical situation since the advertising task may well be of the greatest importance to the company; the fact that the cost of achieving it may not be astronomical does not mean that the media-buying operation should be incompetent.

With any media that overlaps into consumer marketing a good deal of information is likely to be available, but otherwise it is hard to find. The technical press is rarely able to provide reliable readership data and exhibitions are way behind what is done in other countries. Some advertisers set up their own sources of audience information and it may be that in respect of 'data' media choice should be biased towards those channels from which the most reliable facts can be obtained.

13. *Subjective factors* So far, the factors being discussed on media choice have been largely objective or quantitative. In practice of course there are many other sources of influence, apparently trivial, but perhaps of far greater significance in the media-buying decision than many people either realize or are prepared to admit. Why else do advertisers opt for a particular medium? Here are a few reasons:

(a) Good service from the publisher or media house.
(b) Good salesmanship—hard selling—pleasant personality.
(c) The buyer's ego trip—he likes his products to be seen in a particular medium.
(d) Good lunches, Christmas presents, and all forms of what might kindly be termed 'grace and favour'.
(e) Because the managing director says so.
(f) Competitors use it.
(g) The title of a publication, also its format; with exhibitions, location is a factor.
(h) Inertia—we've always done it this way.
(i) Personal prejudice and ignorance.
(j) The good reputation of a medium; with publications, the quality of their editorial.
(k) Hunch.
(l) The agency gets a better service or higher commission.

While the above criteria do not in any way lead to scientific media planning, their evaluation in relation to press advertising and all the other media can lead to a systematic ranking of each of the channels of communication. Figure 4.1 provides a simple grid leading to an effective media mix.

Effectiveness

A very early survey of sources of information, *How British Industry Buys*,[1] indicated that advertisements in the trade press had a relatively small part to play in providing information which influenced the purchase of industrial products. The highest category was 'operating management' of whom 32 per cent cited press advertising as one of the two most important channels of communication. Perhaps the most important category, board members, scored only 14 per cent.

There is good evidence in this survey that respondents are not always willing to admit even to themselves what are the outside factors they allow to influence them in reaching purchasing decisions. Sales engineers' visits for instance were rated at 66 per cent by board members, yet elsewhere in the survey only 18 per cent of board members ever saw a sales engineer! Since the first figure is an expression of opinion and the latter one of fact, 18 per cent is

Figure 4.1   Criteria for media choice

more likely to be the accurate figure. If not from sales engineers, where did board members obtain the information upon which to make decisions? Advertising may well in fact deserve a higher rating than these respondents were prepared to admit.

In the United States a good deal of work has been done to relate on a very broad basis the effectiveness of press advertising to sales.

A survey published by McGraw-Hill[2] showed that in 893 industrial companies, when the ratio of advertising to selling expense, i.e. advertising plus direct selling costs (salespeople's salaries, commission, travel and entertainment), is higher, the ratio of selling expense to sales turnover is lower. On average it was found that 'high advertisers' (where advertising accounted for more than 20 per cent of selling expense) had a 21 per cent lower overall selling cost than 'low advertisers'. The trend was found to be consistent regardless of the volume of sales and of product groups. In the former case, 'high' advertisers in each of four sales size groups had average selling expense 16 to 30 per cent lower than the 'low' advertisers.

For the machinery group (all special industrial machinery such as machine tools and construction machinery, motors, instruments and controls, transport and communications equipment) the sales expense ratio was 25 per cent lower on average among 'high' advertisers than among 'low' advertisers.

For the materials group (raw materials and ingredients such as steel, industrial chemicals, rubber and plastics, structural products) the difference was 27 per cent. For the equipment supplies group (maintenance and operating supplies such as furniture, paper products, lubricants, tyres, valves, machine tool accessories, paint, lighting fixtures, electronic components) the difference was 15 per cent.

It can be argued of course that these data are of a general nature and will hide wide variances. The conclusions, however, are important enough for industrial advertisers to take steps to obtain information relating to their own particular business, maybe through their trade association using inter-firm comparisons.

There are wide differences in the amount of investment in industrial advertising even among firms in the same industry. This is only to be expected but it is unfortunate that the reasons for such differences are often subjective or illogical. They are sometimes based on a philosophy of 'I don't believe in advertising', a comment which has as much rational justification as not believing in raw materials. Or perhaps the sales manager thinks he knows exactly who his customers are, calls upon them at frequent intervals and therefore does not need advertising—a proposition which can almost always be disproved on methodical investigation. Too often sales staff and managers completely underrate the importance of the corroborative function of industrial advertising. Because they may not be able to point to sales or worthwhile prospects obtained by advertising they assume that their advertising is not effective. In fact however a company's generalized reputation is most important; and although advertising is only one factor in building up this reputation it is a vital one. This is discussed further in Chapter 14.

Perhaps the classic summary of advertising effectiveness is to be found in the advertisement by McGraw-Hill which sets out to demonstrate the importance of advertising in the selling process. A surly buyer is illustrated declaiming to an imaginary salesperson:

I don't know who you are
I don't know your company
I don't know your company's product
I don't know what your company stands for

I don't know your company's customers
I don't know your company's record
I don't know your company's reputation
Now—what was it you wanted to sell me?

The industrial and business press

Publications in the United Kingdom can be broken down into six main groups:

1. National dailies
2. Provincial dailies
3. Sunday newspapers
4. Local newspapers (weeklies)
5. General interest and class magazines
6. Trade and technical publications

The primary concern of industrial advertisers is in the two thousand or more trade and technical publications. These journals are diverse and complex. They encompass a comprehensive range of activities, vary greatly in size, scope, authority and in the method of circulation. In recent years there has been a good deal of rationalization in the industry which has led to a large proportion of the total publications being produced by a relatively small number of publishers. Many changes have taken place, some of which have been to the benefit of the advertiser, for example the availability of research services. Fundamentally journals have tended to move away from an editorial basis where a brilliant editor published material about a particular subject in which he was an expert, to a marketing basis where the whole concept of a publication is to provide information and a service to meet the needs of a particular market or specialized group of people. This matter is dealt with in greater detail in Chapter 16 on publishing.

The advertising schedule

The starting point once again must be a written definition of the people it is desired to influence. For example it is not uncommon in the development of a campaign to aim at four groups—the people who specify a product, often the engineers, designers or technologists; the people who have contacts with the suppliers and place the order, usually the purchasing officers; the user; and most important the authorizers, often the board of directors. It is essential to establish at the outset which of these or other groups, it is required to reach. Moreover it is necessary to take the analysis further to include factors such as geographical location, age, sex and so on.

The selection of the most effective publications is vital, for even a poor advertisement in the right journal has some chance of success, whereas a first-rate advertisement in a quite inappropriate publication is absolutely useless. It follows then that time and effort invested in the methodical selection and final evaluation of media is a very worthwhile investment. In practice the data available from publishers is usually grossly inadequate, often misleading and sometimes blatantly inaccurate. Media research is a growing activity in industrial advertising and is dealt with at length in Chapter 13.

Given a potential market, there will be a number, often a large number, of journals whose circulation will cover part or all of it. Circulation, however, is not the real criterion since it is only readership and, in particular, effective readership, that counts. One journal may have a high 'pass on' factor in relation to its circulation, but are the recipients also effective buyers? Furthermore it is not enough for a magazine to appear on a desk, it must be read in order to be effective.

The total circulation or readership of a journal is usually of no great significance in itself. If for example the brief is to reach 1000 chemical engineers in the food industry it will probably be of little value that a journal also reaches 10 000 chemical engineers in plastics, petroleum and other trades in which food has no application. In assessing media and in making comparisons the aim must be to isolate the readership that is directly relevant to the marketing objectives.

Quite often it will be found that there will be numerous publications all having good coverage of the market. The question is whether to concentrate on a limited few, or whether to spread into all publications to secure the widest audience. This judgement must be made in the light of knowledge of readership duplication and also the impact which a campaign is required to achieve. It is generally true in press advertising that after the first two or three publications in a specialized field, any additions will add only a few per cent more to the coverage of a market (see Chapter 13).

COST-EFFECTIVENESS

The cost per thousand total circulation basis, so popular with publishers and agency media departments, is quite inadequate for effective media assessment. Equally unrealistic as a rule is cost per order originating from a given journal, since the number of traceable contracts is usually of such a low order as to be statistically unreliable.

Cost per reader within the defined market segment is probably the most effective basis of assessing a publication, though in some instances cost per enquiry can be an even better guide. This latter factor necessarily depends on whether enquiries are what an advertisement is designed to achieve. A study of packaging media for instance showed the cost per thousand circulation to vary little between one publication and another. When the required readership for a particular type of pack was examined, the cost per reader varied from £1.5 per thousand to £20 per thousand. Moreover, after the top two publications had been added together, further additions made no significant difference to the number of readers reached. In this instance it was found possible to reduce the number of publications from eight to two, increase the concentration and level of advertising, and thus impact, while reducing expenditure.

CIRCULATION AND ADVERTISING RATES

When the overall economics of publishing are considered it is generally found that advertising rates of British publications are reasonably geared to production costs. Within any specialized sector it is usual to find the forces of competition have caused the cost per thousand copies of one journal to be much the same as another. Indeed so far as the absolute level of cost per page is concerned it may be argued that the rates tend to be too low to enable a publisher to provide a good enough all-round service to maximize the marketing efficiency of his publication.

The important differences between rates begin to emerge only when readership 'segmentation' is considered and here the advertiser is at a great disadvantage. Accurate and authentic data on total circulations are beginning to emerge, but circulation breakdowns are usually no more than a publisher's statement and the bitter fact is that these must be treated with reserve. Until circulation breakdowns are subject to independent audit it is unwise to pay any serious regard to them since the basis on which they are compiled is unknown and they cannot be subject to comparative study. Nevertheless the work done by the Audit Bureau of Circulation in developing and promoting Media Data Forms represents a very important advance in providing a quantitative basis for media selection (see Fig. 4.2).

Given the difficulty of determining cost/readership effectiveness, there are still opportunities for significant savings on the basis of rates alone. For instance in determining how many publications to place on a schedule in relation to how many insertions in each, graduated scales of charges are worth examining since quantity reductions in page rates can effect major economies. Long-term contracts can enable further savings to be made, and notwithstanding the existence of published rate cards, many publishers are prepared to negotiate prices in order to increase their share of business.

A growing trend among publishers is to offer discount rates based on the total business placed in certain groups of publications. Another variation is to consider financial concessions related to the time of year.

An alternative to looking for special rate reductions is to look for special

Building Products

|ABC|

MEDIA DATA FORM

13th Series

Valid to 30th April, 1987

GENERAL DATA

Year Founded ...1977........... Changes of publication name/ownership in past 5 years ...None...

To which Group of companies (if any) does the Publisher belong? ....Patey Doyle (Publishing) Ltd.................

If the publication is an official organ of any Society/Association state which and when appointed...Not applicable..

Advertisement Manager

Name ...... David Honeyman ....

Address ...... Wilmington House ....
.... Church Hill, Wilmington ....
.... Dartford, Kent DA2 7EF ....

Tel. No. .(0322) 77788. Fax No. ...76474.............................

Telex No. ...894737.......

Editor

Name ...... Joe Simpson ....

Address ...Wilmington House ....
.... Church Hill, Wilmington ....
.... Dartford, Kent DA2 7EF ....

Tel. No. ..(0322) 77788. Fax No. ...76474·.........

Telex No. ..894737...........

ADVERTISEMENT DATA SEE RATE CARD FOR FULL DETAILS

Rate of standard b & w page, single insertion ..£1,040... sc. cm .£13. Effective date ...August 1986...........

Frequency of publication .....Monthly.......... Publishing Day/Date ....25th prior month.........

Copy Day/Date – Black & White ...One month prior.......... Colour ....6 weeks prior.......................

Any issues during period additional to normal frequency? ...No...... if Yes give details ....

Do you operate a Reader Enquiry Service? ....Yes..... Can your circulation list be inspected by space

buyers? ....Yes..... Do you accept inserts? ....Yes...... If Yes, bound in and/or loose ....Both...............

Do you provide any other special services? ....Yes..... if Yes give details ...Direct mail.............................

MECHANICAL DATA

Type page size ...280mm x 196mm.......................... Normal method(s) of printing Sheet fed cover balance

Method of binding ..Perfect............................ Format – Magazine or Newspaper ...Web offset Magazine....

METHOD OF DISTRIBUTION News Trade ....% Addressed Copies ......100....% based

on a normal issue.

If addressed copies exceed 25% state percentage addressed by

(a) Name ...100...% (b) Job Title only ....% (c) Establishment Address only ....%

Are you able to provide percentage of subscription renewals? ...No...... If yes state ....%

MARKETS SERVED BY JOURNAL

Building industry – areas include: architects, quantity surveyors, building contractors, house builders and developers, industrial and commercial firms with their own building departments, local authorities, specifiers and purchasers, consulting engineers, sub-contractors.

Figure 4.2 Media Data Form

services from a publisher. There are many facilities which can be placed at the disposal of an advertiser which will help to make his campaign more effective. Progressive publishers are recognizing this and are prepared to co-operate, for instance in split runs, inserts, and joint research. One questionable service is the occasional offer of editorial preference in consideration of the placing of advertising. If a journal is willing to do business on this basis it can only mean that it is prepared to forfeit its editorial independence in order to make short-term gains at the expense of the reader and therefore the advertiser.

An interesting term in the publishing business is the 'numbers game'. It is a reflection on the gullibility of some advertisers that the journal most likely to be chosen as number one on a schedule is that having the greatest total circulation. Before the introduction of free-circulation journals, this might have been a valid criterion in a homogeneous market, but where it represents, as is now sometimes the case, simply an expression of the print order, its claims are quite misleading.

Over the past decade a large number of publications have appeared, almost always given away, with circulation methods which are sometimes not controlled with any degree of effectiveness. Such journals have had circulations inflated by a factor first of two, then three and then four—each publisher going one better in quoting a higher number. Rates for such journals expressed in relation to circulation totals have seemed reasonable, but any company librarian will quote example after example of the inflow of duplicate copies of such journals which serve to benefit the printer, paper-maker and publisher, but not the advertiser.

In numerous readership surveys there is ample evidence of magazines quoting massive circulation figures but receiving extraordinarily low readership ratings. The moral, as always, is let the buyer beware, and verify all facts by independent audit.

While page rates in relation to circulation may be fairly standard, this is by no means so of special positions, rates and concessions. The advertising value of such positions may be questionable, but all the same, there is a good deal of scope for skilled media buying.

Wide variations between one publisher and another will be found in respect of facing matter, covers, additional colours, bound-in and loose inserts, and bleed pages. The combination of these factors can entirely change the economics of an advertising schedule and this points the need for a very close liaison between media buyers and the creative staff of agencies in order to achieve the maximum cost-effectiveness. Some journals for example make no charge for bleed whereas others have a high premium: cover positions in particular are susceptible to variations quite unrelated to their advertising value which in itself is questionable.

Skilful media buying is therefore a high priority though many advertising agencies greatly underrate it for technical advertising. This is often because with the complexity of the task the client's 'intimate' knowledge of the trade is allowed to predominate without a critical examination.

Media selection

Intra-media comparisons in the trade and technical press are particularly difficult with the relevant facts often unknown and sometimes misleading. Although this makes the task more difficult, it does not provide a reason for ignoring it. Some of the principal criteria in selecting media are:

1. Total circulation
2. Total readership
3. Segmented circulation
4. Segmented readership
5. Standard rates in relation to 1, 2, 3 and 4
6. Reductions and premiums in relation to special circumstances
7. Credibility of publisher's data
8. Editorial excellence
9. Journal's reputation
10. Format, paper, printing
11. Method of circulation
12. Frequency
13. Special services from publisher
14. Readership duplication

In the limit, of course, given adequate research, and feedback of information, the sole criterion is the extent to which a publication serves as a means of achieving the written specific advertising objectives in terms of the market to be influenced. This hinges largely on the extent to which an advertiser has access to reliable research data. Chapters 12 and 13 deal with this in some detail.

It is necessary at this stage to touch briefly on other criteria which are often employed but which in general are less helpful in assessing media.

Probably the biggest single misleading factor in media selection is the use of reader reply cards. This is a service introduced largely by 'controlled circulation' journals as a means of securing a maximum of enquiries. Viewed in this light alone, and provided the specific campaign objective is to secure the maximum of enquiries without qualification, then these cards can be said to provide a useful service. However, from an examination of advertisements in the technical press the conclusion must be reached that the principal purpose of many advertisements is not to secure enquiries, since so few offer an incentive, either specific or implied, to make an enquiry. If this is so, reader reply response is not specially valuable.

It is the quality of enquiries which is of prime importance in most cases of a campaign to obtain sales leads. Here reader reply cards will be found to need scrutiny in two respects: firstly there tends to be a higher proportion of enquiries from people lower down the scale of purchasing influence; secondly the very ease with which one can make an enquiry using a reader reply card makes such an enquiry less serious, and more casual than would otherwise be the case. Evidence of this is to take at random returned cards in a publisher's office and examine the number of ticks per card, sometimes so many as to be ludicrous. It is not unknown for a card to be received on which every number has been ticked, including all the spare ones against which no advertisement or editorial item has appeared. While it is important to be cautious, the plain fact is that reply cards on balance provide a valuable service to advertisers and to publishers, but more to the point it is a service which is applauded by the readers as can be seen in Figure 4.3.

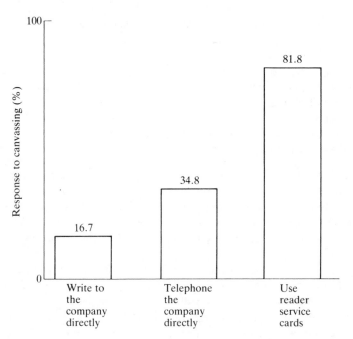

Figure 4.3   Use of reader service cards (*Source:* Cahners Research Report No. 240.1)

Reader reply cards in respect of editorial items are also used as an argument for the advertising effectiveness of a journal. This may be valid in some instances, but it is open to considerable doubt. Consider the timing of an editorial on a new product. The first journal in a specialized field to publish a new product item will tend to mop up the enquiries of those having immediate interest. Subsequent appearance in a competitor journal may pull significantly less because of the later timing. Furthermore a brief notice editorially about a new product giving only a few of the necessary facts will tend to pull more enquiries than an editorial which gives a full and detailed description. Indeed the journal which is so interested in a product as to give a full-scale article on the subject can be fairly sure of pulling virtually no enquiries at all. This interesting fact should be considered in relation to copywriting for an enquiry-getting advertisement.

The number of advertisements carried by a journal is by and large evidence neither for nor against its value as an advertising medium. The argument that many advertisements mean less exposure of one's own advertisement, or conversely that few advertisements mean greater exposure and therefore greater effectiveness, is unsupported by evidence. Likewise the inclusion of competitors' advertisements in a publication is only indicative of its value in advertising terms if an advertiser is confident that his own assessment of media is inferior to that of his competitors!

The list of irrational reasons for selecting media is long. It includes personal views influenced by the salesmanship of the media representative, the views of company employees assessing editorial content from an entirely different viewpoint than the customer, the opinion of the sales force or any other department.

There is in fact no substitute for objective media readership analysis and since this requires an investment in terms of formal research, whether desk or field, it is unlikely that an advertising budget which does not set aside a significant sum of money to evaluate its advertising will secure maximum value for its total advertising investment. It can be argued that in industrial advertising, a research budget of say 10 per cent total publicity expenditure is the minimum required to explore methods for maximum efficacy.

Impact in press advertising

The first requirement of an advertisement is to have the power to stop the reader—to secure attention. From that point on there occurs a series of mental processes which determine the degree of impact achieved. Factors such as advertisement size, novelty, position, frequency and subject matter will affect the impact on a person's mind. It is all too easy for advertisers who are very conscious of their own advertisements to suppose that their impact is likely to be of a much higher order than is actually the fact. From the research work carried out in the United States and to some degree in the United Kingdom there is evidence that advertisements in the trade and technical press are noticed, on average, by only a relatively small percentage of readers and that real impact is achieved with perhaps as few as 2 or 3 per cent. In some studies described in Chapter 13 on research there are indeed instances of advertisements consistently scoring zero in their readership rating. It is essential therefore to examine continuously methods of obtaining maximum effectiveness, and here the following criteria have some bearing.

CREATIVE EXPRESSION

There can be little doubt that all other factors being equal, the creative expression of the sales message—the consumer benefit—is paramount. Equally this factor is the most difficult to evaluate and quantify. As an example of this a new range of fluid power equipment was produced for which six selling features were identified. These were thought to be equally important in terms of satisfying buyers' needs, but applying the 'single selling idea' a series of six advertisements was designed, each featuring one sales point. The advertisements were couponed and designed specifically to pull enquiries. The result was that one advertisement pulled far more enquiries than any other and from this the conclusion was drawn that this selling feature must be the most important to buyers. A new campaign was designed centring on this one feature, but the result was a disastrous failure. The simple fact was that the successful advertisement had achieved its success due to its creative excellence in attracting attention, not to the selling feature.

The advertiser therefore must look to the copywriter and visualizer for those touches of inspiration which cannot be defined and yet are so decisive in the success of a campaign. There may be little an advertiser can do to stimulate such inspiration, but at least a serious effort can be made to establish a good rapport with the creative team, and to provide a full and adequate brief.

Many attempts have been made to effect some measurement of 'creative expression', particularly as perceived by readers of advertisements, namely, buyers. One of the most extensive was by G. McAleer of Florida Technological University. This examined four industry groups to determine the extent to which specific advertising propositions were regarded as valid by advertisers on the one hand and purchasers on the other. The market segments selected for study were consulting engineers, electrical contractors, architects and building contractors. A list of 48 advertising appeals was drawn up in a questionnaire and mailed to both parties in the four groupings. Respondents were asked to use a numerical scaling between $+5$ and -5 to indicate the extent to which they felt that each proposition had validity to them personally in their professional capacity.

Clearly if both parties showed a similar score (as indicated by comparing arithmetic averages) then there would be a good understanding by advertisers of the needs of their customers. Alternatively, if the ratings for a particular proposition were significantly different then there was good reason to suppose that advertisers were not as aware as they should be of the motivating factors relating to their customers. Table 4.1 is an extract from a very comprehensive listing of items, some of which have similar ratings between the two groups, and others differences which are significant.

The conclusion of the survey was 'that advertisers to each of the market segments studied did not correctly perceive the influence of advertising appeals upon the market concerned'. Such a conclusion does not imply that all companies are operating with such a lack of understanding of their customers nor indeed that in the United Kingdom market the data has a direct validity. It does, however, lead one to give consideration to carrying out a review of selling propositions to check their correct relevance.

Table 4.1 Creative expression as perceived by advertisers and buyers

Advertising appeal	Advertiser (av. mean)	Customer (av. mean)
Ease of installation	2.05	1.87
Low maintenance cost	2.30	2.61
Physical features	2.88	2.40
Reliability of the seller	2.35	2.34
Ability to keep delivery promises	1.67	2.32
Newness of product	0.63	−0.43
It is widely specified	2.53	−0.53
Testimonial by a supplier of the product	1.96	−1.08
Easy to repair	0.40	2.65
Announcement of new installation	1.51	−0.24
Automatic operation	−1.00	2.52
Increasing output	−0.48	2.76

PRE-TESTING ADVERTISEMENTS

The wider implications of advertising research will be considered later in Chapters 12 and 13. At this stage, however, serious consideration should be given to testing the 'creative proposition' to ensure that what may appear to be highly compelling and lucidly persuasive copy really is just that.

It is commonplace in consumer campaigns to pre-test advertisements, and experience has shown that there is a good correlation between such research findings and actual performance. With industrial advertising there is a widespread point of view that pre-testing is unnecessary, too complicated, and anyway costs too much. Such an argument is fallacious in that the task of an advertisement is to communicate a selling message to a potential market irrespective of cost, and if that message is not adequately received then a vital part of the marketing communications process is missing, perhaps with a disastrous effect on sales.

SIZE

The size of an advertisement must clearly influence the impact it produces. Research in this field gives some evidence, however, that this is not a linear relationship, and thus large and particularly multi-page advertisements need to be justified by other considerations. Factors which properly enter into the selection of large spaces are the nature of the sales message, the pictorial content required, prestige, and the nature of the publication and the advertisements it carries. There is no doubt that for some products and services a quarter page can be as effective as a whole page.

The importance of bleed has often been neglected. The additional cost is minimal whereas the additional area available is substantially greater. There is some indication from field research work that bleed advertisements score disproportionately higher than non-bleed, perhaps because they are so rare. Another option to consider is the use of a loose insert. Some will hold that with more than, say, one insert the readers become antagonized to the extent that they either ignore the advertising message or even build up resentment to the advertiser. Again looking to American research data, there is some evidence as in Figure 4.4 that advertising readership increases significantly by the use of inserts.

POSITION

A great deal of inconclusive and misleading research has been conducted on the importance of the position of an advertisement in a publication. In newspapers there is probably scope for being particularly selective in the positioning of an advertisement. In the trade and technical press there is little evidence to justify paying the premiums demanded for special positions even where a journal is carrying a hundred or more pages of advertising. The same doubts should also be raised about cover positions which, while undoubtedly having a high prestige connotation, may turn out to have a very low page traffic rating, particularly front covers where so often a circulation slip is attached by the librarian before a journal is circulated in a company.

FREQUENCY AND DUPLICATION

Once again there has been research in the United States which seems to indicate that if the first appearance of an advertisement is seen by, say, 10 per cent of readers, the second appearance will also be seen by 10 per cent but of substantially different readers.

This is probably an area in which a great deal more research should be carried out, particularly to establish how often an advertisement should be changed. There is a general consensus that three appearances is a good minimum and that up to six can be justified. This is borne out by

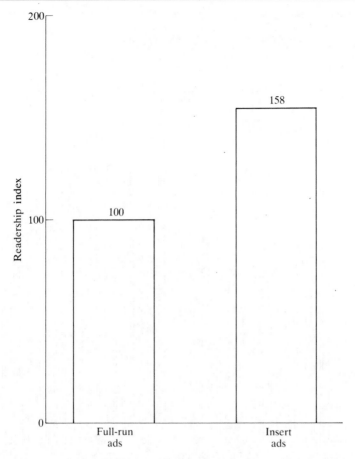

Figure 4.4   The influence of inserts (*Source:* Cahners Research Report No. 117.1)

advertisements which set out to get enquiries and therefore enable a response rate to be traced.

Frequency and duplication must often, at this stage in advertising knowledge, depend upon experience and intelligent guesswork having regard to the market share aimed for, the speed with which the message needs to be delivered, activities in other media, the frequency with which orders are placed, reminder advertising and the overall impact which it is desired to achieve. Some hard evidence is provided by an example[3] from the States of an advertisement which was repeated 41 times over a period of eleven years and produced an apparently ever-increasing number of enquiries as shown in Figure 4.5.

**Ad repeated 41 times
and still working**

The Ludlow Corporation has demonstrated, by counting enquiries,
and by running the same ad over eleven years in
Engineering News-Record that an ad can be successfully
repeated at least 41 times.

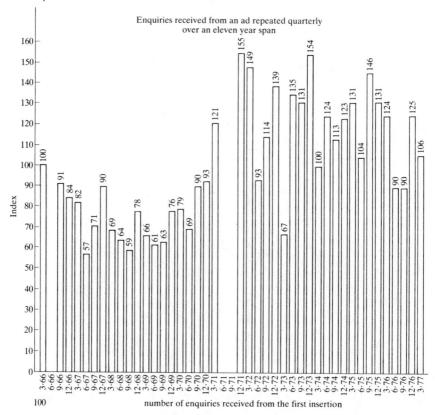

Figure 4.5 Repeat of advertisement (*Source:* McGraw-Hill Research Report No.
3043.2)

COLOUR

The effect on impact of colour depends very much upon the circumstances
and as a general rule is not nearly so important as creative expression and
product illustration. In a magazine full of colour advertisements a black-and-
white design can obtain a very high score. In a publication with no colour at
all, a multicoloured advertisement will clearly have an advantage.

Limitations and advantages

The limitation of press advertising is that, due to the excessive number of publications and the lack of precision in defining readerships, there is a strong risk of wasting large sums of money without ever realizing it.

The advantage is that extensive coverage, even saturation, of a market can be obtained with a minimum of effort—often influencing purchasing units which cannot be reached easily in any other way; which are often indeed not even known to exist.

Checklist

1. Has the potential audience for an advertisement been defined in terms of
   - (a) Size (numbers of DMUs and their purchasing powers)?
   - (b) Location?
   - (c) Market segments?
   - (d) Individual's job categories?
   - (e) Special characteristics?
   - (f) Purchasing motivation?
2. Have the proposed media been selected (a) on the basis of the information from item one and (b) in relation to authenticated readership data?
3. Has readership duplication been considered?
4. Does a particular advertisement or series (a) have a tangible objective, (b) can this be measured, (c) does it fit in with the overall marketing strategy?
5. Has a full and written brief been prepared?
6. Does the brief include
   - (a) Advertisement size?
   - (b) Frequency?
   - (c) Position?
   - (d) Number of colours?
   - (e) Essential illustrations?
   - (f) Action required?
   - (g) A means of media identification?
   - (h) Provision for measuring effectiveness?
7. Has the number, frequency and timing of advertisements been scheduled in reation to other parts of the marketing mix?

References

1. Hugh Buckner, *How British Industry Buys*, (Hutchinson, London, 1967), tables 8 and 9.
2. McGraw-Hill, *How Advertising Affects the Cost of Selling*.
3. McGraw-Hill Research Report No. 3043.2.

5.

DIRECT MAIL

Direct mail means the use of the postal services to carry a persuasive message, in any form, to a prospect. The mailing piece can be as simple as a sales letter, or a postcard. Alternatively it can be as sophisticated as a major catalogue, a complex gimmick or an expensive sample. For practical purposes, items which are distributed door to door by a commercial organization will be included under the term direct mail.

Referring back to the basic impact diagram in Chapter 2 (Fig. 2.2), direct mail is one of the major channels of persuasion available to a company for reaching a prospect and achieving maximum impact. Its importance in the marketing mix will clearly vary, depending on the nature of the product and market, from being of paramount significance (e.g. drug promotions to doctors) to being almost useless (e.g. promotion of nuclear power plants to the Central Electricity Generating Board).

Special advantages

Direct mail enables the user to aim a message at a precisely defined prospect, and to place the mailing piece in front of that prospect at the exact time required, and, indeed, as soon and as often as is wished. Moreover a mailing piece has an advantage over a press advertisement or editorial item in that for a moment at least it occupies a solus position, gains greater attention and therefore greater impact. There is no absolute restriction on size, number of words, colour, illustrations or quality of reproduction. Hence there is a good opportunity to put across an argument in full. A further benefit is that since it can be addressed directly and personally it can be so designed as to produce a response, and where this is a particular objective a very high rate of replies can be obtained.

Direct mail is a versatile tool which can be varied widely in magnitude, direction and frequency; can be brought into use virtually overnight and, sometimes most important of all, can be an extremely cheap method of communication.

Disadvantages

The advantage of direct mail, that it aims at a precise target, is also one of its limitations. In Chapter 2, dealing with strategy, the importance of defining the market in detail was stressed as was the large number of purchasing influences likely to be involved in the placement of an order. For direct mail to be fully effective it is essential to be able to define precisely the audience to be influenced. This means broad market categories, companies within these categories, plants within the companies and people within the plants.

Definition of target audiences cannot be overstressed. Just as with press advertising, it is pointless to develop a first-class proposition if it is placed in front of a non-prospect.

A further limiting factor in practice is the lack of experience which promotion people in general have of direct mail, coupled with the fact that it is complex, difficult to set up, easy to go wrong, and perhaps not yet developed to the state of relative sophistication found in other media. While this generalization cannot be applied, say, to the promotion of pharmaceuticals or to certain specific products, for instance *Reader's Digest*, it is nevertheless true of most industrial operations. Here, however, is the opportunity to gain the edge on competition. There can be little doubt that in trade and technical campaigns, direct mail is going to play an increasingly important role.

Mailing lists

Establishment of an effective mailing list is the prerequisite of a mailing campaign, and upon it will rest the success or failure of a promotion.

The marketing strategy will have defined the markets, their sizes and locations, their relative importance, and the key people to influence. The promotion strategy will have defined the role of direct mail and which of the various targets it is to be used to attack and with what intensity. Most important it will also have defined exactly and quantitatively the objectives of the direct mail operation.

It will be useful to identify the principal sources of direct mail lists, but while doing so it is important to stress that there are usually available in any campaign a wide range of special sources which a creative mind can explore. Careful thought and consultation can be most rewarding here.

SALESPEOPLE'S CALL LISTS

Where a direct mail campaign is required to support a field selling drive it is vital to incorporate the salespeople's call lists. Indeed with some product groups in which the market is compact and easy to define, the call list may be all that is required. If so, however, it is still necessary to have a foolproof system of feedback from the sales force covering changes immediately they occur, and to achieve this the full co-operation and sympathy both of sales managers and sales representatives is required.

The limitation of such a list is that salespeople, however good, cannot always unearth all prospective companies, far less determine accurately which individuals in an organization influence purchasing decisions. Even if such people can be identified, a salesperson may not be able to make contact with them and accordingly they may not be on the call list.

ENQUIRIES

From the publicity activities in which a company engages come a variety of enquiries. These are usually obtained at considerable cost and are a major source of contacts for a mailing campaign. They often serve to supplement the sales call list by identifying within a prospect company individuals who, while not strictly 'purchasers', are very much 'influencers'.

It is not uncommon to include the need for enquiries as a means of list building as one of the objectives of a campaign. An example in press advertising is to include a specific offer of a brochure or a sample; similarly at exhibitions to record meticulously all callers on a stand whether they have some immediate requirement or not.

CUSTOMERS

The nature of a campaign may not require that existing customers shall be included but in other circumstances they must head the list as a top priority. Once again, it is not just the person that signs the order who must be reached, but all the other individuals who contribute to the purchasing decision.

DIRECTORIES

These are particularly useful when entering a new market where a body of knowledge and a range of contacts do not already exist. There may be severe limitations since all directories are well out of date before they are published, many of them are not comprehensive, and some of them are substantially inaccurate. An example of how easy it is to waste money here is with the use of what is probably the best-known business directory to promote a particular training programme to marketing directors and the like. In one of the lists supplied 53 per cent of the names and addresses had an error in them, ranging from a wrong spelling to a person who had left the company five years previously.

Where names of executives are included, this can be of great value: where they are not, a good deal of research is probably going to be necessary to personalize the list in order to make it effective.

EXHIBITIONS

A list of exhibitors is an excellent supplementary source of prospects within a given market. This can very usefully and easily be extended by setting up a survey in which visits are made to each stand and representatives questioned as to who in a certain company is likely to be interested in a particular product. The degree of co-operation that can be achieved, particularly at a slack time, can be very high, almost total.

A new opportunity which is being created by certain exhibition organizers is to invite each visitor to identify himself by filling out an enquiry card. This builds a bank of purchasing influences which is likely to be more extensive than any other method, but a fairly disciplined scrutiny of job category is necessary here.

HOUSE MAGAZINES

From the point of view of direct mail a benefit of external house magazines is that over a period of time they build up a circulation list which often includes many people behind the purchasing scenes whom a company wishes to influence. Additions to the circulation of a house magazine should automatically be considered for addition to the promotional mailing list.

PUBLISHERS

An increasing number of publishers are exploiting their circulation lists by hiring them to advertisers and others for direct mail. As with all lists it is important to be cautious about their value and, as far as trade and technical journals are concerned, the circulation lists are not always as extensive and accurate as is sometimes thought. Many are often directed to libraries, academics, students—indeed to all manner of non-commercial people.

TRADE ASSOCIATIONS AND INSTITUTIONS

Such bodies often publish, or will provide, a comprehensive list of members.

NEW APPOINTMENTS AND NEWS

A large number of publications carry news items of new appointments which clearly identify prospects for a mailing list.

There are a number of commercial organizations which provide an extensive service for direct mail users. The service usually offers some hundreds of specialized lists which are in effect available for hire; the mechanics of addressing, enclosing, franking and posting the mailing pieces; a creative design studio; also sometimes a research unit to help in list building if one is not already in existence.

There is little doubt that with the right degree of co-operation and understanding, a direct mail house is very useful: indeed sometimes almost essential. It is necessary, however, for a client to realize that with many campaigns in hand at any one moment it is not possible for a direct mail company to give the kind of attention to minute detail that the client would himself, and it is therefore important to give a most thorough briefing with written confirmation in order to avoid misunderstandings.

Finally it should be realized that with very few exceptions a mailing house has access to only the same sources of lists as anyone else. Given time a company can usually produce a better list itself. What it probably cannot do is process it more efficiently.

COMPUTER SERVICES AND LIST BROKERS

With the widespread availability of computers and word-processing machines it is likely that direct mail will become more widespread in use. This is because the development and maintenance of in-house mailing lists has become much more simple, as has the reproduction of personalized letters. Coding and fast retrieval is now available to companies with only the most elementary equipment.

Computers have also become part of the standard equipment for direct mail houses which have become more sophisticated in the storage of and access to, their mailing lists. Some outside services have specialized to the extent that they handle only mailing lists. Such list brokers in practice are in the business of simply selling labels.

UNUSUAL SOURCES

For each product group and each market there may well be a variety of unusual sources of lists. Announcements of births and marriages for instance, or graduations at university. Co-operation with complementary trades can provide a source such as the names of people buying turfs as a sales lead to a company selling lawn-mowers. Other useful sources might be shareholders, rating lists, return guarantee cards and records of companies.

Campaign planning

Having defined the market and identified the names and addresses of people who will influence the purchasing decision, it is now necessary to consider the form which the campaign should take. A number of factors need to be examined in order to formulate the most effective campaign mix. The number of shots is going to depend on how complex the sales message is and also the percentage return which is set as a target. If 3 per cent is required (a common but highly misleading norm) then one shot may be adequate. Two shots would possibly bring 6 per cent, or maybe 5 per cent, since the law of diminishing returns clearly applies, particularly on a short time base. If there are six major selling features, and these are not well known, it will be necessary perhaps to send out six shots.

The same general guidelines as used in a press advertising campaign clearly apply but with the additional opportunities of attention, space and colour. In the end it is experience which determines the final plan. This is not the subjective experience of whim or fancy, but rather the building up of a set of data relating to the reaction of prospects to a given mailing technique. One of the interesting characteristics of a direct mail operation is the opportunity to carry out test mailings to small samples of a given list. In this way the likely reaction of the entire list can be determined before becoming committed to the total campaign or indeed the total expenditure.

A direct mail shot can vary from a cheaply duplicated circular to a personally signed letter, to an impressive colour brochure, to a bottle of whisky, to a quarter-sectioned hydraulic cylinder weighing fifty pounds and costing rather more. It is all a matter of deciding what impact it is required to achieve and what is necessary in order to achieve it. Given adequately experienced and able creative people, there is considerable scope for novelty and therefore impact, particularly in comparison with press advertising which is limited in size and material. In direct mail, one can select from a number of materials, choose from a variety of sizes, use three dimensions, and even sound, smell and chemical reaction. A further extremely useful aspect of mailing is that an actual sample can be sent out of the product itself.

The use of the mail is not fundamentally a requirement of direct mail. Circular distribution has already been mentioned though this is clearly more relevant to consumer promotions. Maybe the industrial equivalent is to use telex, or even fax, for distributing an advertising message. This is fast, accurate and likely to have high impact. Care needs to be exercised as recipients could regard this as intruding on their privacy, much as they react to telephone selling.

Whatever form a shot may take, however, it must be emphasized that it does not begin to achieve purchasing impact until it reaches the right person.

An undirected leaflet in a personally addressed envelope may be put in the right file in the mailing room, but without the envelope the leaflet is directionless and will end up who knows where? An individually typed letter addressed to ICI and starting Dear Sirs, may just as well not be sent at all. Similarly a letter to the Chief Buyer of Unilever is hardly likely to reach the person one is trying to influence. It is essential to determine carefully and precisely whom the message is to reach, whether by name or job title, then to address both the envelope and the enclosure to that person.

TIMING

As with press advertising there is an opportunity to achieve a cumulative build up of awareness by sending out a series of shots. The actual number will be determined by factors mentioned earlier. A further consideration is the period of time over which the campaign is likely to extend. If for a year, and if continuity is required, then it may emerge that a monthly interval is an optimum time. If for a longer period, say several years, then perhaps a quarterly interval is adequate, as with a house magazine. Even less frequent mailings can be effective: for instance a calendar or a diary once a year.

It may be necessary to achieve results quickly and in this case the campaign can comprise a series of rapid shots at weekly or even at daily intervals. When considering this kind of saturation it is useful to recall the personal nature of direct mail. One of the pitfalls, which is also one of the strengths, is the fact that the recipient of a direct mail piece tends, rightly, to regard it as an individual and personal communication from the sender. Consequently the receipt of five letters from the same firm on the same subject on five consecutive days may achieve impact, but may well alienate the prospect. Similarly a generalization which does not apply to a particular person in a press advertisement may well cause offence if written into a letter. For instance, a letter inviting an existing customer to try out a product which he or she has been using for years is a good way of losing the business which already exists.

In calculating timing it is useful to put oneself in the place of the buyer and consider the most likely reaction to a proposed plan.

A good deal of emphasis is sometimes placed on the best day of the week and the best time of the year to send out direct mail. It is argued for instance that Monday is a bad day both psychologically and because it is a heavy day for incoming post; also that Friday is a bad day because people's minds are turning towards the weekend. Another argument is that August is a bad month and, of course Christmas time is poor. In modern marketing there is little place for conjecture. It is the function of a direct mail practitioner to accept such theories as possible, but to test them, to verify them or reject them; Christmas time after all is a very good time for Christmas trees.

COSTS

Costs, absolute and relative, are vital factors when establishing the advertising and indeed the marketing mix.

A full page in a technical magazine for instance might cost £1000 given a circulation of 10 000. This would be a cost per copy of 10p.

There may well be more than one reader per copy which brings the cost down to say 4p per reader. It is known, however, that a 10 per cent 'noted' rating is a reasonable average, i.e. only one in ten readers will actually notice the advertisement, and of these perhaps a third will read most of the copy. This can put the cost of real communication up to £1.20 per prospect.

Going to the other extreme, the cost of getting a selling argument across by means of a salesperson may well be £100 per prospect, or more. An exhibition may produce results at a slightly lower figure, but both these situations afford the opportunity of face-to-face selling, which is likely to be more effective.

How does direct mail stand up in comparison with other channels of communication? Distribution of a cheap circular to households can be done at around 30p per unit. Using the postal services and a well-produced letter, maybe including a simple leaflet, the cost is going to be of the order of 50p. Thereafter the costs rise as the mailing increases in quality and sophistication.

If a campaign is designed largely to obtain sales leads a different set of figures will be obtained. It is not uncommon in press advertising of capital goods to find the cost of an enquiry ranging between £5 and £50. With direct mail a 5 per cent response where the unit mailing cost was 40p would result in a cost per enquiry of £8.

It may fairly be said that, all things being equal, there is not much to choose between press advertising and direct mail in terms of cost. If this is so, however, it is strange that so many promotional budgets allocate very much larger sums of money to press. One reason may be that direct mail is a good deal more complex and difficult to set up and that it is far more likely to go wrong. Another reason is simply that insufficient attention has been given to the value of this medium in relation to others and that its results have not been so carefully measured and analysed.

Setting targets

Before the position of measuring and assessing results can be reached, it is necessary to set targets. Just as, in an efficient business, management by objectives is an accepted way of operating, so in direct mail the starting point must be to define the objectives—in measurable, meaningful terms.

As with press advertising the objectives must be realistic. There will be occasions when an increase in sales can result directly from a mailing operation, but more often in industrial promotions the effect on sales is going to be indirect and less tangible. Thus it is necessary to set a target which can be more directly related. Perhaps the intention is to get sales leads which, in turn, will enable the sales force to convert them into orders. In this situation it may be unrealistic to measure the efficacy of the direct mail campaign in terms of sales. The product may not be right, or the price; alternatively the leads may not be followed up efficiently. If the primary objective is to secure sales leads, then the campaign must be assessed in these terms.

In the course of time it will be possible, for a given type of campaign, to establish norms of performance. These will vary considerably between one product group and another, and between markets, but even if a norm has not been established it is nevertheless valuable to set a figure against which performance can be measured.

A mailing campaign to a thousand prospects may take as an objective 'to secure a hundred sales leads'. This gives to the executive concerned, and the copywriter and visualizer, a clear statement of what the operation is all about. It also indicates to sales management exactly the role this campaign is intended to play. It facilitates a cost comparison with other media and this has a long-term value in shaping future media mixes. As the campaign proceeds it becomes apparent whether or not the objective is likely to be achieved or whether the operation needs to be strengthened, cut back, or indeed stopped, to avoid wasting money either because it is totally successful or a complete failure.

Obtaining sales leads is, perhaps, easy: a campaign designed to strengthen a company's reputation may be more difficult. This does not, however, lessen the need for setting targets. Indeed, with image-building campaigns, unless a plan is made beforehand to measure the results, it will be impossible to begin to evaluate the effect of the expenditure. In the case of such a campaign the objective must be quantified even if very broadly, for instance 'to be rated among the top three suppliers of industrial paints'. This will necessitate a minimum of two investigations: first to find out the present rating and then in due course the change in position after the campaign.

A campaign may set out to establish a realization among buyers that a certain brand-name connotes a particular product—and often a product with pre-defined benefits. This is a classic softening-up operation before the field force goes in, and calls for a saturation campaign which will continue until the objective has been achieved.

For every direct mail campaign then there must be a specific purpose, formally stated and in terms which can be measured. The methods of measurement to be adopted will be an integral part of the plan.

There is some confusion as to the difference between direct mail (DM) and direct response marketing (DRM): indeed some people regard the terms as synonymous. This is unfortunate since they are fundamentally different.

Direct response marketing is an activity in which prospects are invited to place an order directly as a response to an offer in an advertisement or a direct mail shot. The order is placed directly with the marketing organization without a salesperson as intermediary, and it is dispatched directly to the customer by post or freight without the intermediary of a retail outlet. There is also another term in use, direct response advertising, which refers to any advertisement that seeks to secure an order directly.

Direct response marketing is said to be the fastest growing sector of marketing activities, and many examples are to be found in the Sunday colour magazines and in the Saturday editions of national newspapers. These, however, are all in the consumer goods field and so far there is not much evidence of its suitability for industrial goods.

Checklist

1. Have the target audiences been defined?
2. Are adequate mailing lists available?
3. Can the people be (a) named, or (b) designated?
4. Do you plan to use a direct mail agency. If so, have you checked (a) the origin and (b) the nature of their lists, and (c) whether they are up to date, accurate and comprehensive?
5. In producing the brief have you defined

   (a) The objective of the campaign?
   (b) The number of shots?
   (c) The form they should take?
   (d) Frequency and timing?
   (e) Use of reply-paid material?
   (f) A follow-up to a reply?

6. Is there a system for names to be deleted from the list as replies are received?
7. Have quantified targets been set?
8. Are the means for comparison of performance clearly specified?
9. Has the field force been given advance notice of the campaign?
10. Has consideration been given to an initial test mailing?

6.

EXHIBITIONS

In the United Kingdom there are hundreds of exhibitions of interest to industrial companies and, if overseas opportunities are taken into account, the number extends into the thousands. These vary considerably in size and scope from a small show with perhaps twenty or thirty modest stands to vast international fairs with a thousand or more exhibitors covering a product range across the entire industrial sector.

The significance of exhibitions in the industrial promotional budget may not be great but, looking at some of the larger events, it is evident that the individual expenditure on many stands is of a high order indeed. While a budget of a hundred or so pounds may be possible with some of the smaller exhibitions, the costs rise easily into tens of thousands with the bigger shows.

It is strange to find that so little is known about the usefulness of exhibitions, that they are so often an expression of faith rather than fact, with such factors as size of stand and budget determined intuitively by some senior executive. Evidence of this is to be found by discussing the matter with exhibitors and is confirmed by the random way in which in one year a company invests in a substantial stand, next year pulls out altogether, then later comes back with an even larger display.

There tends to be a progression in the evolution of a particular exhibition rather like the life-cycle of a new product. Initially an exhibition satisfies a need which as it grows causes the exhibition to expand. This attracts more visitors and thus more exhibitors, producing a cumulative growth. A further variable at work, at least in the United Kingdom, is the force of competitive prestige. In order to impress customers, exhibitors vie with each other to have the grandest and largest stands and, as this factor develops, so the expense rises until a few of the leaders suddenly realize that the whole thing is uneconomical, and drop out. The example having been set, others follow suit, and the exhibition goes into a period of decline in which it may stagnate, disintegrate, fragment or disappear altogether.

There is probably more money wasted at exhibitions than in any other medium, a paradox since fundamentally the concept of an exhibition is to save money by getting face to face with large numbers of buyers in greater numbers per salesperson-day than could ever be achieved on the road.

The exhibition industry itself may be partly to blame. It breaks down into three broad groups: the organizers, the venue proprietors and the contractors.

Exhibitions are arranged by a wide variety of organizations ranging from commercial exhibition companies to trade associations, publishers and learned bodies. Their function is to hire a hall, then let out spaces to exhibitors at a rate which will bring a profit. Beyond this they may involve themselves in conducting pre-publicity and providing some service during the show. Only the most progressive organizers will set up facilities for providing intelligence for exhibitors on the number and nature of visitors, their length of stay, their attitudes towards different stands and exhibits, their wants and criticisms. Furthermore there is little effort to discipline exhibitors into containing costs by, for instance, restricting stand sizes or imposing shell schemes, as in common practice in the United States. Exhibition organizers sometimes play a passive and short-term role which is not helpful to exhibitors and in the long term does not help themselves.

Exhibition halls in the United Kingdom are often inadequate, and this, though perhaps not the fault of anyone in particular, points the need for exhibitors to assess carefully the value of each venue. Exhibition contractors, the people who construct the stands, are involved in very high labour costs, with the result that a stand built to last for a week will often cost more than a luxury house. There is considerable room for improving the cost-effectiveness of exhibitions and there is little doubt that the exhibition industry as a whole could make an important contribution. This is largely outside the control of an individual exhibitor, but this should not preclude collective action by groups of companies. Moreover, to be aware of areas of high expense at least enables a company to exert maximum control and scrutiny in obtaining good value for money.

Exhibitors

Before turning to the positive role of exhibitions in the marketing operation, it is unfortunately necessary to press this negative theme a little further by extending it to the exhibitor. Earlier in this book it has been pointed out that much in marketing communications has hitherto been intuitive, without any logical objective, and without any data to support decisions. Exhibitions are equally susceptible to this danger, as is borne out by a booklet from the Institute of Directors[1] in which what it terms dangers and temptations to exhibitors are set out.

1. An exhibition should not be looked upon as an isolated event.
2. Never enter an exhibition—no matter how inexpensive it appears to be— unless it fulfils some clearly defined marketing objective.

3. An exhibition is not the occasion for giving a once-off opportunity to polish up a tarnished corporate image.
4. Prestige is never a sufficient reason for appearing at exhibitions.
5. Don't base exhibition plans on the theory 'if the competitors are there we have to be'.
6. Don't try one exhibition just 'to see how it goes'.
7. An exhibition should not be looked upon as an opportunity for senior members of the company to have a free holiday or a booze-up with their old cronies—it is an occasion for the people in the firing line, no matter how junior they may be, to do a hard-hitting job of work.
8. Don't exhibit at all if you have to do it on the cheap—in money or executive time. This is not to say that many exhibitions are not inexpensive—but be sure you assign adequate money for the job expected to be done.
9. Remember—it's ten times easier to start exhibiting than to stop, once you have an exhibition programme under way.

To the above 'rules' there are a number of other points worthy of consideration with a view to increasing the effectiveness of an exhibition.

10. Regard an exhibition stand as a three-dimensional advertisement.
11. Build in really effective corporate identification.
12. Pay special attention to lighting the key points of the stand and to the writing of copy panels.
13. Design a single focal point visually and in terms of traffic flow.
14. Allow for staffing at the level of approximately two people per 10 square metres.
15. Plan in advance for fast post-exhibition follow-up.
16. At each show make a formal evaluation of competitors' activities.

Inter-media comparisons

An exhibition is simply a channel of persuasion which is available as an ingredient in the marketing mix. It must therefore fit into the marketing plan and have a specific purpose, or not be used at all. It has certain characteristics which make it more or less attractive depending upon the requirements of the campaign. It is useful to examine these and in so doing relate them to other media with which it will be required to combine.

SELLING EFFICIENCY

Fundamentally an exhibition should be highly efficient in selling terms since it assembles in one place maybe tens of thousands of buyers who if they can be attracted to a stand will facilitate a 'call rate' far in excess of normal. A salesman on a stand may well talk to forty or fifty buyers in the course of a day—a factor ten times greater than the norm.

IMPACT

Compared for instance with press advertising, impact is obviously higher, since an exhibition has the opportunity to compress into one activity the whole selling operation—attention, interest, persuasion, desire to purchase and indeed the placing of an order.

DEMONSTRATION

Here an exhibition scores even over sales visits, since with heavy equipment in particular the opportunity exists to give far more comprehensive demonstrations than can ever be achieved by a travelling salesperson.

TIME-SCALE

This acts in two ways: firstly one may well have to wait a year or two for an exhibition to take place; secondly, setting this factor aside, an exhibition can provide the chance to influence a very large part of a market in a very short space of time.

MARKET PENETRATION

Having regard to the complex nature of the decision-making units in industrial companies, exhibitions often bring to the surface many of the hidden influences in the purchasing process—the engineer, chemist, designer, factory manager, as well as directors.

COMPANY IMAGE

The company can be presented in all its aspects at one and the same time, enabling a customer to see it as a whole—its products, manufacturing facilities, subsidiaries and associates, and most important its senior management.

MARKET DEVELOPMENT

A unique opportunity is presented for uncovering a wide variety of uses for products which lead to the identification of new markets. Similarly an interchange of views on products often leads to modifications which give rise to the development of new products.

COST

It is important to cost an exhibition fully, to add together rental, stand construction, staff, promotional material, entertaining, pre-publicity and so on. An unsophisticated show of a few hundred pounds can have a very high degree of cost-effectiveness. One costing say seventy or eighty thousand pounds needs a great deal of justification. The real cost however is the unit cost, that is, the cost per enquiry or the cost per contact and this in relation to the unit costs of other media.

Setting the objectives

These must be set down in writing as part of the overall promotional strategy and must incorporate targets that are precise, and capable of being attained and measured. For instance an exhibition may be chosen as the launching platform for a new product, say a piece of equipment for food processing. There may be 500 companies who could buy this product and, with perhaps four people likely to be involved in the buying decision, one arrives at a total of 2000 people to be contacted. The setting of the target will in fact be determined by the nature of the exhibition, in that a popular and well-established one may well be visited by representatives of half the industry or more whereas a smaller or untried one may attract only a very small percentage.

Further factors in setting targets in this instance are the interest of the product or service itself and the prestige of the company. These will determine the willingness of people to put themselves out to attend the show and visit the stand.

In the light of such factors and perhaps with previous experience the first target may be to make face-to-face contact with 500 people who represent potential customers and to secure an entrée for a subsequent sales visit. A secondary goal could be to obtain the general goodwill of the industry as a whole by distributing to interested parties 5000 leaflets describing a new piece of equipment.

Over and above the primary objective of an exhibition stand will be a number of supplementary requirements which should be catered for only so long as they do not act as a distraction or as a negative influence. The broad range of company activities may need to be put across to show how it backs up a new product. The extent to which modern plant and machinery is used may be another feature, with examples of accuracy, reliability and quality control. Provision may be made for conducting marketing research; perhaps entertaining facilities are needed for customers in other product categories.

At the other extreme, the need may be to provide first-class entertainment for only a small number of very large customers. Such an example could be the Farnborough Air Show where, frequently, there is little emphasis on products, but rather a very well set up 'soft sell' operation in which VIP customers are provided with pleasant facilities to relax and enjoy the display with hard business left to another time and place. The objective in this instance may be to provide an opportunity for 150 top customers to meet the chairman and to spend one of a number of agreeable afternoons with him.

Planning an exhibition

Having defined the objectives of an exhibition in quantitative terms it is necessary to build into the event a maximum of efficiency in order to achieve the required result at least cost. This can be planned by examining every stage in the development of an exhibition promotion.

Certainly a primary factor in participating in an exhibition is to capitalize on what may be described as a captive audience. The audience, however, is rarely captive in the sense that cinema viewers are; indeed their movements along a gangway are often fleeting and transitory; an attractive stand helps somewhat to overcome this.

It is worth while to regard the established visitors, who will come anyway, as a bonus which adds to the effectiveness of the operation, but the essential task for an exhibitor is to take all possible steps to ensure that his key prospective customers are notified in advance of what will be on show, how much their presence will be welcomed, and the ways in which they will stand to benefit.

An exhibition stand can justify a separate campaign of its own, designed to obtain visits by the right people defined in the marketing plan. This calls for the usual letter stickers, advertisement inserts, preview editorials and a plan showing where the stand is located, but this is what everyone else is already doing. A good deal more is required if the full benefits are to be obtained, and this calls for a campaign of its own using all suitable channels of persuasion—invitations from a director, backed up by personal contact from the sales force, special press advertising, a direct mail build-up and some special incentive.

The fact is however that many firms do little individually to publicize their events. Evidence of this is to be found in a piece of research conducted in the United States but with general application anywhere (Fig. 6.1).

Just what is required will depend on the objectives of the exhibition stand, and as has been said earlier these will be quantified, thus providing a basis for developing the campaign plan, and also eventually a market against which the exhibition can be evaluated.

It is only when 'to have 500 potential buyers call upon our stand' has been written down and agreed that the size of the task becomes apparent. The

Pre-show promotion techniques (83% of all companies did some pre-show promotion)

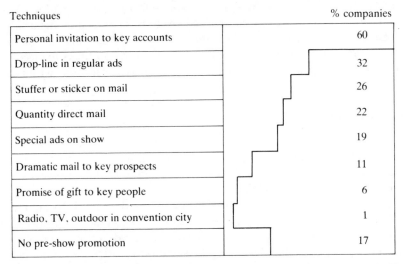

Techniques	% companies
Personal invitation to key accounts	60
Drop-line in regular ads	32
Stuffer or sticker on mail	26
Quantity direct mail	22
Special ads on show	19
Dramatic mail to key prospects	11
Promise of gift to key people	6
Radio. TV. outdoor in convention city	1
No pre-show promotion	17

Figure 6.1   Pre-show promotion techniques in the United States (*Source:* Trade Show Bureau Research Report Study No 4 (United States, 1980)

exhibition campaign plan can only then be put in hand and tailored carefully to match the need—no more and no less.

SITE AND SIZE

An examination of any exhibition hall will bring to light the fact that some areas are popular while others are not. What is missing is factual data on the traffic flow at various places in a hall at various times. This is vital and one should look to exhibition organizers to supply this information. In its absence, it must rest with the exhibitor to extract his own information, such as traffic flow in main and subsidiary gangways, and in upper floors as compared with the ground floor. Interviews with visitors can for instance establish whether they visited the gallery, how much time they spent in the hall altogether and how valuable they found the exhibition. Research can easily be extended into determining what other channels of persuasion they are exposed to, for instance which trade magazines they read. Such information enables one to judge the relationship between a given exhibition and other media including, of course, other exhibitions.

As to the size of a stand, the answer is simply to make it as small as possible consistent with the laid-down objectives. Too much regard is probably paid to highly subjective comparisons with the size and appearance of competitors' stands, a factor which is probably much less significant to the visitor than the exhibitor. If, of course, the objective is primarily to impress upon people that a company is the largest and most important in the industry, then a large and impressive stand could be justified.

It is important to begin by listing what facilities are essential and what are the minimum areas required, rather than first determining the square footage and then fitting things in as best one can. The shape of available sites is often an important consideration, and the number of open sides can be a vital factor, if only because an island stand has up to four times the display area of a wall stand.

DESIGN

Closely related to size and site is the design of a stand: indeed it is difficult to see how a stand can be efficiently conceived without some regard first being given to layout if not design.

It has been said that an exhibition stand should be regarded as a three-dimensional advertisement. It follows that the design should be tested in the same way, having regard to the fact that its cost can well be considerably greater than that of an advertisement. What is the 'single selling idea', what eye-catching headline is needed, what should the body copy say, and who should write it, and what illustration should be used? It is strange that the layout of a stand, the words on copy panels and the products and illustrations are often left to in-company staff to determine and produce, whereas for an advertisement a whole battalion of specialists will be employed.

A number of skills therefore need to be brought to bear since a stand involves construction, décor, advertising messages or selling copy, display, as well as an optimum environment for face-to-face selling. Too often it is evident that only a number of these aspects has received adequate consideration, for example, the large number of people who will walk past the stand, but will not be prepared to step on it and thus become exposed to the attention of sales staff. For these people, usually the majority, it is vital that the design be in the form of a three-dimensional advertisement. It must incorporate a means of attracting attention, it must convey at a distance, and at a glance, a good selling message which will stimulate interest, and it must follow this with descriptive and selling copy which will cause a person to want to read more and to enquire for further information. To a person concerned with advertisement design, such an approach may be second nature and in any case there will be close co-operation with a copywriter whose very function it is to express selling messages in a crisp compelling manner. Exhibition designers may sometimes be primarily specialists in architecture and décor rather than advertising, and the copy is more often than not written by a sales manager or a member of the advertising department who would not lay claim to being an expert copywriter. Yet the space to be filled will cost considerably more than an equivalent press advertisement, or even a campaign.

The layout of a stand is critical to its success in terms of its laid down objectives. Does the stand need to be designed so as to attract a maximum of visitors to it? In which case it must be open and inviting. Does it alternatively have to function primarily as a meeting point for important customers who will relax and refresh themselves in the convivial company of senior members of staff? That may call for a largely closed-in stand where access is open to a carefully selected and screened number of people. Perhaps a major objective is to distribute a large number of leaflets to visitors, in which case it just isn't good enough to lay out the leaflets in whatever vacant space there happens to be. No, the whole stand design in that case must be centred around making it as easy as possible for the passer-by to pick up a leaflet. It's the equivalent of a reply-paid coupon in an advertisement.

For designers to have the best chance of producing a stand which will be effective it is important that their briefing should be brought fully into the overall objectives of the exhibition and be provided with a complete list of facilities required, products to be exhibited, displays to be featured, and finally every single word of copy with an indication of emphasis and dominance of each part.

The sequence of events which should be followed is agreement on layout, visuals, a model if necessary, then working drawings and specification. Each stage must be considered and approved in detail if extra costs are to be avoided. If top management are going to express a point of view, it is now that this should take place before any construction is started.

STAND ADMINISTRATION AND STAFFING

It will be found most effective to designate one senior executive as stand manager for the whole period of the show, and for that person to have a written brief. The job will entail achieving the written objectives and it is only fair therefore that he or she should be involved at an early stage in the development of the stand. Such a person will in effect be the captain of the ship, responsible for motivating sales staff, maintaining discipline, looking to stand cleanliness and maintenance, ensuring an adequate supply of literature, and the hundred and one things that go to make the stand a dynamic part of a marketing operation.

It is surprising how often the staff are not given an adequate briefing on their responsibilities and functions. It is enlightening to go to any exhibition and visit a series of stands in order to assess the level of sales service. It is unlikely that any attention will be given in anything other than a minority of cases and generally speaking the larger the stand the poorer the service. Yet it is elementary to include in the exhibition briefing the instruction (always assuming this is desirable) that everyone stepping on to a stand should be greeted with an offer of help, indeed that anyone even showing an interest from the gangway should be given some attention.

The failure of sales staff to perform effectively on an exhibition stand has been well explained in a feature published by *Industrial Marketing*.[2]

> The sales situation at a trade show is the reverse of a field sales call—the prospect comes to you. You have a fraction of the normal time to present your facts. The salesperson has to make more presentations per hour than he or she might make in a day in the field.
>
> Trade show selling is a different sell, and many salespeople simply don't know how to sell in a trade show. They feel like salt water fish that have been placed in a fresh water lake and have difficulty adapting in order to survive.
>
> It's a frightening change. A rapid presentation style has to be adopted. An adjustment must be made to the environmental change. There is seldom the security of an appointment call or sales schedule. A change in priorities must be made. A seasoned salesperson with a good list of steady clients is suddenly faced with a new 'cold call' fear.
>
> Is it any wonder that when the sales rep's regular customer comes into the exhibit, the sales rep may expand the visiting time in order to avoid the unpleasantness of the trade show's difficult environment?

Exhibitionitis

This is an illness that everyone visiting an exhibition has had but without realizing that it had a name and was well recognized by exhibition professionals. It not only affects visitors, it can also play havoc with exhibitors.

Simply stated, anyone at an exhibition will, after the first hour or so, begin to feel weary of standing or walking to such an extent that his or her normal business drive will give way to an increasingly urgent desire to sit down.

This is an important threat, and an even more important opportunity. The stand can be designed in such a way that staff members can be seated without appearing to have withdrawn from giving service to customers. Alternatively a roster can be drawn up which allows for periods of relaxation. And then for customers a seating arrangement can be made such that without feeling committed or cornered a visitor can sit and relax while discussing his or her particular interest.

'Are you sitting comfortably?' is a slogan which is well worth considering seriously at any exhibition, large or small.

Budgeting

Arriving at an effective and yet economic budget for an exhibition is both difficult and complex. There are of course some short cuts but these do not necessarily produce the best results. They include:

1. What can we afford?
2. What did we spend last year?
3. How much are our competitors spending?
4. Percentage of anticipated sales.

These and other factors are all worthy of consideration, but perhaps the most logical approach is what is known as the task method of budgeting as described in Chapter 3. Here the 'task' to be achieved is analysed in some detail, i.e. a listing of specific objectives. Then in conjunction with the stand designer an outline is produced of what is essential for the achievement of those objectives. This outline covers stand location, size of stand, type of construction, style of presentation, special features and any other requirements. This then gives the minimum requirement and provides the basis of competitive quotations for stand construction.

From research conducted on behalf of British Business Press (1987) a very interesting breakdown of typical exhibition costs was produced. These are given in Table 6.1.

Table 6.1 Typical exhibition costs. Example 1 is a 30 m² shell-scheme stand, portable exhibits. Example 2 is a 60 m² purpose-built stand, heavy exhibits

	Example 1	Example 2
1. Stand space	3600	6000
2. Stand construction	400	6000
3. Transporting and erecting exhibits	200	1000
4. Stand graphics	800	1500
5. Furniture, flowers, power, telephone, drinks, cleaning, etc.	700	1200
6. Invitations/mailings to prospects	300	500
7. Catalogue and other advertising	1000	2000
8. Leaflets for distribution from stand	500	1500
9. Entertaining costs	500	1000
10. Staff travel subsistence	2000	4000
11. Temporary staff	200	400
12. Unforeseen extras	500	1000
13. Internal meeting hours	1000	2000
Total costs per exhibition	£11 700	£28 100

Memorability

Some very interesting work has been done in the United States on the memorability of an exhibition stand.[3] Its purpose has been to measure just how long an exhibit will remain in the memory of a visitor: also to find what factors affect the degree of memorability.

As can be seen from Figure 6.2 an exhibit is remembered long after the event and indeed it can probably be concluded that exhibitions have a longer retention time than any other medium.

Memorability drops off to around 70 per cent at about five or six weeks but then increases to 75 per cent and remains at that level from eight weeks through fourteen weeks. Exhibitors probably are following up on their enquiries with literature and personal sales calls which reinforce the exhibit memorability.

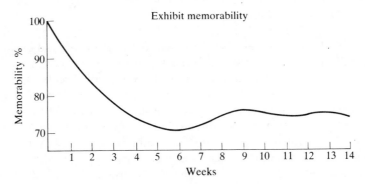

Figure 6.2   Exhibit memorability

Stand staff performance affects memorability the most because the personal contact with visitors creates a strong impact. Stands achieving a high degree of person-to-person contact had higher memorability scores than others. Also the level of awareness of a company was a strong influence on the degree to which visitors remembered visiting an exhibit. In separate analyses of companies considered leaders in their industry or field and companies that spend more money on advertising, their level of memorability was considerably higher than the average.

The type of exhibit approach used is the third major factor affecting memorability. Exhibits using formal or informal product demonstrations generally had higher memorability than static displays.

Perhaps the most important message to come out of this piece of research is that an exhibition investment has a potential value for way outside the duration of the exhibition. The pre-exhibition opportunity to publicize a forthcoming event has always been recognized and exploited to some degree. It may be that exhibitors have not fully capitalized on the favourable opportunity for doing business that exists for many weeks after an exhibition has closed.

Exhibition data form

The exhibition data form (EDF) brings to business, industrial and technical exhibitions the independent, professional auditing procedures which have long been available to the United Kingdom press. Through EDFs, exhibitors have access to accurate, standardized information on exhibition attendance, stand space sold and other useful data on which to appraise exhibitions in the light of their own marketing objectives.

The EDF evolved from the activities of three organizations—the Audit Bureau of Circulation, the Incorporated Society of British Advertisers and the Association of Exhibition Organisers. The scheme is under the overall control of the Council of the ABC which is advised by a Joint Industry Committee (JIC) whose members represent both organizers and exhibitors.

The following details give the broad scope of the data forms. Further information can be obtained from the Audit Bureau of Circulation.

The exhibition data form applies to any business, industrial or technical exhibition which has been accepted for registration by the ABC. The form consists of a basic four pages—three subject to independent audit and one devoted to additional statements by the exhibition organizer. Where space allowed on the printed form is insufficient for the data provided, any section can be expanded and the form enlarged after consultation with the Bureau. All data submitted is subject to further verification by ABC before publication.

MAIN PRODUCT GROUPS/SERVICE

Exhibition organizers are encouraged to give as full a listing as possible of the main product groups and services that were exhibited. This provides a permanent record of the scope of each exhibition and a measure of the success of the exhibition in meeting its original objectives.

TARGET AUDIENCE

The target audience must be defined by the exhibition organizer in advance and the registered free attendance figure includes only those visitors who fall within the target group.

Research at exhibitions

Over and above measurement of the specific value of an exhibition, which is dealt with in the next section, there are many opportunities for research work during an exhibition. Quite simply it can be said that within an exhibition hall for a number of days will be a good sample of a particular market or market segment. There is thus an opportunity to ask questions and obtain answers about any aspect of market opinion, behaviour or motivation that one wishes to pursue. And this at relatively low cost and in a very short space of time.

What are the readership habits of this market segment for instance? A well-tried technique is to compile a short-list of the most likely publications and to compile a flip chart with the front covers of each publication on a separate sheet. Interviewers can then stop people at random, or talk to visitors to the stand, asking them 'which of the following publications are read regularly?' Within a few days one has a profile of readership which is often quite different from an existing media plan based upon circulation data and/or intuition.

Another particularly useful research project for an exhibition is to market test a new product. Here the product is on the stand, having been well publicized in advance, and visitors are asked to comment on certain pre-determined criteria such as size, shape, weight, colour, speed, cost, accuracy, performance, and application. Product prototypes can obviously be evaluated in this way as indeed can mere ideas or concepts. The opportunity is particularly attractive to manufacturers of specialized products where their potential market is widely spread and could only be otherwise contacted at very considerable cost.

In general it can be said that whatever information is required about a market can be obtained from an appropriate exhibition provided due allowance is made for the sample not necessarily being representative of the total market.

Visitors on the whole do not seem to mind answering a modest number of questions: in fact many seem to enjoy it. It is important however to ensure that the exhibition organizers are kept fully informed of any proposed research work where this is to be conducted in the public gangway.

Exhibition evaluation

The setting of objectives and evaluation go hand in hand. Given an objective of securing 200 sales leads, evaluation at its simplest is to ask whether that number was achieved, and if not why not. It will readily be seen how important it is to quantify objectives from the outset.

It is obviously not possible to write down in detail all the ways in which an exhibition can be evaluated. And in any case this must depend on the objectives which were set for a particular exhibition. What must be said, however, is that having decided to make an investment in the form of an exhibition it would be the height of business folly not to make a determined effort to measure the return on the investment.

The question of evaluation is dealt with in a very useful publication by ISBA called *Guide for Exhibitors*.[4] Their many recommendations include:

1. Boxes for visiting cards.
2. Enquiry pads with room for literature/sample requests (literature must be sent out immediately while visitors interest is keen and a reply paid card should be included for further information).
3. Visitors book. Noting of general enquiries—not specifically recorded for follow up purposes. It is advised not to use visitors' books in Eastern European countries.
4. Noting names and number of delegates to lectures and/or film shows at exhibitions. Where one is selling over the counter the total sales less stand/space cost give one the immediate answer.
5. Obtain from the organizers the total number of visitors to the show and compare this with previous years.
6. Note whether your presentation really does stop the crowd.
7. Note the level of activity on your stand compared to others in the near vicinity.

SALES LITERATURE

There are opposing schools of thought on the use of sales literature at exhibitions, some holding that if it is put out, people tend to pick it up indiscriminately, and that if it is not put out people are encouraged to make enquiries; others contend that the more literature distributed the better.

There are good reasons for producing something in the way of an exhibition 'give away' which should be displayed so that people have easy access to it, but which will also include the offer to send on, say, the main catalogue as a means of obtaining future sales leads. Since, however, much of an industrial sales promotion campaign is aimed at getting sales literature into the hands of prospective buyers, it is important that this opportunity be used to the full on a properly planned basis. A jumble of sales leaflets scattered around on a few tables can hardly be said to be maximizing a selling opportunity.

Private exhibitions

An important trend in this field is to mount an exhibition on an individual basis, sometimes to coincide with a public one in the near vicinity, sometimes entirely independently. A further variation is for a number of firms with complementary product ranges to combine and share expenses, a particularly attractive solution where they share common markets.

The reason for the development of private exhibitions lies partly in the spiralling costs of participating in a public exhibition and partly in the degree of attention which can be given to visitors in surroundings which are usually a good deal more comfortable than an exhibition hall, without the distractions of hundreds of other exhibitors, and avoiding the physical and mental exhaustion which most visitors experience at any major show.

Consider for example a medium-sized stand at a national exhibition. The total cost for an area of, say 100–150 m² may well be of the order of £50 000. Such an event if staged in a nearby hotel may provide three or four times the area for half the cost in a relaxed atmosphere, with far superior reception and entertainment facilities. Moreover, the layout could be such that each visitor is greeted personally, conducted around the entire display, and questioned in depth to find out particular interests and to determine future sales action.

Where a company has a limited market, large numbers of people at a public exhibition looking around for general interest can seriously impair the efficiency of the sales staff on duty. The staff at a private show are able to relax, are more likely to be able to carry out an effective selling job, and can give special attention to major customers and to the press, perhaps in a private suite adjoining the exhibition area. Furthermore, competitors cannot easily intrude to probe for details of new products and new selling approaches.

Partisans of the private exhibition will point to more and more advantages such as not having to contend with the difficulties of restrictive labour practices at exhibition halls, being able to set up a show at a time to suit oneself, not having to pay officials to obtain special services. Certainly there are important advantages.

There is, however, one basic benefit of a trade show that does not apply to a private one, namely that with very little effort on the part of an exhibitor a good proportion of a potential market may have the opportunity of coming face to face with one's products.

It would seem, therefore, that to justify a private exhibition instead of a public one, the potential market will be relatively small, say a few hundred, and certainly no more than a few thousand, with all the purchasing influences within that market well defined. Furthermore, there must be sufficient incentive to persuade buyers to make the effort of a special call, even though the venue is fairly close to the exhibition hall.

If, for example, a new company were launching a range of resistors which had a very wide potential application in the electrical and electronic industries, it would probably benefit by using the established audience of one of the major national or international exhibitions to secure a maximum of sales leads, and indeed to gain valuable market intelligence on the reaction to the new range.

Alternatively if the product were a new piece of equipment for carton manufacturers of whom there were only a few hundred prospects, and these very well defined, a private show might be much the most effective method of exhibiting.

Travelling exhibitions

There may be advantages in moving away from the idea of attaching a private exhibition to a public one, and simply setting up an exhibition in its own right. It might be in one location or, more likely, it would be staged in a number of places near the major potential sources of business. The operation can be efficient since, once the exhibition equipment has been assembled, it is a relatively easy matter to move on to another location. Hotels are generally co-operative in accommodating such ventures and provincial rates can be very competitive. A disadvantage is that a good deal of sales force time, and management, is tied down by these events, and this time must be justified by an adequate level of visitors of worthwhile calibre. Once again it is necessary to set targets, compare costs, and as soon as an operation begins to fail, either take corrective action or put a stop to the project.

Trailers and caravans can provide an alternative or sometimes a supplement to the staging of round-the-country exhibitions. They are also of particular value for export promotions. Indeed there is a good deal of scope for initiative in the field of travelling exhibitions, and the use of railways, barges, ships and aeroplanes has not been anything like exploited to the full. The sheer novelty of such ventures can do much to ensure the success of the operation.

Checklist

The checklist has been divided into two parts for convenience—pre-exhibition and post-exhibition.

PRE-EXHIBITION

1. Has a proposed exhibition been examined from the point of view of:
   (a) The likely audience to be reached
   (b) The extent of competition
   (c) Location and accessibility of the site
   (d) Promotional activities by the organizers
   (e) Entertainment facilities?
2. Does the exhibition form part of an integrated marketing plan?
3. Has a written objective been produced for the intended exhibition stand?
4. Have all the relevant people been brought into the planning of the exhibition, for instance; sales management, advertising agency, designer, copywriter, R&D and transport department?
5. Has consideration been given to:
   (a) Site, location and size
   (b) Display requirements

(c) Own entertaining facilities
(d) Sales literature dispensers
(e) Exhibits
(f) Construction
(g) Stand management
(h) Staffing
(i) Planned approach to visitors
(j) Sales follow-up?

6. Has pre-publicity been organized to ensure a maximum attendance?
7. Has special provision been made for receiving:

(a) The press
(b) Overseas visitors?

8. Has a detailed schedule been produced of all activities leading up to the show, including the necessary action for its duration, and termination?
9. In budgeting for an exhibition, have all the costs been included, for example sales staff's time, preparation of exhibits and their transportation?
10. Have you considered how best to exploit photography in:

(a) Products
(b) Product applications
(c) Own factory and processes
(d) News and events
(e) People and personalities
(f) Prestige?

11. Has the use of editorial publicity been established as an integral part of the organizer's press office operation?

POST-EXHIBITION

1. Was the attendance up to target in terms of total numbers, industry category, job status, buying power, etc?
2. What was the cost per 'sales call' or demonstration?
3. Were the numbers entertained satisfactory in quantity and quality?
4. Were any sales objectives met?
5. How many new sales leads were obtained and have these been followed up?
6. How much sales literature was distributed and did this meet the set targets?
7. Did you gain any new contacts regarding decision-makers 'behind the scenes'?
8. What did you learn about your competitors' activities?
9. Was editorial coverage up to target?

10. Were the exhibits delivered, installed and removed on time?
11. Was the stand construction completed on time and did it in every way function to your satisfaction?
12. How did the stand compare with competitors in overall effectiveness, in visitor traffic and in cost?
13. What new market/product knowledge did you gain out of the show?
14. Were you within budget? If not, why not?
15. How did all the above factors compare with the last time you were at this show, and with any other relevant exhibitions?

References

1. Institute of Directors, *Exhibiting for Profit* (London, 1969).
2. A. Konopacki, Why Johnny can't sell at Trade Shows', *Industrial Marketing*, 1981.
3. USA Trade Show Bureau Report.
4. ISBA (London 1986).

7.

LITERATURE

It is a common failing that people believe that others outside their company know far more about it and its products than in fact they do. They also expect customers to have a well-balanced and well-informed view of the company's business as a matter of course and to have an intense interest in even the most trivial aspects of a company's operations.

The preparation of a publications or literature strategy can do much to ensure that there is full information about every important aspect of a company's operations and its products or services.

Planning, production and distribution

It is an unfortunate fact that the publication of company literature is often *ad hoc*, unplanned, hurried, ill-conceived and sometimes quite inappropriate. To be effective and efficient, literature must be part of the marketing and corporate strategy. This means quite simply that every single publication must stem from a defined objective which starts with an outline of the audience to be reached, the method of distribution to be employed, and the basic message which it is required to deliver.

It is, however, wrong to suppose that given this start, the production of a well-conceived range of literature will solve the communications problems. It is more than likely that less than 25 per cent of literature, however efficiently distributed, is ever read at all, and certainly page traffic studies of magazines confirm this proportion. With these discouraging statistics, more and more importance centres on what is produced and its quality.

PLANNING

Publications in industry often run late, and even when a production schedule exists it is gradually compressed so that the final printing stage—in a sense the most important of all, and certainly the most expensive—is rushed to the extent that quality suffers and errors creep in. The reason is nearly always bad planning, or at least planning which has lost direction.

The first stage in effective planning is to ensure that the preparation of a piece of literature is carried out in exactly the right sequence. The objectives must be written and agreed before a writer is briefed. A synopsis or outline must be produced before the copy is started and, finally, every single word of copy must be approved before a designer takes over. This is not to say that the designer does not enter the procedure until this stage. The designer should be an integral part of the team from the outset and must work in closest co-operation with writer and executive. But layout, as a general rule, does not start until writing is both complete and fully agreed with everyone who is required to express an opinion.

Presentation of design must vary according to the nature of a job, but it is important in maintaining a time schedule that design work is progressive in the sense that ideas and treatments receive general agreement before the preparation of finished visuals, and policy matters such as style, visual treatment, size, colours, typography and so on are defined to produce work which will meet the specific objectives.

Following this sequence of operations is the type mark-up which must be read as an engineer would read a blueprint before production begins. It is wasteful and unnecessary to wait until proofs are available before deciding that 8 point is not really large enough or Times New Roman is too traditional a typeface. The proofs when they come should be an agreeable conclusion to a well-planned exercise. There should be no unpleasant surprises, no radical changes—the job should be exactly what had been envisaged throughout the phases of production.

The second stage in effective planning is to establish from the outset a realistic time schedule and to take steps to enforce it. This is easy to say but sometimes difficult to implement: nevertheless it must be done. If, from past experience, the managing director is likely to require a complete rewrite at a certain stage, the possibility must be included in the schedule, and to do so is probably the surest way of bringing home to him or her just what effect a change of mind can have on a project.

Table 7.1 may serve to underline the value of scheduling. It has been constructed as a typical time-scale for the preparation and production of a sixteen-page, three-colour brochure. Note that no provision has been made for the commissioning of special photography or technical drawings for instance.

There could well be situations in which a piece of print is required within a week or even less, but to work to high standards it is essential to allow adequate time for a publication which will, after all, last for perhaps a year and sometimes considerably longer.

PREPARATION AND PRODUCTION

The production of good industrial literature is often complex and almost

Table 7.1 Print schedule

Produce written objectives and obtain approval	1 week
Brief writer, obtain synopsis and get approval	2 weeks
Write copy	2 weeks
Obtain complete approval	1 week
Visual treatment	2 weeks
Finished visual	2 weeks
Final approval	1 week
Type mark-up and artwork	1 week
Proofs	2 weeks
Printing	3 weeks
Total—17 weeks	

always difficult. The subject matter is usually of a technical nature, it is specialized, and, moreover, must be written with an authority which demonstrates to the reader the expertise of the company issuing it. This maybe indicates that it should be written by an expert but the chances of the writing being interesting and dynamic are then frequently diminished.

Careful choice of the best available writer is therefore of paramount importance. If the technical nature requires that it be written by an engineer, then perhaps it will be necessary for it to be rewritten as a matter of deliberate policy by an expert and stylish writer. Similarly with design, when illustrations are of a highly specialized nature a visualizer will require considerable guidance by experts on precisely which items are of most importance.

In the production of literature there are a large number of variables which perhaps are not encountered with so much force in other media, for instance how many pages, what kind of paper, what size, how many colours, what style of design and typography.

It is reasonable to argue that having hired the best or most appropriate creative people to do the job, they should be left to get on with it. This will only be true if the initial briefing has been full and comprehensive.

Literature must fit into the general company style, shape and size; if not it should be different for a good reason. The creative team must know if cost is the overriding consideration, or if prestige; whether an item is to fit into an existing catalogue, be carried in the pocket, sent through the post or handed out by sales staff. The nature of the audience must be known: different styles will be required for addressing architects and archaeologists, artists and artisans, scientists and directors. Size of typeface and style becomes important depending upon age groups; but a good creative person if equipped with the right background information will be able to produce work which fits a particular audience's frame of reference.

Similarly the most appropriate printing process will tend to come out of the original definition of objectives, or if not here, from the visual treatment.

Interdependent with this will be the kind of paper to be used, number of colours, degree of finish and method of presentation.

A more difficult matter is in the choice of a printer. The variations which occur between one supplier and another in quality and delivery make price alone an unsatisfactory and incomplete basis on which to select a printer. The soundest basis is to build up a relationship with a few printers with whom the majority of business is placed, establishing from the outset that certain standards of quality, service and, most important, integrity, must be maintained and that any serious defects will result in a termination of the relationship. Even so, it will be necessary to put an occasional job out to tender in order that cost comparisons can be made.

DISTRIBUTION

Experience shows that much industrial literature is produced at considerable expense, then left substantially unused for a few years before being repulped as wastepaper. This underlines the need for a literature strategy which plans its audiences and methods of distribution.

There will no doubt be a primary audience. For example a leaflet about a new electronic device may be aimed primarily at all design engineers within certain defined industries. Secondary audiences may be the technical buyers and production engineers in the same factories. Other audiences for consideration will be the press, one's own staff, wholesalers and retailers or other end users. A prestige brochure, on the other hand, may be directed towards the senior management of customers and prospects, again to employees, but maybe also to suppliers and to shareholders.

A good general rule is that literature in the store room is wasted though, of course, it is necessary for efficient distribution to maintain adequate stocks to meet demand. Here it is most important to install an adequate system of maximum/minimum stock control coupled with a procedure which ensures that before re-ordering takes places, the full 'pass for press' procedure is used to ensure that the reprint is completely up to date.

Prestige publications

Jargon in marketing has brought down upon itself connotations which are both unfortunate and inaccurate. 'Prestige', for instance, tends to be equated in the minds of many managements with waste of money. If, alternatively, such publications were described as 'image building', the reaction would be even less favourable.

The fact is, however, that when a company name is mentioned to a buyer, if she or he has heard of it at all, a certain image is conjured up. It may be favourable or unfavourable. Indeed it may be highly biased or completely erroneous. Yet is it possible to produce literature which if read will help to create the kind of image that a company hopes to possess. This, of course, presupposes that there exists a plan which defines the company image. Given this objective there are numerous types of publications which can be produced having a sound business basis other than just a general feeling that this is something which ought to be published.

A general company or corporate brochure, for instance, can bring together all the activities of a company expressed in terms which the key audience can recognize as valuable. Such a publication may be preceded by research to establish the level of knowledge about the company and where gaps exist. It is important to avoid being introspective and writing about the company for the sake of it. At the other extreme, if the capability of top management or the existence of modern buildings are outstanding, they are worth publicizing. The first step in such a publication calls for an objective analysis of a company's strengths in relation to competitors and the nature of the audience, and their interest.

A number of companies publish books about their histories, but the important question here seems to be 'who cares?' If the company has had an outstandingly interesting history there may well be justification for such a book. The growth and development may reflect very creditably upon the business as a whole; there may have been outstanding personalities in the business who are characters with an intrinsic interest of their own; there may have been a number of innovations which people in general do not know about—inventions, or new management techniques. On the other hand a company may be in a fast-developing industry where little regard is paid to the past and in which the future—long- and short-term—is all that seems to matter. Perhaps the criterion to be adopted is to demonstrate the need and value of such a publication, and if this cannot be done then not to publish.

Often a company will be in an industry which itself is of wide general interest and can therefore justify a special publication about it. Certain industries producing basic materials such as paper and steel come into this category, along with, for example, textiles, soap, aircraft, electronics, railways and very many others. Sometimes this aspect of literature is covered by an educational programme or classed under the heading of public relations. In the context of this chapter it is enough to apply the question 'will this help to achieve our defined overall objective?' Providing the answer is yes, then the job is worth doing.

It may not be inappropriate at this juncture to emphasize that much industrial purchasing is done on a subjective basis and that attitudes, as well as the placement of orders for capital goods, have an average gestation period of some years. The long-term building of a good reputation is therefore an important activity which is part of the marketing plan. It is no longer inevitable that providing a good product is produced a good reputation will follow without further effort. Customer satisfaction must not only be given, but must be seen to be given.

In much the same way as company publications about an industry can enhance a reputation, so also can literature dealing with other matters which bear on a company's activities. Statistics about an industry as a whole, for example, can prove to be of great value to buyers, suppliers and other interested people. If no other source of such data is readily available many people may take advantage of the statistics and in turn equate the value and reliability of this service with the performance of the company as a whole.

Some marketing principles may be misleading; for instance the proposition that one does not sell product performance, but rather consumer satisfaction, is fine but it can lead to missing quite real selling propositions. The fact is that, no matter how well a customer's identified needs are met by the specification of the product and its performance, there are intangible influences on all human behaviour which will affect decision-making. The task is to uncover these hidden motivations and to take action to satisfy them. Knowledge of the existence of very modern and sophisticated machinery may well be an important factor in a purchasing decision even though it actually makes not the slightest difference to the quality or performance of a product.

Technical publications

In the field of industrial publicity there almost always exists the need for technical publications which range from specification and data sheets to servicing and operating manuals. To have technical validity and authority these must be written by engineers, technicians or scientists who frequently do not wish to undertake the task and anyway are not able to express themselves clearly.

The result is often a compromise, the outcome of which is that the job is not as good as it might be. There are of course technical writers, but good ones are few and it is not a profession which attracts talented specialists. A solution which is often adopted is to sub-contract the writing to an outside organization which specializes in the production of technical publications. This can be satisfactory, particularly for the smaller firm which may not have a constant demand to maintain a well-balanced workload for its own technical writers. Considerable caution must be exercised in using an outside organization: quality and capability vary considerably, and there is often a high staff turnover which makes continuity of style and quality difficult.

As with many other publicity activities the right solution is perhaps to establish and then pursue exactly those publicity services which are essential. It should then follow that a technical leaflet or a maintenance manual is no more an undesirable but necessary evil than the raw material from which the product is made or the machine that makes it. Thus, if the product warrants first-class materials it also warrants first-class literature and the rate for the job must be paid to the few good technical writers available.

Where a company has a wide range of complementary products it is usually necessary to provide a catalogue, with all the difficulties this involves. Catalogues are expensive to produce, impossible to keep up to date, and never meet the requirements of everyone. Nevertheless, with many technical products they are so essential a part of the marketing operation that they are used by the customer's design department to specify a certain type number, and thus predetermine the brand of product ultimately to be purchased. Interesting catalogue developments are taking place particularly in the development of microfilm storage units and various other systems of information retrieval, and there is every indication that this technique will continue to develop. A further but quite different system is one in which a specialist distributor arranges to send out staff to a given market on behalf of a number of clients and actually place into customers' catalogue files the latest material. This scheme is certainly working successfully in some fields, but its application may be limited.

Sales publications

Sales literature represents the opportunity for placing in front of a prospect the complete selling proposition. Even if such material will not always be read, it is nevertheless a good chance to set down in detail a considered view on the merits of the product and the satisfactions it will provide.

A disadvantage is that it is difficult to be specific to an individual's needs in the way in which a salesperson can. A salesperson, however, while having the chance to modify a presentation to suit the circumstances, and to counter objections and doubts by the buyer, does not have unlimited time during a visit and therefore may miss out certain features. Overall, the considered and consolidated argument contained in a piece of sales literature ought to be better than that of any one salesperson.

This is not to suggest the replacement of sales staff by sales literature. Rather it is to emphasize that in technical selling, sales literature has a powerful role to play providing it is carefully produced and used in a planned and purposeful manner.

A sales leaflet or brochure can be regarded as the back-up material to a salesperson's visit during which the buyer will have been taken carefully through each item, relating it to his or her special requirements. Such literature will not be simply an enumeration of product attributes, but a summary of the benefits to the customer. It should probably not be sent out in advance or in lieu of a visit, since it might enable a prospect to conclude that he or she did not require the product, thus creating an unnecessary sales block.

Alternatively, other forms of sales literature, such as direct mailing pieces which are designed simply to create interest but not to call for a yes/no judgement to be made, are an excellent preliminary to a sales call. The contents of a piece of literature or any other item of publicity should not be based solely on what a buyer wants to know. This is only the starting point. The contents must be planned deliberately to provide a prospect with what the selling company wishes him or her to know, no less and no more.

Various other items of print can come under the heading of sales literature. Some of these are covered under direct mail, and others under point of sale. Two that are not used as much as they might be are reprints of advertisements and of editorial mentions or articles. It seems likely that if an advertisement is worth while, it is wasteful to rely simply on its being seen in a magazine. From readership data, it can be reliably forecast that perhaps only a third of a potential market will ever notice it, let alone read it. The exposure must be increased if it is mailed out to the prospect list, and the cost of doing so is very low.

House magazines

In this section of the book dealing with marketing communications, consideration is given only to external house magazines (i.e. for customers and prospects) as opposed to those which are produced primarily for internal circulation to employees. Sometimes one magazine is produced to serve both functions, but it is rare for this to be successful since the interests of the two groups are so different.

External house magazines are certainly a valid means of persuasive communications: their selling role is sometimes rather remote and in fact more nearly related to a long-range image-building operation.

One of the difficulties facing a would-be publisher is that, once started, a house magazine is difficult to stop. As the cost of launching such a venture can be quite high a major policy decision is required at this stage. Again the solution is to define audiences and objectives and then to produce something which is modest and infrequent but can be strengthened if it succeeds.

The acid test must be whether it can prove to be of sufficient interest to cause recipients to look at it and even read it. Unless continuity of really interesting material can be assured it must become of declining value. It is akin to a new product launch without the possibility of a test marketing operation.

Against the idea of a house magazine is the situation that already too many trade and technical journals are produced commercially and this must restrict the available reading time by prospective buyers. Secondly, it is only natural that the sponsors of a house magazine will view it with a great deal more interest and initial enthusiasm than its potential readership. In the balance against the idea, much more than a printing operation is involved: this is publishing and it includes producing to a deadline and the most difficult matter of distribution—of a growing uncontrollable mailing list which becomes out of date at a rate of at least 10 per cent each year and therefore requires very thorough procedures for maintaining its accuracy. The overall cost of a well-produced house magazine can become very high indeed.

If the advantages predominate, the job must be done well, since this magazine will contribute in very large measure to the image of the company in the minds of the readers.

There are often good reasons for placing the publishing of a magazine in the hands of an outside organization. This is clearly not so if the format is simply a few duplicated pages of 'company newsheet', but if the work is substantial it is difficult to justify employing a staff with adequate expertise to produce something which must compete with the best commercial journals. The very fact of having an independent editor will help to ensure that the subject matter is written to interest people outside the business, and without the kind of introverted jargon and detailed trivia which easily creep into an inside production.

Goals must be set, not only quantitative, but also in terms of reader interest. In Chapter 13 on media research, page traffic studies are dealt with. This same technique can be applied to house magazines to establish the percentage interest in each page, and in the magazine as a whole. The objective should be stated in terms of readership, not circulation. One goal, for example, may be to obtain a readership of say, 500 hospital engineers within a year of publication. A formal readership study may subsequently show that only 10 per cent of the circulation of 1000 is read, the remainder discarded. In such a clear-cut situation the course of action ought not to be difficult to determine; for instance, cease publication.

Checklist

1. Have you a long-term plan for literature?
2. Does this plan fit into the company marketing strategy?
3. In the preparation of a new piece of literature
   (a) Has the object been defined?
   (b) Is the potential audience agreed?
   (c) Has the method of distribution been determined?
   (d) Has a production schedule been produced?
   (e) Does the schedule make provision for
       (i) briefing?
       (ii) writing?

    (iii)   visual treatment?
    (iv)   quotation?
    (v)   finished visual?
    (vi)   artwork?
    (vii) proofing?
    (viii) revisions?
    (ix)   printing?

4. In briefing a designer has guidance been given on

    (a)   Number and size of pages?
    (b)   Paper and board?
    (c)   Illustrations?
    (d)   Style of design?
    (e)   Number of colours?
    (f)   Typeface and sizes?
    (g)   Expense?
    (h)   Printing process?
    (i)   Quantity?

5. Has provision been made for (a) storage (b) stock control and continuous updating?

8.

PHOTOGRAPHY

Still photography is part of the raw material which serves as the basis for promotion and other persuasive communications activities. A good deal of photography is carried out for a specific purpose and is used subsequently for other purposes. Much of the work, however, is done speculatively when the opportunity presents itself in anticipation of future uses.

Subjects

Consideration will be given later to the care which must be exercised in order to match the photographer to the job in hand. Before doing so, it is perhaps useful to examine some of the variety of subjects which can be included in what is part of the promotion programme. This classification of subjects is not exhaustive, but is presented rather to show that a disciplined and analytical approach is possible and indeed necessary even in such a creative area as photography.

PRODUCTS

It goes without saying that there are numerous products which, as such, cannot usefully be photographed—usefully that is in a promotional sense. A management consultancy may be said to fit into this category, and to a lesser extent industrial chemicals, or even for that matter steel strip.

In practice there are many products where illustrations are vital, for instance where appearance counts, as in packaging, and others which cannot be taken to a buyer because of size, as with heavy capital equipment.

Product photographs to a greater or lesser extent form the basis of press advertising, literature, sales aids, press releases, and direct mail, but there can be rather more to product photography than merely presenting a factual static representation of what the product looks like. There is much creative scope for interpretation by the photographer in order that the picture portrays the product benefit rather than only the product itself. Take, for example, a new type of fibreboard box designed to provide extra strength; itself a most mundane subject. Now stand an elephant on it and the picture may well prove to be of interest to a daily newspaper, and certainly to trade outlets. Another example might be a sheet of cardboard which is particularly water resistant. Here the product benefit could be demonstrated by constructing a boat from it and then photographing it being rowed across the Thames by an Olympic oarsman.

PRODUCT APPLICATIONS

It follows naturally from the above section that an outstanding way of showing product benefits is to photograph them in use. A radiation monitor maybe is not much to look at and could well be mistaken for a valve voltmeter or a pH meter, but when put into the radiotherapy unit of a nationally known hospital its use is immediately apparent, as well as the added value of implied endorsement by the user. An industrial pump designed to withstand the most rugged of conditions has difficulty in making this point until it is photographed *in situ* on a massive paper machine with water and stock jetting all over it.

To ask a photographer to produce a 'dramatic' picture of an industrial product may be a cliché (a dramatic cucumber was once called for), but a top-rate photographer with an adequate brief will produce photographs which sell the goods, sometimes more effectively than written or spoken words, since here is pictorial evidence of a product providing a service or satisfaction which is claimed of it. It is a credible demonstration of a manufacturer's claim.

INDUSTRIAL PROCESSES

It has been argued elsewhere in this book that the nature of the manufacturing process can be a powerful support to the selling proposition of a product. This factor can be utilized by building up a library of the principal or interesting features of a process.

In photographing the operations of a factory it is necessary in the first instance to produce a shooting schedule and to confirm this in advance with everyone likely to be involved. The works manager will be of special importance, since his or her staff will be needed to give maximum co-operation by repainting machinery, providing clean overalls, pacifying the operatives who are concerned at losing bonus pay, and providing electricians, labourers and technical advisers to help the photographer. It is a matter of communicating to staff that an industrial photograph is a far cry from a seaside snap and is making an important contribution to the future of the business.

Some photographers on a large assignment prefer to carry out an initial survey, sometimes with a hand-held camera, to ensure that possible difficulties are anticipated and that any major work the client needs notice of can be put in hand in good time. A photographer may, for instance, wish to work at night in order to have pure artificial light: this may involve bringing in a special night shift.

Top-class photographers have a creativity and sensitivity which enables them to give life to a piece of plant or machinery. More important even than clever composition and lighting, if the brief requires it, they can illustrate what a machine *does* rather than what it *is*. Furthermore a photographer can build in a feeling of quality and precision which turns a fundamentally passive situation into an active selling picture.

It is not enough to leave things to chance, and hope that the right result will emerge. The briefing for photography must state the specific merits that a series of pictures need to portray: whether it is cleanliness, scale of production, automation, efficiency of factory layout, craftmanship, scientific aids, or quality control.

NEWS PHOTOGRAPHY

This is a separate class of photography and needs certain qualities if it is to be useful—a sense of immediacy, a human interest, an unusual angle.

There is a great danger of producing cliché photography in many news situations—VIP shaking hands with managing director prior to a tour of works; a plaque being unveiled; the mayor shares a joke with one of the workers; or the chairman's wife cuts tape, presses a button or accepts a ceremonial key. These photographs are easy enough to take but are difficult to place with newspapers and tend to be repetitious and uninteresting even for a house magazine.

The best news photographs are probably not planned at all but come out of the persistent trailing of a tour party by a photographer with a news sense. Alternatively news can be created, as for instance when a boat was sawn in half, then stuck together and refloated, to demonstrate the qualities of a new adhesive.

PEOPLE

A basic library of portraits of directors and senior executives is necessary for any firm seriously engaged in marketing communications and public relations activities. This is good reference material and will be used for such events as new appointments and announcements, though such pictures serve little purpose sometimes other than to break up a page of type and provide a sense of satisfaction to the person concerned.

There are opportunities to go further than a straight portrait or a picture of someone sitting at a desk signing a letter or holding a telephone; a happy group of people clutching their cocktail glasses; or those frequently used groups of businessmen with their wives, all in evening dress, standing in the corner of a ballroom looking sometimes self-satisfied, and sometimes embarrassed.

There is now a healthy trend towards photographing people going about their business so as to get across their personalities, functions or features of the products or processes in which they are involved. This is valuable because it is both different and gives the photograph a positive role. It communicates something other than just faces.

PRESTIGE PHOTOGRAPHY

It is not easy to be specific about this since so much depends upon the circumstances. Often it is a matter of looking through photographs which have been taken for other purposes and selecting any which have additional merit. Photographs of industrial processes for instance, apart from showing the equipment and demonstrating its purpose, may be of such a quality in photographic or visual terms that they can be used outside their original intention. Many newspapers and magazines will accept such pictures with a small caption on an exclusive basis.

It is necessary to decide what aspects of a business are likely to be impressive in a general sense. The exterior of a new building, for instance, or an aerial view, a well-equipped surgery, or a fleet of vehicles with a new livery, advanced scientific equipment, or a computer: features of a business which are not directly relevant in a promotional context but tend to be creditable in their own right.

Photographers

Much emphasis has been laid on matching a photograph to its purpose. It follows that the means of achieving such an objective must be to match the photographer to the task. Just as in any other art form, each photographer will have certain strengths and weaknesses, special interests and capabilities. The strength of 'high quality' will probably be matched by the fact that the cost will be high. A photographer who excels at portraiture may be only average at industrial work or news photography.

COMMERCIAL PHOTOGRAPHERS

It is necessary then for a publicity executive to build up a knowledge of sources of supply of various skills and price ranges. Many of the best sources of supply are independent photographers with a small studio and processing unit. Their particular skill is one that is difficult to pass on to an assistant, or to a group of colleagues, and for this reason photographic units tend to be small. The disadvantage is that a one-man firm suffers from peaks and troughs in demand which will sometimes make it difficult to get a particular photographer on to an assignment at a given time. The sporadic nature of the business may also cause the charges to be high since the photographer must fix fees at a level which will cover the costs on a long term and continuous basis, even when there is little work going through.

A top-flight photographer may command a market price of £500 a day or more, and in the context of the job to be done this may represent good value for money. The provision of a good set of photographs of a new £50m plant for example is worth every penny of the £2500 a week's assignment might cost.

There is, of course, room for competitive buying in photography. One of the customs of top photographers (and top designers) is that, apart from being able to command relatively high charges by virtue of their excellence, they sometimes base their fees on the use to which a photograph is to be put. Thus a photograph for record purposes may cost say £50 while the same photograph for an expensive series of newspaper advertisements may be billed at £500. Advertising agencies, particularly large ones, tend to be at a disadvantage here. A good example was of a photographer on a routine assignment at a fee of £200 a day, who was asked independently by the company's advertising agent to take a particular shot, while he was on the spot, for a press advertisement. He billed the agency £400 for the one shot and the art buyer considered he had obtained good value for money. The client took a different view. No doubt photographers will argue that the marketing men, for whom they do much of their work, themselves set product prices on what the market will bear and that they should not complain when they are given the same treatment. It is as well, however, to be aware of the situation.

The larger studios employ a number of photographers, perhaps half a dozen, and there are obvious benefits to be derived. The provision of a news service in particular tends to call for a pool of photographers to be able to meet sudden demands. Shared overheads may enable such units to function more economically, and a group of photographers can consist of a number of people who are specialists in their own right. On the other hand it is difficult for a client to build up such a personal relationship as when dealing with an individual and, since changes in personnel occur from time to time, a continuity of style, technique and quality can be difficult to maintain if there are several photographers on call.

STAFF PHOTOGRAPHERS

Bernard Shaw said: 'The golden rule is that there are no golden rules', and this certainly applies to dogmatism about staff photographers or indeed any creative staff. The odds are weighted heavily against staff photographers being at the very top of their profession. They cannot hope to be a specialist in all the categories of photography that will be required; moreover their skills will not match those of a £500 a day person, or they would themselves be working independently.

Even a very capable staff photographer will tend to get into a rut if he or she always works for one firm, and it is unlikely that there will be the same freedom of creative expression as a freelance has since the work will be controlled by a direct-line boss. The day-to-day operations will be restricted by conventional working hours, by limitations of props and equipment and by general interference, however well-intended.

Nevertheless, for larger companies there is a real value in an internal photographic unit which can cope with the many routine photographic demands which arise. It can supply an essential and very economic service provided its limitations are recognized from the outset.

PROPS AND MODELS

It is so easy, and in industrial publicity so common, to think always in terms of getting work done 'on the cheap'.

If, for example, a home environment is required for a photograph, there is a good chance that someone's actual home will be used rather than a set built at £1000 to match the requirements of the assignment. Similarly it is much easier to look around for the prettiest secretary to stand in front of the camera rather than pay for an expensive model. For a small firm working on a tight budget these improvisations often make sound common sense, but one gets what one pays for, and there is little doubt that the quality of a photograph can be enhanced radically by the use of professional models and exactly appropriate props.

Expensive photography is not always so expensive as it seems since it rarely needs retouching, often finds many other uses, and projects a quality image which can be of a great benefit to both the product and the company.

Processes and production

Most industrial photography is in black and white. While there is a growing trend towards colour there is still little need for it in the majority of literature, direct mail or press advertising, and the requirements of exhibitions and public relations can usually be met with monochrome. The nature of the product can be decisive since a carton manufacturer or a printer may well have a very definite need for colour work, but by and large colour is unnecessary and indeed often unsuitable.

Types of cameras can surely be left to the photographer, although it is as well to be aware of the limitations of filmstock as regards size. For some years past there has been a good deal of controversy around the merits of sizes from 35 mm to 5 in × 4 in and even larger. While some industrial photographers still use large film stock, virtually none use 35 mm, and there is a general consensus that $2\frac{1}{4}$ in^2 is the most suitable. Certainly with fine-grain film and development, very considerable enlargements can be obtained up to 6 × 8 ft without the effect of grain becoming objectionable.

In commissioning photography it is as well to be aware of the importance of lighting, if only to understand and anticipate the needs of the photographer. The hand-held flash unit may be enough for news photography, but for product shots it is frequently necessary to employ a wide variety of sophisticated lighting techniques for the best results. In photographing industrial plant, lighting often becomes the most significant single factor, with high-powered lights located at strategic points often to the inconvenience of the work people. One of the greatest failings among clients is to arrange shooting schedules which do not allow enough time, people, mechanical handling, electricians and power supplies to do justice to the lighting.

SALES AIDS

Obviously black and white prints can be used by sales representatives and sometimes that is all they need. Colour photography here can come into its own since the additional cost may not be great against the realism of the picture.

Consideration should also be given to the use of 35 mm colour film for the provision of slides and film strips and for three-dimensional slides with a special viewer. These visual aids can provide the basis of a very effective sales presentation, sometimes at very low cost.

Checklist

1. Have you made budgetary provision for photography as a separate promotional element?
2. Have you considered how best to exploit photography in
   (a) Products?
   (b) Product applications?
   (c) Own factory and processes?
   (d) News and events?
   (e) People and personalities?
   (f) Prestige?

3. Have you (a) set up an adequate library of prints, (b) with suitable cross referencing? (c) Are there arrangements for updating this material? (d) And preventing people removing them?
4. In arranging a photographic session, is the photographer aware of the purpose and objectives, both (a) immediate and (b) long-term?
5. With photography inside factories and offices are the necessary line management, staff and works fully informed in order to obtain maximum co-operation?

9.

FILMS

The production of an industrial film, whether video or photographic is sometimes the most expensive single item in a publicity budget and yet, paradoxically, once produced it is often the least used because it has few or no pre-planned objectives. It may indeed prove to be the most expensive white elephant in the promotional field.

As with other media it is necessary to refer again to the marketing and promotional strategies which determine the need for a film or not. It is easy to think of good reasons to justify a film, having already decided to make one, but this sequence of thinking often leads to the film being the end in itself rather than simply the beginning of a promotional process.

'What is the objective?' This is the essential question, and the singular is deliberately used in order to avoid the other common failing in film making, that of trying to satisfy the interests of several different audiences with one and the same film. The result is generally a film of no special interest to anyone.

The objective, for instance, may be to demonstrate to farmers the versatility of a new tractor and its range of attachments, to help a salesperson to put across the selling proposition. From the definition of potential market in the marketing strategy, the precise nature of the audience will be known— say farmers having in excess of a certain acreage—and this will determine the method of film distribution and display.

There is usually a case for examining secondary audiences, but this must not cloud the principal objective. In the above example there may well be an overseas potential; schools, agricultural colleges and young farmers' clubs among others may be interested, but they must be regarded as ancillaries and of secondary importance.

Having set a specific objective, the next step is to restate it in quantitative terms, fixing not only a measurement against which performance can be judged, but also an assessment of value for money before production begins. Suppose the total potential market is 50 000 people, can a realistic target audience be set at 5000 a year? If that seems practicable, having regard to the methods of distribution available and the estimated life of the film, is the expenditure justified? The answer is often that, given planned distribution, the cost per viewer is very low. In the above example for instance, a film costing £30 000 would obtain an exposure in the first year at a cost of £6 per viewer. If distribution continued at the same rate for four or five years, the cost would come down to around a pound per head. At the other extreme, there are films which have been so little used that the cost per viewer has reached hundreds of pounds or even more.

Advantages and disadvantages

In terms of the 'impact diagram' in Chapter 2 (Fig. 2.2), the film can be regarded as one of a number of co-ordinated media which impress a common message upon the mind of a prospect. It is useful to consider the merits of a film in relation to other media.

IMPACT

This is clearly of a high order, arguably even higher than a salesperson's visit, due to the complete absence of distractions. This is not necessarily so, since there is no opportunity with a film for varying the argument to suit the circumstances, or to counter an objection. Obviously, however, a film has a much higher impact than press advertising.

COST

Initial costs very high, maybe between £10 000 and £100 000. Organizational and distribution costs must be added. Cost per viewer may be low.

COVERAGE OF POTENTIAL MARKET

Depends very much on how precisely the purchasing influences can be defined and how willing they are likely to be to view the film. This probably is the biggest problem and the biggest challenge. Video films are obviously easier to show than photographic.

COMPLEXITY OF SALES MESSAGE

In press advertising, for example, the sales message is subject to severe limitation. In a film there is virtually no limit and moreover the sales argument is presented in two forms—visual and audio—simultaneously and of course in colour.

SPEED

While films can be produced very quickly, it is usually unwise to do so.

Several months may be needed for production alone. Distribution may have to be spread over a number of years.

INTRUSION

Mention has been made with other media that a buyer may feel a sense of intrusion which can build up a resistance, for example in an intensive direct mail campaign. With a film he or she is likely to have gone to a showing as a matter of choice, and will probably at least start with a positive attitude of mind. Also films have a relaxing 'entertainment' connotation, arising from TV or cinema.

Film-making

The decision to make a film having been reached in principle there are a number of stages required in logical sequence to ensure an effective result. In the chapter on literature the need for such a procedure was stressed. In film-making it becomes even more important since changes made, particularly towards the end of production, can not only be very expensive, but can lead to the overall quality depreciating with serious results. It is assumed that the objective, audience and distribution procedure will have already been put down in writing and that the budget, type and length of film have been given some consideration.

The following sequence might then be:

1. Outline synopsis
2. Choice of film unit
3. Briefing
4. Treatment
5. Quotation
6. Script and visual interpretation
7. Shooting schedule
8. Internal organization and liaison
9. Rushes
10. Editing
11. Recording
12. Viewing
13. Completion

It follows that plans will be in train concurrently for distribution, and to secure adequate publicity for the film on its initial launching.

OUTLINE SYNOPSIS

It is usually the task of the publicity department, or maybe the advertising agency, to set down in more detail the points which need to be made verbally and visually in order to communicate the essential sales message.

It is useful at this stage to consider this not so much from a creative point of view, but rather as a factual outline of events which may or may not be in an acceptable creative sequence. This document will in due course be the basis of the briefing and with this in mind it can well be written while negotiations are proceeding with the film units which have already been short-listed.

From the outset it is essential to secure the active support of top management, and a realization that they will need to devote time at each critical stage to give a considered judgement which is unlikely to be changed. Approval of the outline synopsis is one such critical stage.

CHOICE OF FILM UNIT

Without wide experience in the film business it is wise to have the views and advice of other people who have been concerned in the recent past with the making of a film. A preliminary selection is not difficult as film units will usually have gained a reputation in a particular field of activity, or technique, or price range. It will then be advantageous to see a number of their recent productions and to judge these not only from the standpoint of entertainment, but also as audio/visual interpretations of the client's objectives.

This procedure should lead to the choice of one or two units that appear to meet the requirements. Full discussions must take place to give them the data they require for a quotation and to provide an opportunity of discovering whether a good personal rapport can be established and if they, as a unit, seem capable of understanding and interpreting what is required.

BRIEFING

There are a variety of ways of operating. One satisfactory procedure is to commission the chosen film unit to prepare a treatment and maybe a script for a nominal fee, with a full quotation to follow. The justification for this interim action is that to ask for a quotation before a full treatment has been prepared is rather like asking a printer to quote for a job before it has been designed.

The outline synopsis now becomes the basis of briefing the unit, which must be given every facility to ask questions and examine locations. This degree of co-operation will enable them to make the best possible creative contribution. If the film involves technical subject matter, a senior technical person must be assigned from the outset. If the factory is to be filmed, the factory manager must be fully involved.

The client company must treat the briefing as a most serious contribution to the subject. Thereafter the matter moves progressively out of its hands.

TREATMENT

This is the document in which the film-maker feeds back his interpretation of the client's briefing. It will be in effect an expanded and detailed synopsis with a written description of both visual and sound effects added. It will enumerate the various locations, the need for music, commentary and direct speech, and animation for instance.

In engineer's terminology this is the film's specification and blueprint combined into one. It should be read and agreed by everyone concerned and care exercised to ensure that the readers are well enough briefed, even with a verbal explanation by the producer, to understand fully the implications of each item.

QUOTATION

A 'treatment' can be costed accurately and, if the above procedure has been followed, the subsequent quotation is not likely to be very different from that which was foreseen. Items which are likely to have a significant effect on costs will have been discussed at an earlier stage, such as the extent and nature of animation sequences, special music to be composed and so on.

The contractual stage of the film and the detailed points in the contract are important to formalize; for instance, progress payments may be required, and provision for contingencies such as bad weather and lack of access to locations due to plant closedown.

SCRIPT

Good writers are not easy to find and it is worth paying for the best. An extensive briefing must be given to the writer and the script must be scrutinized together with the visual and timing schedules so that every single item is seen to fit. Any alteration hereafter can have most undesirable consequences in terms of both cost and quality.

SHOOTING SCHEDULE AND ORGANIZATION

Many people in a client's organization will need to be co-opted in order to ensure the smooth shooting of the film. The importance of management support has been stressed; it is valuable now to line up alongside the film unit a team of staff with executive authority over the whole internal operation—

to plan the organization and liaison in detail and to anticipate difficulties before they arise.

RUSHES

As the shooting of the film progresses, each sequence will become available for viewing and it is at this stage that the technical advisers should be brought in to ensure that pictorially there is nothing inaccurate.

EDITING AND RECORDING

There is little that can be contributed by the client at this late stage: in fact, the results will probably be better if the experts are allowed to get on with it. The client may want to hear the recording to be reassured that the right emphasis is given to certain passages in the script or that technical words are pronounced correctly.

VIEWING

The final viewing will be to a mixed audience of all those concerned in the client's organization, and they must decide that the result is right from their viewpoint, at least in technical and factual terms. From this stage the film goes to processing, and production is complete.

Distribution

Just as with press advertising there is an inclination to concentrate the main effort on the creation and production of an advertisement and to neglect media selection, so with films there has been a tendency to disregard the need for a plan of action to make maximum use of them commercially. In other words, the production of the film becomes almost an end in itself.

There are many channels of distribution available and it is to be hoped that the distribution plan and budget will have been drawn up and approved well before the film in completed. Such channels include:

1. Cinema circuits
2. Television
3. Film libraries
4. Trade and other associations
5. Clubs and organizations
6. Customers and prospects
7. Central Office of Information
8. Client-sponsored local film shows

9. Education establishments
10. Part of individual sales presentations
11. Exhibitions and conferences

Re-examination of the target audience will help to determine which methods of distribution are likely to be most effective. From the moment a film is completed it is starting to become out of date; therefore action must be prompt and it must be intensive.

Distribution can be expensive, as well as the maintenance and administration that must accompany it; nothing can be worse than a film arriving late, damaged, or even just not rewound.

In promotional terms, a film represents an opportunity of breaking new ground, influencing new people, and getting across a message often with greater impact than can be achieved with other media. The film, however, must not be expected to do this task alone. It must be supported, perhaps with a brochure highlighting the main features, or with posters and handbills, product displays or instructional charts. A personal introduction or demonstration is also very useful.

A film is only one part of the sales promotion armoury and should be treated as such by being linked with other media. It should be advertised. It will clearly be reviewed in a house magazine. If the subject justifies it, say a steel strip mill, the film may be mailed direct to the top fifty prospects throughout the world. The opportunities are limitless.

Pre-distribution publicity

A major event, such as the completion of a new video or photographic film, provides the opportunity for good deal of pre-distribution publicity, valuable both for general public relations and also to help to stimulate the demand for showings.

A particularly useful way of introducing a film is in a series of previews. The first will usually be for the press and provides the chance for journalists to meet company management as well as the film unit itself. Film reviews in the press can lead to a useful demand and, if the reviews are complimentary, they can be used to form the basis of promotional material.

Following the press reception, there are a number of events which should be considered. Important customers will feature largely when planning such functions, and if staged at a high level in congenial surroundings a good deal of hard business can be generated at them. Particular people will have special interests in a film: suppliers of equipment that was featured for instance; general suppliers to the company; officials of trade associations; and of course employees, particularly those who have co-operated and appear in the film.

Finally, pre-release publicity can spread across the entire selling function so that for a period the film is being promoted by the sales force, direct mail, inserts in advertisements, mention in the house magazine, envelope stuffers and so on until every prospect viewer is thoroughly informed and interested to see it.

Film strips, slides and VTR

This chapter would be incomplete without mention of the growing opportunities provided by film strips, slides and video tape recordings, and also, the declining use of photographic film.

The oldest technique here is film strips which go back almost to the beginning of film itself. The process simply involves a series of individual frames, usually on 35 mm stock, each of which portrays part of a story sequence. The setting up of a complex piece of equipment may be the subject, or a comprehensive series of applications in diverse fields. There are also valuable opportunities for a film strip in the educational field and in training for internal staff or for distributors or users. An advantage can be to combine the visual sequence with a taped commentary. This provides a very neat package of a small roll of film plus a cassette which can be used independently of one's own staff, and indeed can be mailed around the world. The cost of a film strip can be held within a few hundred pounds, and additional copies are easy and inexpensive to obtain. Two disadvantages should be considered. The sequence of events is fixed and may not be suitable for every audience. More important perhaps is the fact that a special projector is required, and not all audience groups will have ready access to such equipment.

Colour transparencies are the basis of 35 mm slides which can be put together to form a programme in a similar way to a film strip but with the special advantage of flexbility. Slides can be changed, updated, omitted or used in a different sequence to suit the circumstances. With modern projectors, usually widely available, there are few problems likely to be encountered in setting up for a presentation. Specialists in AV programmes have developed techniques involving multi-projector images coupled with integrated soundtracks which provide an impressive show coming close to that of a cine film. As with still photography it is important not to fall into the trap of expecting such a programme to be produced for a few tens of pounds. Top-quality photography is essential and, if sound is to be used, a thoroughly professional recording. Even so, there is no doubt that if the subject is suitable for this form of treatment it can be produced for very considerably less than a film.

Video tape recording (VTR), already widespread in television and in consumer advertising, has yet to be fully exploited in the industrial field though for high quality presentation, 35 mm film is still significantly better. Given that the film might cost 10 times that of the video there is clearly a temptation to change over whenever possible.

It is not only the cost of video that is an advantage. The equipment costs less, special lighting is hardly necessary, 'production' is easier and can be done in-house, and the editing is faster and simpler. As against this, the quality is not as good, and generally the picture is screened on to a small CRT monitor which can be seen by maybe a dozen people.

For certain specific applications, video wins on all counts. For instance a new pension scheme to be explained to employees; for an industrial process to be demonstrated to a potential customer; for educational purposes; for training; or for public relations activities—in all of these cases a photographic film whether 16 mm or 35 mm would be hard to justify, both in terms of cost and time. Increasingly, video is taking over in spite of the constraint of 3 non-compatible recording systems.

Checklist

1. Has the objective been set?
2. Has the target audience been defined?
3. Have the relative merits of video and photographic films been carefully assessed in relation to the objective and audience?
4. Have the methods of (a) distribution and (b) presentation been decided?
5. Has provision been made for checking and maintaining copies?
6. Has the budget been agreed together with the type and length of the film required?
7. Has a comprehensive production schedule been (a) produced, and (b) distributed to every person likely to be affected?
8. Has a date been put on each of the following stages?
   (a) Synopsis
   (b) Choice of film unit
   (c) Briefing
   (d) Treatment
   (e) Quotation
   (f) Signing of contract
   (g) Approval of script and visual interpretation
   (h) Shooting schedule
   (i) View rushes
   (j) Approval of complete film
   (k) Press show and launch
   (l) Publicity
   (m) Distribution
9. Has consideration been given to film strips, slides and VTR?

10.

EDITORIAL PUBLICITY

As a preliminary to this chapter it is necessary to discuss a term in publicity which is possibly misunderstood more than any other, namely PR. What does it mean and arising out of this just what are the functions of a PRO and a press officer?

The first point is of course that PR can mean either public relations or press relations—two quite different subjects. Furthermore, either may or may not be viewed in the context of the marketing function or of the business as a whole.

In this book the term public relations is used in its widest context, that of building and sustaining good relations between an organization and its various publics which include customers and prospects equally with employees and shareholders. The means by which good public relations are maintained include press advertising and direct mail just as much as editorial publicity.

The term press relations is used here to indicate the building up of good relationships between an organization and the various journalists who are likely to be concerned with it in order to secure good editorial publicity about any aspect of a company's operations, whether news about products, or new management techniques or strikes. It should also be noted that 'media relations' is being used increasingly to replace 'press relations'. This is in order that radio and TV shall not be overlooked. Similarly 'news release' may replace 'press release'. On the other hand there continue to be 'press officers' who in turn hold 'press conferences'.

In this chapter the subject of editorial publicity is dealt with only in so far as it contributes to the promotion of sales and is strictly within the confines of marketing activities and objectives.

Of the channels of persuasion which are available to bring to bear a sales message upon the mind of a prospect, the editorial columns of the press, television and radio are powerful media to include and integrate in the overall marketing communication mix. Again it is important to start with objectives and where possible to quantify these, both in order to determine the amount of effort needed to achieve the target, and as a means of subsequently measuring performance. It is not good enough to aim at 'securing a maximum of editorial coverage about a new type of industrial fire extinguisher'. It is necessary rather to define all the audiences which represent buying influences, to categorize and enumerate them, then specify which should be the target of an editorial message covering the new product. From this point the publications needed to make contact with this audience can be listed and a strategy developed for obtaining editorial coverage.

For example, suppose there are a total of fifty publications reaching the potential market for fire extinguishers of 50 000 people. The duplication of readership can be determined from readership surveys (see Chapter 13) as will be the average page traffic of the types of publication in question. It may be that by a combination of data, experience and judgement, it is concluded that to register with 75 per cent of the total potential market, editorial mention must be secured in twenty of the publications. If the news value is high this may be easy to achieve. If not, then perhaps some special activities will be necessary to create interest amongst the journalists. Alternatively the answer may be that the objective is not capable of achievement through editorial publicity, in which case other channels of persuasion must be strengthened in order that the total sales promotional impact provides adequate support for the selling effort.

The media, be it national, local, technical or special interest, is concerned primarily with providing information of interest to its readers or audiences, within of course the framework of a given editorial policy. The editor's job is to provide editorial material which will result in the readers' approbation and will influence the prestige of the publication. In due course this will influence its circulation, readership and thus advertising revenue. Editors can select from a wide range of sources: items of news, features, specialized stories, off-beat pieces, illustrations and so on. They must provide a good editorial mix. The function of a publicity executive is to think in terms of the ultimate audience, and to write in a way that will fit in with editorial criteria. To do otherwise is both a waste of time and an insult to the intelligence of an editor. The goal which must be aimed at then is to write a story which an editor will regard as a worthwhile item for his publication and which at the same time does a first-class selling job.

Editorial subjects

Approaching the matter with a journalist's eye, there are often too many subjects in industrial publicity: too many for the available staff to write about and, more important, too many for the press (particularly the monthlies) to assimilate. For many companies, having a variety of product lines and markets and applications, it is not difficult to produce, say, one story a week. It is expecting too much of the trade press to hope that all these will be published; even weeklies and dailies have many hundreds or thousands of other sources of news to call upon and regardless of any other consideration they must maintain a good editorial balance.

Thus the release of stories, even very good ones, may have to be rationed and this leads to the discipline (so often missing in press relations activities) of advance planning. It should be possible for the publicity officer concerned to have an outline plan of releases to the press covering at least several months ahead. Obviously unforeseen news stories will emerge but this does not invalidate the need for planning the basic framework of editorial publicity. Within the promotional strategy it is known well in advance which products are to be promoted and when. It follows that editorial stories would be planned to coincide with publicity in other media. A new product, for example, only becomes news when it is released to the outside world. It might have been produced months before and indeed been in service on a restricted basis for weeks, but it is only news as and when a company decides to make it so.

NEW PRODUCTS AND SERVICES

When exactly does a product or service qualify to be called new? It could be argued that for a firm producing plastic bottles or mouldings, every new order is likely to be a new product. But there may be a thousand of these each year. The criterion then should not be, is it new, but does it have news value? A small modification to a well-established moisture meter which results in an improvement of accuracy from ± 5 per cent error to ± 2 per cent has a far greater news value than a new style of lettering on a plastic bottle, even though the moisture meter can hardly claim to be a new product.

The degree of news value must also be assessed, since this will determine the way in which the story is written and presented. For example, the substitution of nylon bearings for metal in industrial castors has news value, though somewhat limited, whereas a process control system to automate a paper mill for the first time in the world is likely to justify major international press coverage.

When integrating editorial publicity with other promotional activities, it is important to emphasize that an item is only news as long as it is not known. Pre-planning must ensure that advertisements do not start appearing before an editor has had the opportunity to publish the contents of a press release.

PRODUCT AND SERVICE APPLICATIONS

Even where a product range is not undergoing a continuous change, a good basis for industrial and business news is the variety and novelty of product applications or new uses for a service. A thickness gauge may be developed and established for use on steel strip. Adaptations may well lead to its application in measuring paper, plastics, rubber, foil and fabric. A radiological dosemeter may seem to lack a very broad audience interest, but applications could well include detecting radioactive minerals in Cornwall, equipping a civil defence force in Sweden, finding a lost isotope through police action, or locating the blockage in a sewer.

The difficulty with application stories is to find them, and there is no easy solution here. The answer lies in the progressive building up among company staff of an awareness of the value of such stories. This is a target at which publicity executives must aim. It can be aided by continually probing and asking questions, by participation in sales conferences, by visiting customers, and by subsequently distributing press cuttings to all concerned. Top management can help by indicating that they regard time identifying and sifting out application stories well spent. This attitude of mind is easier to cultivate if such stories are planned to fit into the overall strategy. The possibility of a substantial financial incentive to employees contributing stories should be considered.

NON-PRODUCT INNOVATION

If a piece of editorial publicity is to contribute directly to the promotion of sales, it follows that it must have a direct reference to whatever is being sold. There are, however, a number of editorial subjects which, while not having a direct selling value, act as a reminder of the company and its products. Many innovations fall into this category, such as the installation of a new type of machine to produce a product not only faster but to closer tolerances, or a more efficient way of storing a product, or a way of processing waste to enable it to be reused. These items do not offer a 'consumer benefit' but they have reminder value coupled with a contribution to the building up of company reputation which is probably one of the set objectives of the public relations campaign.

OTHER NEWS ITEMS

Appointments of new people, staff promotions, new literature, exhibitions, large contracts, new factory openings, visits by VIPs, setting new records (the thousandth order), anniversaries—all these items can be turned with advantage to assist the promotional campaign. Even staff achievements are worth publicizing, like registering patents, lectures, learned papers or even election to the local council.

No listing of news subjects can be comprehensive: rather it is necessary to build up a news awareness throughout the company, a process which is helped a great deal by a perceptive reading of periodicals as well as talking to journalists and continually monitoring their needs. For example, in Chapter

8 we mentioned a very boring but very strong fibreboard box that had been taken into Billy Smart's Circus where an elephant stood on it. The resulting photograph was used not only by the packaging press, but also by the nationals.

FEATURE ARTICLES

Over and above news stories there are many opportunities for having a single subject dealt with in depth, either by offering a journalist exclusive coverage of some item, or by getting a member of staff to write an article dealing with a subject more extensively than is possible in a press release.

Many feature articles which have no direct sales connection fall into the category of public relations but others can be quite deliberately part of the sales plan. For instance, the complexities of the production process, the planning and launching of a product and the marketing research which preceded it.

The big problem is always to find someone with the time and ability to do the writing, maybe one or two thousand words, or even more. For a busy and senior executive to find the time is partly a matter of motivation. Apart from the 'ego trip' it is worth considering actually paying a fee for the job. In addition to this, many publications will also pay a fee for a contributed article, in which case the writer benefits from two sources. Not all people have the ability to write well for the press. In this case the publicity executive may take on the task of editing or rewriting. Alternatively it may be necessary to employ an outside specialist writer; for instance a feelance journalist. Even so the effort and the expense will be well worth the publicity which will be achieved.

Press (or news) releases

THE PRESS LIST

Before beginning to write a press release it is essential to define the audience to whom it is addressed. This may be for instance the decision-makers in a particular market segment plus a number of other categories who are known to have an influence on purchasing decisions. A useful starting point is to compile a list of all publications, people and other media which can conceivably be interested in news from the company or organization, and use it as the basic checklist for each proposed press release.

Over a period of time the list will be extended by the inclusion of contacts such as freelance journalists, trade organizations, specialist news agencies, house magazine editors, named journalists with a special interest, as well as overseas publishers and agencies. Names will be deleted as publications change or the business is modified.

WRITING THE RELEASE

Editors receive far too many press releases for them to handle or sometimes even read, and few hit the mark. Most often, releases are introspective about 'me' and 'us' and 'how proud we are' rather than about 'you' and 'how your company stands to benefit'. They are acceptable neither to the reader nor to the editor.

It follows that writing a press release is not a job which can be delegated to a junior. Securing adequate editorial publicity is a major part of a publicity programme and needs to be placed in the hands of a specialist. The publicity value of a press release is to be judged on the same terms as an advertisement in the same medium. A release of high interest value may result in an area of editorial space equivalent in impact to several pages of advertisements. The same technique and effort is justified for a press release as for an advertisement.

On the actual writing of the release, the maxim should be: 'If in doubt, leave it out', but generally a story should run to between 100 and 300 words. It should be written in the same style as a journalist would write it, i.e. giving the news as it will interest the reader. And it should be written in a factual, authoritative manner; it should be lively and interesting, but without the smallest trace of the hard sell.

A good rule to follow is to adopt the style of the inverted triangle with the really important news at the top and the supporting information coming further down. This enables a news editor to sub from the bottom and still leave intact the main thrust of the story.

Structure

As with any piece of writing, it must have a beginning, a middle, and an end.

1. *Headline*   This is vital. It is the signal to the journalists which must at a glance cause them to pause and read on rather than discard the release into the bin. So put in the essential news in three or four words. And play it straight. Other journalists will not use your headline. If they did, they might find some competitive journal doing the same thing to them, so they just won't take the risk.

2. *1st paragraph*   The release stands or falls on the first paragraph. It must therefore contain the main news angle written from the reader's point of view, not from yours. The basic marketing concept—identify the consumer benefit.

3. *2nd and 3rd paragraphs* If these are necessary, then they are there to elaborate on the main story already told in the first paragraph. But even so, they must give the highlights only of what you are trying to put across. It is not nearly so interesting to the reader as it is to you.

4. *4th paragraph* Consider putting in a quote from someone in authority, preferably outside the organization and therefore more credible.

5. *5th paragraph* Include facts and data here such as price, delivery, the date an event will happen, and so on.

6. *Further information* Always offer this: give two names to contact, with office and home telephone numbers.

Points to note

1. Keep sentences short; avoid jargon and abbreviations.
2. Have a clear attractive layout, typed double-spaced, on one side only.
3. Send the release only to publications that will really find it of interest.
4. Use a photograph wherever possible and always caption it so that the caption can be seen at the same time as the photograph.
5. Any amplification of the story should be on a separate sheet or accompanying publication which can be used or discarded depending on its relevance to the journalist.
6. Ask journalists to criticize your release. That's the way to learn.

PHOTOGRAPHS

Most press releases should be accompanied by a photograph. The reasons are varied. A photograph can illustrate special features: it helps to result in an editorial which is different and stands out; it may secure additional column centimetres; lastly it may be published even though the release is ignored.

Something has been said in an earlier chapter on the way in which photography is used in publicity. A paradoxical situation often exists between photography for press advertisements and photography for press releases. In the former the contents and composition are given considerable thought and closely debated by creative people at the agency even before a visual reaches the client who once again examines and scrutinizes the material. A photographer is commissioned, briefed, directed by a visualizer, possibly accompanied by the copywriter or the creative director, and fifty or sixty shots are taken. From these maybe half a dozen enlargements are examined until the desired visual solution is found.

Unfortunately the procedure for a press photograph is likely to be very different—a print from the file, or a quick shot by the work's photographer with a word from the press officer as a briefing. This makes no sense at all since whether a picture is used by an editor or not will depend in large measure upon its excellence and, after all, the illustrations both for advertisements and editorial are seen by the same audience. Second-rate photographs are a very false economy.

TIMING

Editorial publicity must be timed to fit the promotional plan but it must also fit in with the publishers' requirements. Copy dates in industrial publicity range from a few hours for nationals to a month and even more for some periodicals, and this is one of the reasons why it is sometimes necessary to place an embargo on publication. As an example of the need for planning, a press release on one particularly important news event, concerning the opening of a new factory, had to be supplied to a quarterly magazine two months in advance in order that the editorial mention should coincide with the coverage to be given by the dailies.

If the time of appearance of an editorial item is of special importance, a close study is necessary of copy dates of all the major publications involved, perhaps coupled with a personal contact with the editors concerned.

Press receptions

A major piece of business or industrial news will frequently be publicized by holding a press reception, or by taking the press to the factory, or alternatively to see a product being used by a customer. Such an event usually does not involve a very high expense in relation to the overall selling cost, or indeed the value of the resulting publicity.

A press reception enables a subject to be explained in depth and with greater impact than can be achieved by a press release. It enables senior company officials to make personal contact with journalists, to their mutual benefit, and in particular enables an enquiring reporter to get an individual angle on a story which will be much appreciated. Questions are facilitated and these help to avoid misunderstandings, while at the same time a good deal of general company philosophy rubs off on to one of the most influential of a company's publics, the press. Probably most important of all is that for an hour or so, maybe even a day, each journalist is thinking and acting within the company's environment. The company therefore becomes more than a mere name; it assumes an identity, a personality. This is an investment for the future which will have continuing repercussions and almost certainly affect the way in which press releases and other contacts are received subsequently, generally for good.

Journalists, however, do not have unlimited time and cannot be expected to react favourably to giving hours to a reception where it is dramatically announced that the southern area sales manager has been promoted to national accounts manager. Receptions must be reserved for worthwhile events judged in the terms of editors and their audiences.

Personal relationships

Journalists have a difficult task in sorting the multitude of news items which pour into them: in deciding which represent genuine news, which make technical sense and are appropriate to their readers' interests, and which should be set aside because they are merely product puffs, misleading or badly written.

It is valuable for publicity executives to build up good personal relationships with members of the press, not in order to influence them into accepting poor-quality material, but to keep them accurately informed about progress and developments in their section of industry. Journalists rely heavily on such personal relationships; they provide a means of obtaining news from a source on which they can rely both for accuracy and speedy action.

There are occasions when the press should meet senior executives of a company: a personal interview can be interesting editorially and valuable in sales promotion terms but as a general rule the press officer must be sufficiently senior and well-informed to deal with the press as an executive voicing the view of the company. If this is not so a journalist could be justified in regarding the latter as an obstacle in the communications process rather than an instrument.

A few executives still hold the view that even though editorial publicity may be useful, journalists themselves cannot be trusted. There are hair-raising stories about badly reported events, breaches of confidences and the need for advertisements as bribes. No doubt such things have happened but they are now mostly part of the folklore of the past. Journalists by and large are trustworthy and sincere professionals. Where they get a story wrong or report on a company unfairly it is generally because the firm failed to supply adequate material.

Measuring results

Every release to the press must be scrutinized in terms of each and every publication's needs. Therefore, a presupposition in the measurement of results is that most publications receiving a release may be expected to carry the story. It is tempting to send a standard press release to an entire mailing list in the hope that one or two extra mentions might be gained in this way, but this is clearly lazy and expensive and the press quickly learns to ignore the sender. One method of measurement is to determine the percentage of publications using a story, expressed on a base of the total number circularized. One hundred per cent response is sometimes attained but 50 per cent can be regarded as a good achievement. Twenty per cent or lower implies that the release was sent to too many publications or was wrongly written: at any rate it points to the need for enquiry. If a publication consistently fails to use a company's material, there should be an adequate record system to indicate this fact and the editor should be contacted diplomatically to find out why.

Measuring results in terms of sales leads can be misleading. It is well known in technical journalism that reader enquiries can be increased significantly by the simple expedient of missing out certain key data, thus forcing people to write to a company to obtain it. It is true that this provides sales leads and might meet a company's short-term requirements, but reader enquiries will tend to be, say, in tens, whereas readership of an item may well be in thousands, or considerably more. Looking at this particular matter in reverse, if an editor puts himself out to cover a story in depth and publishes a comprehensive feature article, few enquiries may be generated, yet the value of the editorial is many times greater than a short column mention. If response were to be the criterion, the opposite conclusion might be reached.

A technique which is used extensively, but has been subject to a good deal of criticism, is to measure by column centimetres. The disadvantage is that to add the number of centimetres in, say, *The Financial Times* to that in *Production Equipment Digest* is like trying to add apples and pears. This is certainly a valid limitation. Nevertheless, for a given firm or a particular campaign, the results can be sufficiently homogeneous to be assessed in this way. A refinement which is sometimes adopted is to express column centimetres in terms of equivalent advertising space, and this may well provide useful information on value for money spent.

As a research exercise an investigation of reader impact may be made following a particular piece of editorial publicity. This can hardly be a continuous measure of editorial efficiency since the expense would be too high. Where a certain item of news is restricted to editorial publicity only, the percentage audience reached of a defined potential market can be measured by carrying out a subsequent recall research.

Press cuttings

To carry out an editorial publicity campaign without evaluating the press cuttings is rather like an artillery bombardment without observation of the fall of shot. Not all mentions will be identified, but this can be partly made good by using two cuttings agencies, and by following up publications where no mention is recorded to find out what the reason might be.

Press cuttings can be circulated with effect among top management and sales staff. They are often of great interest to employees in general and can be used in house magazines. They may even form the basis of sales literature.

Moreover the widespread circulation of cuttings, apart from improving morale, enables employees to see for themselves the type of story which interests the press and stimulates them to originate ideas for further stories.

Limitations and advantages

While it is by no means true that editorial publicity is free publicity, the fact is that it is not only very good value for money but that it is also in some respect the most effective form of publicity available. Its particular strength derives from the implied endorsement of the publication in which a particular item appears, or, if not endorsement, at least an apparently independent appraisal of a product or service now being offered. As against this, an advertisement for the same product will be seen as partisan and much of its message will be discounted for this reason. And quite apart from credibility it is known from page traffic studies (see Chapter 13) that editorials have far more readers than advertisements: maybe as many as a factor of five. A further benefit to come from editorial publicity is the opportunity for inexpensive reprints, and quotations of extracts.

There are a number of important limitations, the most significant of which is the uncertainty of when a particular piece of news will appear, whether in fact it will ever appear at all, and if so whether it will be an accurate representation of the story. In an extreme case it could well be a negative report and cast doubts upon the value of a product. It is difficult to see editorial publicity as the main component of a promotional campaign since once a story has been reported it cannot be repeated, whereas a requirement of a campaign is likely to be continuity over a protracted period of time, and to satisfy this requirement is going to call for the deployment of a multi-media mix.

Checklist

1. Has the use of editorial publicity been established as an integral part of the selling operation?
2. Is there a plan of action covering the same period of time as the marketing strategy?
3. Have quantified objectives been set for editorial publicity?
4. Are the sales staff aware of the value of this form of publicity, and the extent to which they can contribute?
5. Have press lists been drawn up which relate specifically to (a) the company's activities (b) its markets and (c) its products?
6. Has attention been given to the importance of producing press releases which are tailored to the needs of the particular audience and media concerned?

7. Is photography used wherever possible, and is the same attention given to its creative treatment and production as for press advertising?

8. Are press releases timed so as to fit in with (a) editorial press dates and (b) the overall promotional campaign?

9. Have good personal relationships been built up between the relevant journalists and the key company staff?

10. Has provision been made (a) for measuring results and (b) for corrective action to be taken if necessary?

11. Are press cuttings used as a means of evaluation?

12. Are they comprehensive?

13. Are they circulated to personnel who might be interested?

11.

TELEVISION ADVERTISING

During the second half of the eighties television has become a far more important medium for business-to-business advertising. Many companies selling products and services to business people have discovered the creative value that television can add to their message. In fact some of the most creative advertisements seen on television today are for business-to-business products and this is not surprising when it it considered that 19 out of the top 20 advertising agencies have at least one business-to-business client.

Many business and industrial advertisers are no longer worried by the fact that many of the people watching the ad are not interested in their products. They are offsetting this fact against the added communication value of TV to their specific target. Because ITV and Channel Four are sold on a regional basis, the advertisers can of course choose geographical targets. When Channel Four was introduced it brought with it a much greater consciousness by marketing and advertising people of the need to look at the make-up of the audience to any one of the many different programmes. Now, television audiences are analysed both by media buyers and sellers in terms of their subgroup ratings, ratings of ABC1 men or 16–24 adults for example. The value of individual commercial spots is now analysed carefully according to their audience profile.

Some of the television companies themselves have taken particular interest in trying to help business-to-business advertisers find their special target market. Granada Television for example has analysed the normal BARB viewing panel, selected what they consider are business people and then tracked their viewing across certain days and certain weeks (Figs 11.1, 11.2).

The weekly reach of ITV for business people for the four weeks ending 1 November 1987 was 94 per cent; for Channel Four it was 80 per cent. The top four programmes on ITV were *The Charmer, The Bill, The Dame Edna Experience* and *The New Statesman*; while on Channel Four they were, *The Last Resort, Golden Girls, Worldwise* and *American Football*.

A traditional target market for business advertisers is AB men. One way to build a campaign that will reach AB men effectively is to look at the top AB men viewing programmes (see Table 11.1).

Another form of analysis, especially when looking at efficiency, is to

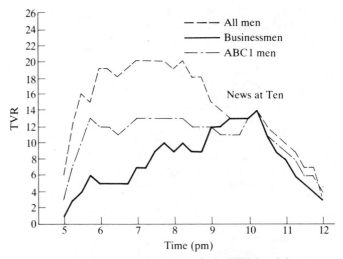

Figure 11.1 Businessman viewing analysis, ITV (weekday averages)

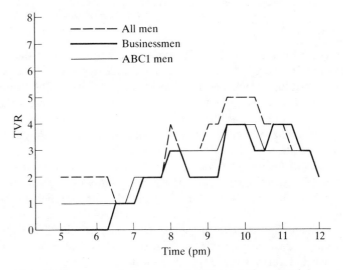

Figure 11.2 Businessman viewing analysis, Channel Four (weekday averages)

choose spots with a high **AB** men profile. The top five programmes in October 1987 across the network, in terms of index of **AB** men over all men are shown in Table 11.2

TVS Television has gone further and conducted a study to show how many people are actually involved in the buying decision-making process within

Table 11.1 Top AB men programmes
11 October–1 November 1987, ITV (rating)

	TVR
Bruno vs. Bugner	36
Spitting Image	32
News on Saturday	26
News at Ten	23
The Charmer	22

Table 11.2 Top AB men programmes,
October 1987, across the network (index)

	Index
Book Choice	347
What the Papers Say	338
Booker Prize 1987	336
Comment	295
Channel Four News	293

companies for business products. The object was to show that there is rarely one person alone who needs to be communicated with by advertising. Therefore, the target market is wider than first originally thought and advertisers may be losing out if they do not consider these others. The research then went on to analyse these sample people's viewing according to which products they are either buying or influencing the buying decision on, i.e. the composition of the Decision Making Unit.

The results of the work undertaken by TVS show, for example, that in the buying of office equipment, an engineering company with a turnover in excess of £20 million had at least four people who played a part in the buying decision (the director and general manager, the admin director, the office systems manager and the chairperson of the group's Guidelines Committee). The viewing of these people was then tracked and all four people were shown to have selected various programmes to watch.

The growth of business-to-business advertising

Table 11.3 shows the increasing importance of business-to-business advertising for the television companies and, while still small as a percentage of their total revenue, it is growing fast (see Table 11.3). A closer look at specific markets will help quantify the extent to which business advertisers are moving towards television advertising (see Table 11.4).

Table 11.3   Television expenditure at rate card costs (£'000s Jan–Dec 1986) (*Source:* MEAL)

	£'000s	TV %	Press %	Radio %
Office cleaning/services	791	6	93	1
Car/truck rental	5 926	47	43	10
Calculators	531	0	100	0
Typewriters/word processors	5 365	28	71	1
Photocopiers	1 835	23	77	0
Phones, communication systems	49 001	53	45	2
Stationery/office supplies	4 699	52	40	8
Vending machines	92	85	15	0
Corporate/sponsorship	140 880	52	47	1
Motor trucks/vans	15 755	18	82	0
Computers	22 302	38	60	2
City and financial services	42 396	8	91	1
British development corporations	14 079	34	7	58
Shipping agents	5 446	32	17	52
Agricultural feeds	78	30	70	—
Cultivators/hoes	32	0	100	0
Fertilizers, compost, chemicals	4 196	74	26	0
Portable buildings	2 223	0	100	0
Steel storage furniture	284	0	100	0

At this stage of the chapter it may be worth taking time to explain how a television commercial works in the United Kingdom.

The Independent Broadcasting Authority (IBA) is the central body appointed by the Home Office to provide Independent Television (ITV), Channel Four and independent local radio services in the United Kingdom.

The IBA is given authority to award contracts to companies which will best serve the programming needs of a particular area of the United Kingdom for a specified franchise period.

The ITV companies obtain their revenue from the sale of advertising. Controls over the advertising are among the most comprehensive in the world. The frequency, amount and nature of commercials must be in accordance with the Broadcasting Act and the extensive rules and principles laid down by the Authority. There must be a total distinction between programme and commercials. The frequency and duration of commercial breaks are strictly regulated by the IBA—an average of 6 minutes per hour with a maximum of 7 minutes in any one clock-hour.

The Broadcasting Act provides for the insertion of breaks between programmes and within programmes. Natural breaks within programmes often occur in light entertainment, quiz shows, sport, etc. No internal advertising is allowed in many different types of programming, e.g. selected

Table 11.4   Profile of business television (1980 and 1987)

	1980 %	1987 %
Agricultural/horticultural	0.4	0.4
Charity/educational	—	—
Drink	8.7	9.1
Entertainment	1.8	1.5
Financial	*3.0*	*7.3*
Food	27.0	24.0
Government and service	2.9	2.7
Holidays/travel	2.8	2.7
Household appliances	3.8	3.9
Household equipment	2.4	1.2
Household stores	8.2	8.3
Institutional/industrial	*1.5*	*4.6*
Leisure equipment	6.7	4.5
Motors	5.6	7.2
Office equipment	*0.2*	*1.1*
Pharmaceutical	3.0	2.9
Publishing	3.3	4.3
Retail/mail order	6.1	4.5
Tobacco	0.9	0.7
Toiletries and cosmetics	6.3	5.8
Wearing apparel	1.6	0.6
Local	3.9	2.6
Total	100%	100%

current affairs and documentaries, religious services, half-hour children's programmes, formal Royal occasions, parliamentary broadcasts and programmes lasting less than 20 minutes.

In addition to the mainstream television companies, Channel Four Television Company was established in 1981 as a wholly owned subsidiary of the IBA. Eight-seven per cent of the population were able to view it from the outset. Programme schedules are devised by Channel Four in accordance with the IBA, although the existing contractors sell its advertising. The country is broken down into 15 areas as shown in Table 11.5.

It is important to examine closely the nature of each television area, especially in relation to sales or potential sales. Some, like London and TVS, have a much more upmarket audience and a more high-tech business environment. Others are more biased towards traditional heavy manufacturing. Information on each contractor's area is available from them on request.

Table 11.5 Commercial television in the United Kingdom

Area	Company	Transmission hours	Potential audience
London	Thames	Monday–Friday	10 998 000
London	LWT	Friday–Sunday	10 998 000
East and West Midlands	Central	All week	8 924 000
North-West	Granada	All week	6 638 000
Yorkshire	Yorks	All week	5 822 000
North-East	Tyne-Tees	All week	3 028 000
Wales West	HTV	All week	4 697 000
South and South-East	TVS	All week	5 121 000
East	Anglia	All week	3 942 000
South-West	TSW	All week	1 526 000
Central Scotland	Scottish	All week	3 480 000
North Scotland	Grampian	All week	1 135 000
The Borders/Isle of Man	Border	All week	656 000
Northern Ireland	Ulster	All week	1 389 000

The cost of advertising on commercial television

Because commercial television offers a range of rates dependent upon supply and demand it is difficult to provide exact costs. However, a network 30 second *peaktime* commercial on ITV and Channel Four combined could cost in the region of £40 000 if that spot got a TVR (television rating—i.e. percentage of viewers) of 30. Within that cost, buying the spot in London (with the same TVR) would be in the region of £13 000, on Central £6000, on Television South £6000, and on Border £300 (1987 average estimates).

Channel Four allows, on its own, new advertisers with limited budgets to experiment with television advertising. That is not to say that Channel Four is not a medium in its own right. Equally, advertising on ITV 1 need not be a prohibitively expensive exercise. Buying a campaign which does not depend on high-demand peaktime spots may reach exactly the target audience that a business advertiser wishes to reach.

In assessing which area(s) to advertise a product the same questions must be asked that are asked in other media. Which area best reflects my market profile? Which areas are heavy users of this type of product? Which areas have the greatest market potential? And of course who and where are the decision-makers? A television area like London or TVS may appear to be more expensive; however, the success of a campaign can only be quantified in terms of results and the size of the potential market must be ascertained from the outset.

How to advertise on television

The advertiser will obviously consult with his agency initially from a budget point of view. He will then establish the creative approach and the weight of the TV campaign, the latter, of course, being directly related to budget. With the advice of copywriters and the TV production department a commercial is generally fed out to an independent production house at an agreed cost. Alternatively, if industrial advertisers do not have an agency they may go direct to the television company who will advise and help make the commercial. In this case it is common practice for the advertiser to use a time buying shop at no extra cost.

THE COST OF MAKING A COMMERCIAL

While a commercial may cost as little as £100 it is likely that larger sums of money will be involved. Below are some ball-park figures on just how much it can cost to advertise on television.

1. *5 or 10 second commercials—£200–£2000*   Within this price range, production values will range from the most basic and cheapest slide presentation of a simple message with a station announcer's voice over it, to a multi-slide presentation accompanied by pre-recorded sound on a separate audio cassette. At the upper end of this price bracket, a director and/or producer should also be provided, as well as some editing facilities.
2. *5 or 10 second commercials—£2000–£5000*   Advertisers requiring high production values can add extra facilities such as special visual effects, or the addition of music, pack-shots of the product; studio use plus colour camera, as well as more of the director's and producer's time.
3. *30 second commercials—£5000–£15 000*   Productions within this range will enable the advertiser to be more ambitious in his presentation. A budget at the top end should be adequate to cover a full day's studio use, editing time, special effects, casting, lighting, make-up and art direction, simple set construction and props, and all necessary crewing and transportation and artwork costs and insurances.
4. *30 second commercials and longer from £15 000*   Commercials that require location shooting, as well as studio time, synchronized sound, the use of several artists as well as the necessary technical and staffing facilities, can be expected to cost anything from this figure up to £40–£50 000. Many factors determine price: the stature of the lead artist or artists; the cost of music; where and if location shooting is required; the complexities of set design; how much editing time is needed—and so on.
5. *Repeat fees and other ancillary costs*   In addition to the performance fee paid an artist or artists to appear in a television commercial, 'repeat' fees

are due to performers when the commercial is transmitted. The scale of these fees is related to the area(s) in which the commercial is shown, and to the number of times it is repeated.

TYPICAL BUSINESS-TO-BUSINESS ADVERTISERS USING TELEVISION: ADDITIONAL SERVICES

The television contractors not only help the advertiser with commercial production facilities. They offer a range of other services including:

1. *Ansafone*   Offering a simple and efficient direct response facility on behalf of the advertiser.
2. *Television telegrams*   A message printed on a telegram format communicating promotional news to relevant markets.
3. *Television sales force*   Which supplements an advertiser's own sales force and offers the skills of direct selling, merchandising, distribution checks, demonstrations etc.

Commercial television in the future

The state of broadcasting in Britain at this time is one of great flux and new legislation could well change the structure of the industry completely. The most exciting development for television broadcasting in Europe will be the introduction of high powered satellites. One example is a new medium-powered satellite to transmit 16 channels over a footprint of most of Europe receivable by homes (and cable operators) who have reception dishes of 85 cm.

Many of these 16 channels could be of interest to the business-to-business advertiser. A further development is a satellite transmitting three channels over a footprint covering the United Kingdom receivable by dishes smaller than 85 mm and which even now are declining in cost at a great rate.

No doubt in the coming years we will see a proliferation of both satellite and maybe terrestrial channels all of which will provide increased television opportunities and improved target marketing for the business-to-business advertiser.

12

OTHER MEANS OF PROMOTION

In this Marketing communications section of the book, the reader has been taken progressively from the initial strategy through each major channel of persuasive communications—press advertising, direct mail, exhibitions, literature, photography, films, TV and editorial publicity. One of the problems facing publicity executives is that as each of these media is used more efficiently, its competitive edge is blunted. Maybe this is countered by ingenuity in creative presentation, but nevertheless competition is intense. An advertisement is fighting for attention amidst thousands of others; an exhibition stand may be in a hall amongst hundreds of others, an editorial mention is only a drop in an ocean of words.

The impact of a sales message depends a great deal upon the novelty with which it is presented, but novelty becomes increasingly hard to find as a particular medium is more widely used by industrial advertisers. Each seeks as a result to find more unconventional ways of presenting a message. For instance, the first time a national newspaper was distributed at an exhibition with a special front page entirely devoted to one of the exhibitors it must have created a remarkable effect, as no doubt did the first aerial advertisement to be towed behind an aircraft.

This chapter examines some of the lesser-used industrial publicity techniques as well as some of the peripheral activities which tend to be classed under the publicity function. It cannot hope to be exhaustive, but it will underline the importance of applying creative imagination to new or less used techniques which can give a powerful stimulus to a campaign or even becomes its focal point.

Radio advertising

Radio is a mass medium in much the same way as television and newspapers. It has a variable audience profile as does television and there will be times when listeners will comprise a higher than usual AB content. Even with this narrow profile, use of radio will be a blunderbuss approach to communicating with businessmen, though there are certain time slots in which listeners become highly segmented, and the opportunity to reach businessmen can be available for instance during the immediate pre- and post-work driving hours.

The geographical segmentation which can be achieved with local radio stations may be of interest if a firm is setting about a moving sales campaign or road show: it can also help on the rare occasion when test marketing an industrial product. Generally its usefulness is in direct proportion to its number of prospects, i.e the total number of companies who may buy a product multiplied by the average number of people in the decision-making units. On a national scale it is probably not worth while for target prospects less than the order of 100 000, though in many other countries radio has for long had an important role to play in what might be regarded broadly as the corporate communications function.

On the credit side, a radio commercial is fast to produce and relatively cheap. Small slots of time can be bought to give tactical support to the sales force. And there are minor spin-offs like reaching out to non-buying audiences (which even so are important in PR terms) such as employees and their families, shareholders, local communities, opinion formers and potential recruits—schools.

A starting point after obtaining audience profiles at various times of day is to conduct a small research amongst existing customers. Get the sales force to ask people they call on for a week if and when they listen to local radio.

Sponsorship

A major new activity in the promotion of companies and products is sponsorship. Simple and effective this can involve paying for or subsidizing such things as sports, the arts, books, conferences, exhibitions, flower shows, ballroom dances: the list is endless. A clear distinction must be made with patronage which can be applied to any of these activities, but is concerned only with giving suport to the event regardless of any possible reward or benefit. Sponsorship on the other hand is the deliberate financial support given to an event in order to achieve a specific commercial objective. Typical objectives might be:

1. To increase brand awareness among customers.
2. To improve perception of company in terms of modernity, warmth, concern etc.
3. To increase goodwill and understanding among trade customers.
4. To enhance company's image in local community.
5. To raise employees' morale and company loyalty.
6. To create favourable awareness of the company among young potential future consumers.

The staging of numerous 'high visibility' sponsorship schemes by major consumer goods companies tends to imply that there is little going on in the industrial sector. The opposite is probably the case: it is simply that they tend to be specialized, or educational, or at a local level. So their visibility is not very great but in practice they not only do a useful job, but are also very cost effective.

The whole business of sponsorship has been very well summarized by the Incorporated Society of British Advertisers in a booklet[1] which puts up 10 points:

1. Sponsorship is a tool of company communication. Its prime purpose is the achievement of favourable publicity for the company or its brands within a relevant target audience by the support of an activity (or some aspect thereof) which is not directly linked to the company's normal business.

2. It should not be confused with patronage, advertising or sales promotion, although they have some elements and objects in common. Sponsorship can prove an important additional ingredient in the marketing communication programme.

3. Sponsorship provides great flexibility—*in the choice of activity sponsored*; the arts, sport, leisure, social or communal activities; *the form the sponsorship may take*—tournaments, events, support of teams or individual competitors; *scale of participation*, from international golf to awards at the local flower show. Terms, conditions and level of financial contributions are invariably open to negotiation.

4. Sponsorship is normally undertaken for one (or more) of the following reasons:
   (a) To enhance the company name/brand image.
   (b) Improve trade relations.
   (c) Foster company's 'good citizen' image.
   (d) Boost employee morale.

5. Sponsorship is unlikely to achieve significant results used on a 'one-off' basis. It should be regarded in the long term, both in setting objectives and budgets. (The possibility of escalating costs should be borne in mind, as should the 'risk' factor in sponsoring a team or individual over a lengthy period.)

6. Setting realistic objectives is imperative; both when deciding the area, nature, level and duration of sponsorhip, and in formulating strategy once participation has been decided upon.

7. Sponsorship is a business deal; a written contract is essential. It is important to establish a good relationship, with mutual recognition of the responsibilities and expectations of both parties.

8. The full benefits of the sponsorship will be achieved only if it is integrated with the company's other publicity activities; e.g., advertising, PR, sales promotion, staff and customer relations etc.

9. Procedures should be established for the control (including budgetary), monitoring and evaluation of the sponsorship programme.
10. First-time sponsors should consider obtaining advice and guidance— from relevant statutory bodies and/or a specialist consultancy or agency.

Sponsored books

The sponsored book is an excellent method of promotion and, if the editorial theme is carefully devised in association with a publisher, it can prove to be a significant instrument of marketing policy. The book usually relates to subject matter close to the firm's products or markets and should be practical and authoritative. (*The Industrial Applications of the Diamond* by N. R. Smith, Director of the diamond tool specialists, Van Moppes and Sons Ltd is a good example.) The author is usually a senior member of the firm and his or her name appears on the title page, linked with the name of his/her company. This is the only reference to the firm but all examples, pictures etc. are drawn from the firm's products and customers. The firm underwrites the cost of the book but takes an agreed percentage of all revenue from all copies sold. It can thus be a self-liquidating exercise, but if it is not, there is always some financial return as libraries take the book, and the promotional cost is low. It should also be remembered that a published book is the most permanent and deeply penetrating method of communication yet devised.

Telemarketing

A new range of uses for the telephone has grown up over the past few years and looks likely to develop further. Already in the United States direct marketing by telephone is said to have exceeded that by mail. In a United States survey of industrial companies two-thirds of the respondents said they used the telephone for selling or lead generation.

In the United Kingdom the use of the telephone for selling has been slow to get off the ground due perhaps to the reaction by customers that such calls are intrusive and an unwarranted, and certainly undesirable, invasion of their privacy.

The function of telemarketing has grown in the United States into a highly disciplined activity by people having a natural aptitude for telephone conversation. They are well trained and usually work to a structured brief on what to say.

One of the most useful applications of the telephone in marketing is in market research where at least simple answers can be obtained in a very short space of time. There is little doubt however that other business uses of the telephone will expand. Campaign evaluation for example is worth considering as are readership surveys in relation to business people and industrial decision-makers.

Posters

Little use is made of posters in industrial publicity, and this may be a good reason for using them. They represent a first-class medium for getting across the basic sales message but the problem is in finding suitable site locations. Some obvious opportunities exist: exhibition halls, conferences, key railway stations, airports and even railway and underground trains. There are the company's own vehicles, sites adjacent to exhibition halls and hotels where visitors are likely to stay, taxis or even sandwich-board men. Posters can be used as direct mail pieces: they even occasionally reach the office wall if the design is outstanding enough.

Point of sale

Many industrial products, especially components, have a retail market and, however small, this is worth supporting. Consideration can therefore be given to showcards, dispensers, display units, give-away leaflets as well as posters. Point of sale material can also be of value in industrial merchandising, for instance, by agricultural merchants, electrical contractors or industrial wholesalers.

Packaging

With very many consumer products, food, toiletries and cigarettes, packaging may lay fair claim to be at least as important as the product itself. Apart from other factors, it preconditions a buyer to adopt a favourable attitude towards the contents: it is a vital part of building up a favourable brand image.

Professional buyers are not immune to subjective forces. A well-packaged or presented product will have the edge on one for which no trouble at all has been taken. It is equally true as with consumer goods that an over-packaged product may set up a resistance.

Most industrial products must be packaged in some way. A wooden crate with wood wool packing can be improved by including around the product a well-fitted polythene bag with a brand name on it. In place of a cardboard box an attractively printed carton can be used. Functional packaging also has a part to play: shrinkwrapping of gear wheels to prevent corrosion, a dust cover for an inspection microscope, expanded plastic case inserts for delicate machinery. A well-produced and appropriate piece of packing confirms the supplier's belief that his product is good enough to be carefully protected.

Gifts

The question of giving business gifts is more likely to set a boardroom alight than the most expensive advertising campaign. Does it establish a dangerous precedent? Will competitors follow suit? Where should the line be drawn and what of those who do not receive a gift, or worse still, get one this year but not next? These questions are answered only by a careful consideration of what to give, how and when to give it, and what repercussions are likely.

There can be few guidelines on gifts since the circumstances vary so much. The criterion is: does the gift make a maximum contribution to the promotion of sales at minimum cost? If to emboss the trade mark will provide additional publicity, for example with an item to stand on a desk or hang on an office wall, then it should be used. If it is likely to be out of place, say on something for the home, then it should not be used. Guidance on what not to give can usually be found in the multitude of business gift catalogues. The items in these are most likely to be what other firms will be choosing and there is a limit to the number of penknives and desk diaries that a buyer can absorb. Choose then something novel, something that sells, is appropriate and in good taste.

Christmas cards

These are included under sales promotion rather than under public relations, because they can be regarded as contributing to the selling effort. Where firms use Christmas cards as another direct mail shot to all and sundry there is a strong case for supposing that they are likely to be either ineffectual or even considered in bad taste and therefore counter-productive.

In industrial selling, however, a close personal relationship is often built up between a buyer and a salesperson—to their mutual advantage—and here an exchange of Christmas cards can surely be regarded as part of the building up of good relationships, and in so far as they contribute to efficient selling, an element of a sales promotional activity.

Brand-names

All products, including industrial, must have names. The buyer, and the user, must identify it and if the selling company does not provide an adequate name or identity, the buyer will invent one.

Furthermore, all products have an image. This may have evolved, or come by chance, or it may have been deliberately planned and promoted. The inescapable fact is that whenever a product is named to a buyer it conjures up a certain image which may be good or bad, cheap or expensive, reliable or unreliable. The brand-name itself is not necessarily a significant factor in determining the image of an industrial product. This would be too much to hope for, rather the image will be created by the product itself in the long run. However, it is the case that a product needs a name to identify it and to enable a buyer to recall it when making the purchase. The essential requirement is that it should be memorable, and the simpler the name is the better, both in the number of letters and the ease of pronunciation.

In determining a brand-name for an industrial product there would seem to be little point in basing it on, say, the raw materials from which it is made, or the process, or the town, or a nearby forest or river. There may be some advantage in a name which emphasizes the 'customer benefit', but if this leads to a word which is exotic, complex and highly contrived, it is better to abandon it and try for something simple. It is possible to aim for both but it will be hard to improve on such classics as OXO or KODAK.

Sales aids

The marketing services or publicity department often finds itself closely involved in a number of sales activities such as sales training, sales conferences and sales manuals. This is to be welcomed since it helps to weld the two functions. These, however, are not considered to be a major part of the promotional operation and for this reason are not dealt with in any detail. They are mentioned, however, because it is important that they are not overlooked in the overall marketing mix. Two matters which perhaps can be considered within the publicity framework are sales aids and samples.

Progressive sales managers will devote considerable time in training their sales staff to present the benefits of a product to a buyer, to overcome points of resistance and to close the deal. In this process a variety of aids can be deployed with advantage.

The product itself is the obvious choice together with the facilities to demonstrate it. This may be a demonstration caravan or a well-fitted show case. Where a product is not demonstrable, use can be made of a photograph album, a slide projector or a self-contained video unit. Samples of raw materials need to be more than just a handful of pieces of sheet metal; these can be presented in such a way as to project their selling features attractively.

A sales presentation requires the skill of a stage show. The development of the argument needs to be planned, using the salesperson to the full, but support needs to be given with every appropriate visual, audio and three-dimensional aid. Pre-presentation material should be sent in advance to prepare the prospect, and the follow-up should make full use of sales literature, advertisement reprints, press cuttings and any other promotional material.

Whatever material is used, it should be geared to the sales arguments and method of visual presentation being used elsewhere, to achieve maximum integrated impact.

Stickers, stuffers and mailings

Correspondence from a company provides at least three opportunities for introducing, or at least reinforcing, a sales argument.

Suppose, for instance, that a new brand of heat-resisting paint is being launched and that all the conventional media of a major campaign are being brought to bear on the potential market. For a specified period of time and with suitable phasing, the brand-name together with the main slogan can be printed on to a mini-leaflet and stuffed into every envelope leaving the company; a small sticker can be affixed to each letter sent out; finally at very low cost all envelopes can be franked with a few key words. In themselves these are small actions, but viewed as a whole they help to give cohesion to a campaign, and have an impressive effect both on potential buyers and one's own staff.

Signboards

Signboards outside a factory are often overlooked, or left to the initiative of an architect or factory manager. A solution is to place the responsibility for company signs firmly on the publicity department. These may include large illuminated signs and neon lights, and range down to signposts and notice boards.

Seminars

Although perhaps part of educational public relations, seminars can have a direct selling function. Indeed in some branches of business, such as hi-tech and financial services, they have become a major selling activity. One company took over the Festival Hall to present a technical seminar on a new range of components having certain novel features. Not only did they fill the hall with prospective buyers, they also charged an entrance fee, and made a profit.

Summary

Finally, an interesting though dated indication of the usage of 'miscellaneous promotion items' is given in a publication by Metalworking Production[2] in relation to a segment of the engineering industry (see Table 12.1).

Checklist

1. Are novel means of sales promotion encouraged in order to get the edge on competition?
2. Is 'brainstorming' or other techniques used in which people are able to

Table 12.1   Expenditure on miscellaneous promotional items

	Percentage
Regular press handouts	54
Christmas gifts	48
Christmas cards	45
Films	34
Calendars	30
Coloured slides and viewers	17
Mobile display vans	8
Diaries	8
Point of sale display panels	6
Press conferences	6
Private film shows/cocktail and theatre parties	4
Technical posters and wall charts	3
Advertising gifts and novelties	3
Works exhibitions and novelties	3

suggest the most unlikely ideas, without fear of criticism, in order to maximize on creative initiative?

3. Does such creative expression extend past headlines, copy angles, sign-offs, slogans and symbols, to include the medium, e.g., size and shape, material, colour, texture, feel, smell, wrapping and presentation?

4. Specifically, has consideration been given to:
   (a)   Radio?
   (b)   Sponsorship?
   (c)   Telemarketing?
   (d)   Seminars and conferences?
   (e)   Christmas cards?
   (f)   Calendars and diaries?
   (g)   Point-of-sale material, posters, or wall charts?
   (h)   Sponsored books and pamphlets?
   (i)   Outgoing mail, stickers, stuffers, franking?
   (j)   Sales aids, manuals, conferences, slides, films?
   (k)   Brand-names and symbols?
   (l)   Packaging and presentation?

References

1. *Guide to Sponsorship* (ISBA, 1982).
2. *Special Report on the Buying and Selling Techniques used in the British Engineering Industry* (McGraw-Hill).

Part 3

RESEARCH

INTRODUCTION

During the past twenty years or so a great deal of progress has been made in applying research techniques to aspects of marketing. Initially this was concentrated in the consumer sector since it was here that the money was most readily available, and in a sense this was an easier area to investigate. The movement into industrial marketing was slow, and often inadequately based because of low budgets, and this in turn resulted in inaccurate results, discouraging further research and leading to yet lower budgets.

Persistence on the part of certain leading companies, publishers, and in particular a few specialist industrial research agencies, has led to a breakthrough to such an extent that sophisticated techniques are nowadays being applied to the marketing of industrial products and services. It may well be that in the future, expenditure on industrial marketing research will exceed that on consumer research.

The distinction should be drawn between market research and marketing research, particularly in the context of his book. Market research is concerned with the investigation of markets, their size, location, purchasing power, growth, capital structure and economics. This is only one aspect of the matter. Marketing research can be regarded as the application of research techniques to any facet of marketing including the market. Thus new product research, concept testing, attitude and motivation studies, patterns of buying behaviour, structure of decision-making units, are all part of the growing science of marketing research. Into this category fit media research and campaign evaluation, the subjects of the next two chapters.

Research processes are not infallible. The aim of any research activity is to reduce to a minimum the areas of uncertainty surrounding management decisions. The application of research techniques, and the use of scientific disciplines do not of themselves eliminate uncertainty. They merely provide a degree of precision to some of the criteria upon which marketing and other business decisions are based. The tendency in some quarters for marketing research to be regarded as wasteful or misleading is more often due to a blind reliance on, or a misinterpretation of, research data than the data itself being at fault. The solution lies in using professional expertise not only to conduct the research but also to interpret its significance.

13

MEDIA RESEARCH

Press advertising

Press advertising represents the largest single item in the industrial publicity budget.

In Chapter 4 emphasis was laid on the need for accurate media selection and the criteria which should be considered were broken down into fourteen categories. Some of these do not require research to evaluate them, for instance 'frequency' or 'special services from publisher'. Others require accurate data for intelligent decisions to be made.

CIRCULATION

It is necessary to be sceptical when considering media data and to examine closely the basis upon which it has been arrived at. Take for example total circulation. If a figure is quoted by a publisher, but unsupported by his membership of the Audit Bureau of Circulation (ABC) an advertiser must draw his own conclusions and at least be doubtful. A good deal of pioneer work has been done by *British Rate and Data* (published by Maclean Hunter) in insisting on data meeting certain standards before they will publish it.

Given that a total circulation figure is validated either by ABC or by postal certificate or perhaps some other acceptable audit, the question arises 'what precisely does this figure mean?'. This at least is an assurance that a certain number of copies went out through the post. But to whom did these copies go? Did they ask for them? And did they pay for them? Suppose in a specialized field there are 4000 separate identifiable purchasing units, and suppose a journal can prove that its specialized circulation is 4000, this is by no means a guarantee that it is addressed to 100 per cent of the market. Where the market for a particular publication is not homogeneous, the variations in coverage between one segment and another can be so great as to make a total circulation figure comparatively useless. Some progress has been made in providing details of circulation by the introduction of the Media Data Form. This enables an advertiser to obtain reliable information on methods of circulation (free, subsidized, or full price), circulation to overseas countries and often a breakdown under United Kingdom geographical regions.

When a breakdown of industries or of occupations is in question, the situation is different. In the first place, such data on the Media Data Form is not audited and it is an unfortunate fact that from some publishers the figures can be little more than uninformed or approximate head-counting. Even where the job is done thoroughly and professionally by a publisher, there are real difficulties in knowing just how to categorize a given recipient, and in how much detail. Since, however, the usual reason for an analysis being required is to enable comparisons to be made between different, competitive publications it is necessary to note that such data is presented in a form which makes a comparison possible only in very few instances.

One basis which is used by publishers for circulation analysis is the Government *Standard Industrial Classification*. This breaks down the whole of British industry with a great deal of detail and provides explanatory notes on what is meant by each sub-classification. This does not enable a conglomerate to be easily classified, but for many requirements it is a valuable starting point.

Finally, it must be appreciated that circulation is continuously changing, with perhaps 20 per cent a year new registrations, offset by 20 per cent lapses. A judgement based on circulation this year, even if it is right, may be wrong after the year has elapsed. It is surprising that to meet the apparent demand of big advertisers, publishers devote their energies increasingly to expanding circulation as an end in itself, when the factor which really has any relevance at all is readership. This, also, should not be regarded as an end in itself since finally it is the impact of an advertisement which really counts, and this will be dealt with in the next chapter on campaign evaluation. In the meantime, there are several techniques which can be employed to measure readership.

TOTAL READERSHIP

Any readership survey is liable to considerable errors from differences in interpretation as to what constitutes 'readership' and how individual respondents react to the term. Accepting an initial margin of error, however, a good deal of progress can be made in measuring the usefulness of a journal in terms of readership as opposed to circulation. The same criticism of total readership applies as with total circulation, namely it tends to be of use only in a homogeneous market, for example hairdressers or market gardeners.

A study of the number of people reading a publication in comparison with its circulation is often most revealing. For instance a magazine distributed only to members of an association or institute may have fewer readers than its circulation because not all members will spend time reading something they receive as a part of their membership. Furthermore they probably do not bother to take it into the office and circulate it. Against this, many publications exist which can fairly claim a readership of eight or more people per copy. Controlled circulation journals probably do not achieve such high reader/copy ratings, partly because they tend to send out individual copies as a matter of policy. Indeed this may be regarded as a strength since, if speed of communication is important, it is not in the best interest of an advertiser to use a publication which takes a month or two to reach out to all its readers.

A research into journals covering the instrumentation and automation industries gave a dramatic example of the differences which can occur between circulation and readership and resulted in quite different assessments in terms of 'cost/1000'. Table 13.1 is an extract from this survey.

Table 13.1   Cost per 1000 circulation compared with readership

Journal	Circulation	Estimated readership	Cost/1000 circulation	Cost/1000 readership
C	10 400	9 700	£6	£6.6
A	11 500	42 000	£7	£1.9
D	8 000	28 000	£7.9	£2.2
F	9 200	8 700	£10.7	£11
E	5 000	27 000	£13.4	£2.5
B	16 300	47 000	£16.5	£5.7

One of the problems facing a researcher into readership by industrial and business personnel is to determine a satisfactory definition of the 'universe' and then to find a reliable method of sampling. Table 13.1 was produced from a series of interviews at an exhibition that, because of its size and importance, could be regarded as counting among its visitors a representative cross-section of the whole industry being surveyed. Such an assumption is of course an immediate source of bias and must be considered when assessing the results.

The use of the interview is particularly important in readership surveys since readers are unable to distinguish between one journal and another without aided recall. The above survey used a flipchart with the front covers of each journal. As can be seen, the ranking order of publication in terms of cost/1000 circulation changes radically compared with cost/1000 readers.

An early survey into the horticultural field concentrated on two magazines *Grower* and the *Commercial Grower*. Initially a postal questionnaire was used and a result obtained. The question then arose of possible confusion of names, as a result of which an interview research was conducted that proved that the original results were quite incorrect.

A more recent study 'Engineering Publications in the UK' by Maclean Hunter, provided a comparison between circulation and readership as shown in Table 13.2.

Without a careful scrutiny of the sample base and the methods involved in obtaining and processing the data, it is not reasonable to take the figures as they stand in Table 13.2 and draw specific conclusions. What can be demonstrated is the extent to which a schedule drawn up on the basis of circulation can be wrong compared with a readership base.

Table 13.2   Readership compared with circulation

	Readership	Circulation	Readers/copy
Engineering	105 000	20 045	5.25
Mechanical Engineering News	89 000	71 767	1.24
The Engineer	87 000	37 964	2.29
Engineers Digest	46 000	15 568	2.95
Engineering Today	44 000	50 932	0.86
Chartered Mechanical Engineer	39 000	47 962	0.81

SEGMENTED READERSHIP

Here the objective is to find the readership habits of a specific group, usually a company's potential market, or a segment of it. Very often a company's own mailing list is not acceptable as being representative of the potential market: it may be for this reason that press advertising is being used to reach purchasing influences which are unknown. Each problem tends to be entirely different, and sampling methods need to be individually planned.

An example of the use of a segmented readership analysis was a survey of buyers of paperboard for carton and box-making. In this case, an examination of the total readership of the packaging press would have been meaningless since the number of converters of cardboard adds up to hundreds, while the number of users of packages as a whole amounts to tens of thousands. The result showed that the most popular and large-circulation journals scored badly, and of course they were expensive whereas certain minor journals did well. The budget was cut by 75 per cent.

DUPLICATION

When compiling a schedule to obtain maximum coverage or 'reach' it is important to examine the overlap of various publications, that is the extent of readership duplication. Researches into this aspect of readership have enabled schedules to be cut significantly, or alternatively for expenditures to be concentrated into significantly fewer publications, achieving much greater impact. A good deal of work on this has been carried out by a leading advertising agency on behalf of its clients. For one product the media department had identified some one hundred journals which, at least from the publishers' claims, could be considered as possible advertising media. A survey showed that one journal alone covered 89 per cent of the potential market while the second most important rated 68 per cent. Added together they amounted to 93 per cent, an exceptionally high coverage by any standards and well above the average. It is interesting to note that the sixth journal out of this massive list scored only 26 per cent.

A similar study carried out by an electronics company showed that there was no gain in advertising in more than three journals since the addition of a fourth added so little additional coverage as to be worthless.

A body of evidence begins to appear which leads to the conclusion that the law of diminishing returns applies in media scheduling wherever more than just two or three publications are available to reach a given market. The same results come from research into American business publications and the graph in Figure 13.1 is typical of many such investigations. As can be seen, if duplication of readership is not required there is little point in advertising in more than three publications—in a homogeneous market.

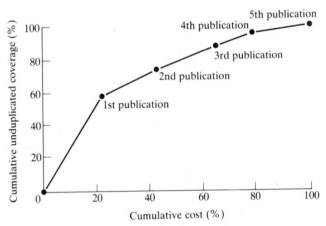

Figure 13.1   Cumulative readership—law of diminishing returns (*Source:* McGraw-Hill Report 1120.4)

It is interesting, though not surprising, that the law of diminishing returns in cumulative audience coverage also applies to consumer publications. In a survey of United Kingdom newspapers a similar phenomenon was to be found, as shown in Table 13.3. In this example, the addition of *The Times* to

Table 13.3 Cumulative unduplicated readership

Publication	Unduplicated readership by businessmen (%)
Sunday Times	39
Daily Telegraph	55
The Financial Times	60
The Times	62

the schedule would add only 2 per cent to the number of businessmen having the opportunity to see (OTS) a particular advertisement.

EDITORIAL EXCELLENCE

This must be regarded as a highly subjective area and one which must pay regard to the views of experts in the subject matter of a particular journal. With subscription magazines it might be considered that circulation is some

Table 13.4 Editorial page traffic

Editorial item	Interest rating (%)
Comment	60
Planning for decimals	91
Mechanical accounting	
Background to reappraisal	53
Visible record accounting computers	44
Special purpose accounting computers	36
Machine detail chart	26
Case history 1 (Burroughs Ltd)	37
Business man and machine in the 70s—a 2-day seminar	36
Case history 2 (Philips Electrologica Ltd)	36
Design flow chart	22
Eat, drink and be wary	43
The greatest show on earth	32
Computerscope	
Wide scope for first Univac 9200 in UK	16
IBM announce magnetic tape keyboard peripherals	19
ICT builds model of optical store	20
Insurance moves into real-time	14
A score for Scottish Honeywell	13
Mintech guide to installing a computer	17
The computer bureau scene	
ITT to introduce a remote access service in the autumn	9
Jobs for the boys	16
Fast start for Inter-Bank	10

measure of the value readers put on the editorial. This concept is clouded by the variety of circulation techniques used, though readership figures tend to overcome this difficulty.

One interesting research technique, which follows the Starch method in the United States, is the measurement of page traffic, i.e. the percentage of readers who claim to have read or noted a particular page or editorial item. A few British publishers are using this technique and although the results must be regarded as being approximate, a good measure of consistency has appeared in relating one type of editorial item with another. Making comparisons between journals is a more difficult task but is not impossible.

An extract from a survey of *Business Systems and Equipment*, published by Maclean Hunter, is reproduced in Table 13.4.

Another type of study on editorial excellence was carried out in connection with *Travel Agency*. This showed that respondents spent an average of 1 hour 12 minutes reading the journal, and that 68 per cent claimed to read every issue: 24 per cent most issues.

A further study[1] looked at the place where journals are read and as is seen in Table 13.5 there can be a wide variation between one journal and another. The journals were all connected with civil engineering. The abbreviations are of the names of the journals. In the case of *NCE*, most of the recipients had the journal mailed to them at home which accounts for its high 'at home' rating.

Table 13.5 Where journals are read

	NCE	CN	CJ	CE	CP&E	PMJ
At home	78%	32%	22%	9%	18%	14%
At work	25%	63%	72%	75%	76%	83%
When travelling	—	—	1%	—	1%	—
Other	1%	10%	6%	16%	5%	3%

Another hitherto ignored factor about readers is their age. Figure 13.2 comes from Cahners Publishing Co. in the States and portrays a fairly typical spread of ages. It is worth noting that the average age was 45 but that varied from one job category to another. Clearly this factor is important for copywriters since it will determine the style of writing.

JOURNALS' REPUTATION

Over and above the intrinsic editorial value, a journal acquires a certain reputation which to some extent reflects on advertisements placed in it. It may be claimed for instance that the quality image of *The Times* tends

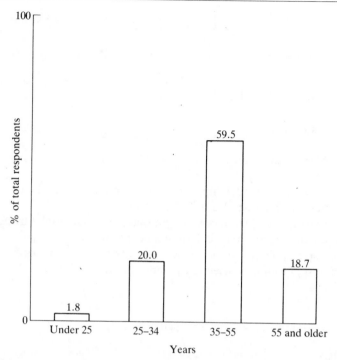

Figure 13.2 Age of recipients of business magazines (*Source:* Cahners Research No. 536.1)

subconsciously to enhance the view a reader takes of a product advertised in it.

There are a variety of techniques which can be used to evaluate 'journal reputation', each depending upon the particular circumstance. An interesting use of a semantic scale has been employed to compare a number of electronic journals. The following is an extract from the questionnaire:

How would you rank the journals listed below for their conciseness, up-to-dateness, etc.?

Here are a set of scales (Figure 13.3). We would like you to mark them as follows: if you find, say, *Wireless World* eminently concise, just as you would like it in fact from this point of view, then tick the scale in the space next to the word 'concise'; if you normally find it extremely long-winded, then tick the other end. You may feel, however, that the magazine ranks somewhere between these extremes; if so, then place your tick accordingly.

A survey into the printing industry was conducted in order to establish readership among managing directors of printing houses. Additionally the question was asked 'which single journal do you find most valuable?'. The point here is that there will sometimes arise a situation in which two journals

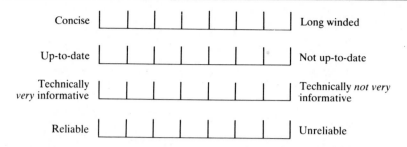

Figure 13.3 Semantic rating scale (*Source:* personal research)

score equally well in readership rating and even in segmented cost/1000, but their reputations may be of a different order.

One company asked readers which journal they would look through first if they were looking for a particular component. While the readership figures varied by up to a factor of two or so, the responses to this specific question were quite significant. A selection is reproduced in Table 13.6 to show the effect.

Table 13.6 'Journal preference' for a particular purpose

Publication	Read regularly (%)	Look at first for a particular component (%)
B	59.0	53.9
D	48.4	67.5
A	48.3	8.2
G	41.6	—
E	34.6	18.3
F	29.5	13.9
C	28.9	4.9

SPECIAL SERVICES TO PUBLISHERS

Some publishers recognize that it is valuable to assist the industries they cover by providing information which, even if not related specifically to the publications themselves, helps their clients to produce more effective advertising. Such a service is not in itself a reason for placing advertising in a sponsoring magazine, but it is reasonable to assume that publishers who try to meet the needs of their clients with supplementary research data might well concern themselves in a similar way with ensuring that their journals are written and distributed with competence and care. One particular service which has been developed extensively is to access the circulation list for direct-mail purposes. This can be a very valuable supplementary channel of communication.

Other media

In dealing with each of the major channels of persuasion in previous chapters, emphasis has been laid on the need for measuring results. This is in effect post-research. The object of media research is pre-research or, alternatively, research which, even if after an event, can be applied to future or similar cases.

Attempts have been made to assess the value placed on various media by buyers and it is surprising to find how few people are prepared to admit to being influenced to any degree by advertising, particularly men.

A survey in the *British Printer* asking printers which means of communication they found the most valuable source of information produced the result shown in Table 13.7.

Table 13.7 Influence of various media on British printing by company size (%)

| | Total | Number of employees | | | | |
		1–24	25–49	50–99	100–199	200+
The trade press	36	28	47	48	50	60
Calls by representatives	40	47	36	31	19	19
Exhibitions and trade fairs	10	8	7	18	25	12
Letters and brochures sent to you through the post	15	19	10	8	9	9

It is interesting to note how the trade press rating changed according to size of company. Indeed the whole mixture changed with company size, which points to another variable in market segmentation and the need to evaluate media against a specific segment whether this be product group, application group, size group, geographical group or whatever.

A similar investigation was included in the *How British Industry Buys* survey from which Table 13.8 was extracted.

Again it is interesting to note the variations which occur between different management functions in a company.

EXHIBITIONS

There is considerable scope for the provision of more data on exhibitions particularly authenticated information which is relevant to an advertiser's needs. Some organizers already record information about visitors as they

Table 13.8 Influence of various media on different types of personnel in British industry.* (*Source*: Hugh Buckner, *How British Industry Buys*)

	Board (general management)	Operating management	Prod. engineering	Des. and dev. engineering	Maint. engineering	Research	Buying	Finance	Sales	Other
Catalogues	39	36	45	64	34	64	52	32	44	76
Direct mail	12	9	14	6	31	21	23	14	5	27
Sales engineers' visits	66	61	60	67	78	64	64	60	73	40
Advertisements in trade press	14	32	28	22	21	15	12	23	24	24
Exhibitions	15	17	11	11	47	15	9	19	14	12
Demonstrations by manufacturers	50	41	35	26	37	21	37	38	45	22
Other	6	4		6				5	5	35

*In industry, personnel with these functions consider, in the percentages shown, these factors to be among the two most important when obtaining information on products. For example: in industry generally board members, who play more than an occasional role in purchasing, in 66 per cent of cases consider sales engineers' visits to be among the two most important methods of obtaining information on products.

enter the exhibition hall. This will lead to exhibitions becoming more effective selling functions and in the long term will benefit the whole exhibition industry. Much remains to be investigated: corridor traffic for instance, the value of an island site or one near an entrance, the gallery versus the ground floor, and shell stands as against elaborate tailor-mades.

As has been indicated, research data on exhibitions are hard to come by, and do not yet represent a consolidated body of evidence. An example of useful information comes from a study of the International Electrical Engineers Exhibition. This showed that visitors stopped or talked at an average of 14 stands, and spent an average of 5.3 hours at the exhibition.

A more recent research showed that 61 per cent of visitors attended the International Wire Exhibition in Basle for more than one day as shown in Figure 13.4. The arithmetic average time spent in the exhibition halls was 5 hours per day, and the average length of stay for all visitors was 2.2 days. The number of stands visited varied widely between 2 or 3 and 30 in any one day: the arithmetic average was 13. The same research investigated the show's value or usefulness. On a scale of 1–7 where 1 represented the lowest

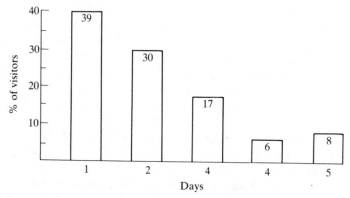

Figure 13.4 Length of stay at exhibition (*Source:* Mack-Brooks Research Report)

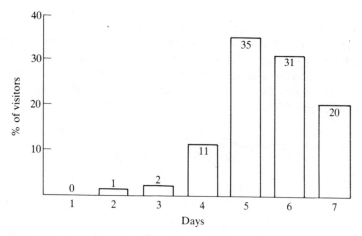

Figure 13.5 Exhibition visitor preference (*Source:* Mack-Brooks Research Report)

perceived value of the exhibition according to the visitor and 7 the highest, the results were shown as in Figure 13.5. Eighty-six per cent rated the exhibition above average and the arithmetic mean was 5.6.

Matching the market

The usefulness of media information—who reads what, who sees what, who is influenced by what—presupposes that a company is able to define its potential market with an adequate degree of accuracy.

A good deal of work has been done in examining who in a firm is responsible for buying decisions and it is evident that there may be up to a dozen people to be reached and sometimes more. An investigation in depth into a large manufacturer established that while a 'yes' decision could be made by four people, a decision not to purchase a given raw material could be made on the basis of a negative report from any one of twenty-three people. Yet the salesperson concerned saw no more than two people.

A frequently quoted average is eight people per company, and this, when multiplied by the number of manufacturing units in Great Britain (in excess of 50 000), brings the number of people involved in industrial purchasing to nearly half a million. And in matching media to market, the industrial press alone consists of over 2000 different publications.

Even so, there is nothing special about the job of matching which cannot be carried out by a normally competent marketing team given adequate support from published and commissioned research and subsequent statistical analysis.

There are two useful reference works which are of particular significance. The first is the Board of Trade's *Standard Industrial Classification* which categorizes in some detail every trade and industry, and second the work pioneered by the Institute of Marketing and Industrial Market Research Ltd, which examined in considerable depth purchasing influence across the whole industrial sector, revealing a number of hitherto unquantified characteristics such as the example shown in Table 13.9

Table 13.9 Purchasing 'decision-makers' showing who decides which supplier gets an order (%) (*Source*: Hugh Buckner, *How British Industry Buys*)

	Board (general management)	Operating management	Prod. engineering	Des. and dev. engineering	Maint. engineering	Research	Buying	Finance	Sales	Others in company	Others outside company
Plant equipment	44	28	10	7	3	—	19	1	—	2	—
Materials	17	25	5	6	1	4	52	1	1	1	1
Components	10	25	6	9	4	4	39	1	1	1	—

The extract from the Buckner study given above has been further amplified by a research now published periodically by *The Financial Times*, entitled *How British Industry Buys*.

A further piece of research on decision-makers is to be found in *Modern*

Purchasing on the influence of purchasing managers in the procurement of a variety of products and services and this is shown in Table 13.10. As can be seen the purchasing authority of buyers appears to be very limited.

Table 13.10 Purchasing responsibilities of buyers. (*Source: Modern Purchasing*)

Product	Actually selects supplier (%)	Has no influence (%)
Computer hardware	8	36
Air freight services	16	50
Vending machines	20	45
Floor cleaning contractors	26	48
Calculators	28	13
Cars	28	29
Fuel oil	44	16
Cartons	63	7
Stationery	74	8
Ball point pens	77	9

Research techniques

The techniques for media assessment are not excessively complex, difficult or expensive: nor are the results any more or less approximate than those from other types of research. It is perhaps surprising that this sector of marketing research has not expanded more rapidly, since the savings which can be achieved are both immediate and large. Given the lack of suitable information on all types of media it must follow that any promotional budget which does not make provision for some form of readership or comparative research is not likely to be utilizing its expenditure to the full.

Commenting on the opportunities in assessing advertising effectiveness Aubrey Wilson, a pioneer in this field, had this to say:

Advertising results, even the most enthusiastic supporters concede, are still largely unpredictable. Thus advertising poses one of the most difficult areas for management decisions and, therefore, one in which the accumulation of any knowledge is disproportionately valuable. Mistakes in advertising strategy and technique are costly and difficult, if not impossible, to rectify and expenditure is almost invariably irrecoverable. A misplaced purchase of a machine tool or vehicle will at worst, yield the second-hand value of the product. Not only can nothing be saved from unsuccessful advertising but often additional monies will be needed to correct the errors made. For these and other reasons advertising research is taking on a new importance as industrial advertising begins to take an increasing part in industrial marketing operations.

Checklist

1. Are your target audiences defined in sufficient detail to enable media readership to be compared with them?
2. Have you made an assessment of each proposed publication in terms of
   (a) Circulation—total and segmented?
   (b) Readership—total and segmented?
   (c) Cost per reader?
   (d) Rates—possible reductions?
   (e) Authenticity of any research data?
   (f) Editorial quality?
   (g) Journal's reputation?
   (h) Method of circulation?
   (i) Frequency of publication?
   (j) Readership duplication?
3. Have you set aside a budget for media research to supplement the available information?
4. Is there evidence to justify using more than three publications to reach a particular audience?
5. Are the publishers you are patronizing prepared to co-operate by way of (a) page traffic studies, (b) split-runs and (c) mailing list?
6. Have you established the relative importance of each channel of communication with your particular potential customers?

References

1. Survey of purchasing and readership (Research Services Ltd, 1982).

14

CAMPAIGN EVALUATION

Campaign evaluation can be difficult and expensive, but this is by no means inevitable. It is true that some campaigns cannot be measured in total, but this does not mean that measurements cannot be made of some of the component parts, which will result in an improvement in cost-effectiveness.

The position has been well stated by L. W. Rodger[1] whose comments on advertising could be taken to apply to the whole range of promotional activities.

The advertising budget probably represents the largest amount of money disbursed by manufacturers with no precise measure of what it can be expected to achieve. The spending of large sums of money on advertising without some system of accountability can be compared to conducting a business without a book-keeping or accounting department. Advertising accountability has lagged far behind general management accountability in that the latter is held responsible for accomplishing certain specific and usually, measurable results in relation to money spent. Sound business operation demands that expenditure and results be related. The idea of holding advertising accountable for accomplishing certain sales results is certainly not new. But there is now a growing body of expert opinion that the sales criterion, as applied to advertising in isolation, is based on a fundamental misconception.

Rodger goes on to develop his theme on the criteria for evaluating a campaign in terms which are relevant to the media and also capable of implementation.

Advertising is a means of communication. Its results can only be measured in terms of communication goals, in terms of the cost per advertising message delivered per customer for a given result. In other words, according to Colley, 'an advertising goal is a specific communication task, to be accomplished among a defined audience to a given degree in a given period of time'.

Lack of progress in the development of campaign evaluation is generally to be put down to the lack of defined specific goals, or alternatively to the setting of goals that are invalid.

It is not only the number of individuals in a company who contribute to a purchasing decision who must be considered, but also the many factors which are likely to influence each person's judgement on where an order should be placed. Typical influences give an idea of the complexity of the operation:

1. Used it in my previous firm.
2. Saw it at an exhibition.
3. Salesman convinced me of its quality.
4. I'd heard of the company's name.
5. Read about it in the press.
6. My MD knows the supplier's MD.
7. Swiss machines are always more reliable.
8. This firm was the only one to supply enough technical data.
9. I always get a bottle of Scotch from this firm.
10. All our other machines are this make.
11. Recommended by a friend.

The list is endless and highly subjective, notwithstanding the usual test of 'price-delivery-quality-service' which so many buyers like to believe is the sole basis for decision-making.

To take expenditure on advertising, or sales promotion, or even on the overall marketing function, and expect to be able to relate it precisely to sales (that is purchasing) is clearly unrealistic. It is made more complicated by the fact that for many industrial products, the gestation period between the original enquiry and an order is often more than a year. One authority has estimated an average time lag, depending on the product, of between one and four years.

Component research

If all influences cannot be researched in total, it is necessary to examine each 'component' of purchasing influence and decide whether it is amenable to scientific evaluation. From the various 'channels of persuasive communications' many criteria, some more detailed than others, can be tested. Copytesting an advertisement, measurement of product awareness, brand-name research, product-company association, attitude studies, and finally, measurement of communications goals are some examples which can be examined here.

An examination of the sales communication process in Figure 14.1 well illustrates how very simple it is to consider each stage from advertisements to repeat business. Clearly each block is amenable to some form of evaluation and a relationship can be established with the next in the process. But equally it can be seen how easy it is for extraneous factors to invalidate conclusions based solely upon such a simplistic flow diagram. If the product performance is unsatisfactory, or the price or delivery, then the conversion factor between quotation and first order will be affected. If competition suddenly becomes

Figure 14.1   Sales schematic diagram

fierce, conversion from enquiry to sales call may change. There are, then, factors quite outside the marketing communications area which prevent a valid relationship between advertising and sales being established as a basis of campaign evaluation.

An analysis of the communications process can be taken further and broken down into more components in order to make monitoring more effective and accurate. Figure 14.2 as a model is perhaps a somewhat academic approach and has been devised quite deliberately in this way so as to allow readers to adopt a system of their own in more practical terms.

In Figure 14.2, known as Sequential Advertising Measurement (SAM), the starting point is with the 'message' (selling proposition) which is then formulated into a 'creative expression' (e.g. advertisement), which appears in a 'medium' (journal) and achieves 'attention' (page traffic noting) and 'impact' (recall). This then changes the 'attitude' of a prospect which arguably changes his or her 'behavioural intent' (what is to be purchased) and ultimately leads to a certain 'behaviour' (the order). Fulfilment of the order leads to 'contentment' as a result of acquiring the 'product' which has a 'performance', representing to the customer a 'benefit' which is the basis of the selling proposition, i.e. the 'message'. And so the circuit is complete.

Now the proposition is that each block can be taken in turn, objectives set,

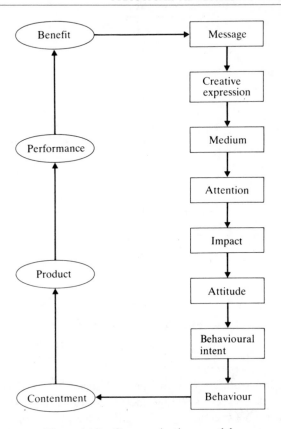

Figure 14.2 Communications model

quantified, measured and adjusted. The diagram has been converted into a
table referred to as an Ad Evaluator Checklist, and showing nine discrete
stages together with suggested sources of data.

From Table 14.1 a somewhat alarming calculation can be made of
communications efficiency. Suppose each stage is 80 per cent efficient, and
this is surely unlikely, then the cumulative efficiency of this particular
communications system would be 17 per cent. This compares interestingly
with a classical work on this subject in which messages from top management
to shop-floor operatives were received by only 7 per cent. This was referred to
as a 'somewhat opaque situation'.[2] Maybe advertising executives would do
well to face up to the opaque screen which screens their products, their
messages and their company.

Table 14.1 Seventeen possible sources of data for the evaluation of advertising within a sales context

Communication component	Data source
1. Customer benefit/message	1.1 Customer needs and wants—group discussion 1.2 Syndicated research
2. Creative expression/advertisement	2.1 Ad. pre-test—group discussion 2.2 Brand name pre-test
3. Transmission/medium	3.1 Readership research
4. Attention/interest	4.1 Page traffic 4.2 Read-most rating
5. Impact/action	5.1 Enquiries 5.2 Recall 5.3 Brand awareness
6. Attitude	6.1 Company/brand reputation
7. Behavioural intent/procurement motivation	7.1 Brand preference 7.2 Test market
8. Behaviour/1st order	8.1 Sales statistics 8.2 Competitor research
9. Satisfaction/repeat purchase	9.1 Sales statistics 9.2 Sales reports

Advertising testing

There are a number of techniques in common usage:

PAGE TRAFFIC

A first requirement of any advertisement is that it should be seen or 'noted'. In the United States it is not uncommon to use Starch ratings obtained by questioning readers by personal interview, on which advertisements they can remember (by 'aided recall'). In the United Kingdom the same idea has been tried by a number of publishers, but usually using a postal questionnaire.

The technique is to send out a second copy of a particular issue, say two weeks after publication, asking a sample readership to cross through any advertisement which they recall having noted in the original issue. An alternative approach is to ask respondents to indicate which advertisements they found of interest.

Such a technique may appear to be subjective and approximate, but a high enough degree of consistency is obtained to enable an advertiser to draw the conclusion that a particular advertisement is not performing as well as is required. Table 14.2, extracted from an interest rating survey by *Modern Purchasing*, indicates the kind of results that can be obtained.

Table 14.2   Advertisement page-traffic. (*Source: Modern Purchasing*)

Product type	Advertisement size	Interest rating (percentage of respondents finding an advertisement of interest)
Raw material	1 page black and white	20.3
Raw material	1 page black and white	5.9
Raw material	¼ page black and white	12.7
Raw material	2 pages black and white	12.7
Electrical goods	1 page 2 colours	3.4
Industrial fasteners	½ page black and white	14.4
Industrial fasteners	1 page 2 colours	6.8
Machinery	2 pages black and white	8.5
Tools	¼ page black and white	16.9
Exhibition	Inset black and white	17.8

In the issue in question, the highest rated advertisement was for storage equipment, a single page which scored 33.1 per cent. It is, however, by no means unknown from other researches for advertisements to score zero, but this does not necessarily mean that the advertisement itself is useless. It may only be in the wrong publication. But it does mean that it is not doing its job.

It is interesting to compare such ratings with those obtained from editorial items. Referring again to the *Modern Purchasing* survey the average score for recall of advertisements was 9.9 per cent whereas for editorial items a figure of 41.4 per cent was obtained.

From data made available by publishers, notably Maclean Hunter, some interesting facts emerge. For instance in Figure 14.3, the percentage of readers showing an interest in a particular ad can be compared with the interest ratings for editorials. The interest profile for ads peaks at around 8 per cent (arithmetic mean is 9.9 per cent), while editorials cover a very wide span, from 10 to 90 per cent, and peak at 35 per cent.

This data comes from an examination of seven different researches covering three particular non-competing business publications and encompasses an evaluation of 484 ads. This number is regarded as sufficiently large for further analysis which at least can be said to be indicative of trends.

Take as an example the widely held assumption that an advertisement will do better if it is positioned facing editorial instead of being drowned in a sea

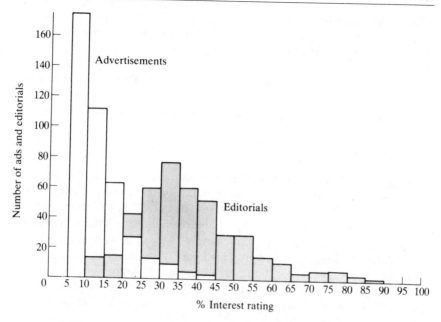

Figure 14.3 Advertisement ratings compared with editorials

of other ads. In terms of interest created, there was no significant difference between the 250 ads involved in this study.

Another commonly held view is that the addition of a second colour will increase the effectiveness of an advertisement. To throw some light on this factor, the ads in the above survey were further analysed and while a few two-colour ads achieved the highest individual scores, the overall effect was of no difference.

This of course does not reflect the attitude or image created, but merely the interest. Even here, the scope of the survey is not sufficiently broad to enable firm conclusions to be drawn. It does, however, call into question the blind acceptance that a second colour must produce better results.

Even when small advertisement spaces are used, it seems that some good performances can be obtained. There is a similarity between interest ratings for quarter pages as against half-page ads. From this it would seem that providing the subject is right, and creatively expressed, the size of the ad doesn't make too much difference.

There must come a stage at which the dominance of an ad is determined by size. Evidence of this comes from a comparison of the average score for two-page and larger ads with the average figure for all ads. The larger ads achieved something like twice the effect of the average.

In order to draw some conclusions about those advertisements with the highest scores, a detailed examination was made of the top 67 ads—those scoring 20 per cent and over. The two highest (over 40 per cent scores) were both two-page black and white, but more than half were single page, of which the bulk were one-colour. The majority of the DPS ads were here, but so also were eight small ads. At the other extreme, several ads received a zero rating and back covers in particular did not seem to do too well.

ADVERTISEMENT READERSHIP

'Noting' an advertisement is only the first step. The Starch research goes on to question which advertisements were read. The criterion is actually to have 'read most' of the copy. Whereas figures for noting an advertisement may range between 10 per cent and 30 per cent, the number of people claiming to have read most of an advertisement is more likely to be only a few per cent. Paradoxically, there are sometimes instances of an advertisement getting a relatively low 'noted' score, but a high 'read most' figure.

Studies in the United States indicate no different in 'read most' as between back and front of a magazine, but bleed ads score 25 per cent higher (McGraw-Hill Report 3066).

ADVERTISEMENT RECALL

Another type of recall test can be to mail out a copy of one specific advertisement as part of a questionnaire and ask the question 'Do you remember seeing the enclosed advertisement?'. This has the merit of assessing the overall effectiveness of the advertisement, having regard to all the publications where it appeared. For example, a research in connection with printing machinery determined that 30.1 per cent respondents remembered seeing the advertisement and 69.9 per cent did not. A similar investigation for computer equipment obtained a recall of 34.6 per cent and a negative response of 65.4 per cent. From such tests, over a period it is possible to determine the effectiveness of one advertisement against another, and the degree of penetration being achieved.

An alternative technique is to telephone a sample of readers and ask questions about a particular advertisement. One such research for a dictating machine produced recalls over a period of time ranging from 40 to 60 per cent.

ADVERTISEMENT ENQUIRIES

In Chapter 4 on press advertising the use of enquiries or sales leads was discussed as a means of advertisement evaluation. This can be a valid criterion and indeed it may be argued that it matters little what 'attention' an advertisement scores; what really matters is what action follows. If action in the form of enquiries is what is required of an advertisement, then this is a reasonable argument, provided the quality of the enquiries can be measured.

ENQUIRIES RELATED TO SIZE

A little publicized but immensely important piece of research was conducted by Cahners Publishing Co. in America. The first, No. 250.1, produced the information shown in Figure 14.4. The data came from an analysis of 500 000 enquiries and can therefore claim a reasonable measure of statistical reliability. It shows that size of advertisement has surprisingly little effect on the number of enquiries generated, and certainly nothing like a linear relationship.

The next step is to plot this data against cost per enquiry (see Fig. 14.5) whereupon it is shown that enquiries from whole page ads cost more than double those from small sizes.

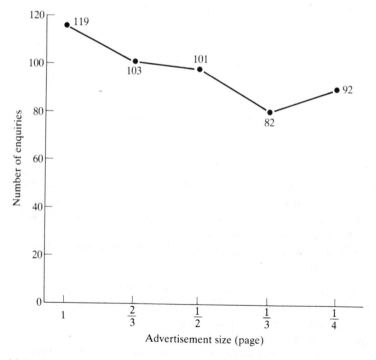

Figure 14.4 Enquiries by advertisement size (*Source:* Cahners Research Report No. 250.1)

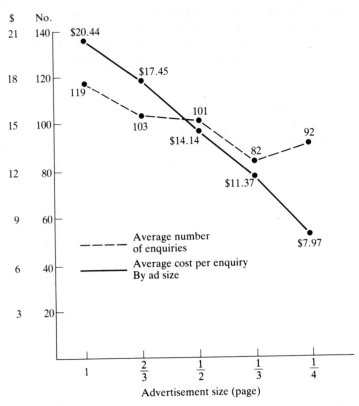

Figure 14.5   Cost per enquiry

Other Cahners Researches show that:

1. Advertising readership (as against enquiries) is not influenced by the use of coupons (Cahners 114.1).
2. Copy set in reverse (white upon black) is read at a 10 per cent slower rate than black on white (Cahners 1310.1).
3. Type set in lower case is read 13 per cent faster than that set in all capitals (Cahners 1310.4).

With some product groups, particularly where repeat business is rare, a series of ratios can be established which, if constant, can enable a campaign to be assessed very effectively. For instance, given the average cost per enquiry, the average conversion into a quotation, the average number of quotations per order and the average value per order, an advertising budget can be calculated directly from the sales budget and targets set for each stage in the process so that any failure in performance can be pinpointed, and corrective action taken. However, few product groups are so simply constituted as to enable this procedure to be implemented with any degree of certainty.

Product awareness

How aware is a potential market of a product's existence? A conventional questionnaire can ask respondents to list the 'top three industrial floor cleaners'. Such an open question will enable a manufacturer to determine whether his product is top of the list, rates number three, or perhaps does not appear at all.

A campaign may very well have as an objective to raise the level of awareness from sixth position to being among the top three. The plan of action will estimate the cost of achieving this result and will indicate the time-scale. By monitoring progress, it can be determined to what extent a campaign is achieving its objective. This procedure is particularly useful for a new product launch since at the outset product awareness will be zero, and by progressive researches the real value for money derived from promotional activities can be gauged with accuracy.

This is still of course 'component research' since a product can be pushed up to the top of the awareness charts and still not sell, but at least one factor has been identified. The market knows about the product and further investigation must now be made to establish why sales are not being achieved.

An example of product awareness, and indeed company awareness comes from an American study of a campaign for Sta-flow, a plastic produced by Air Products. Table 14.3 shows how after an advertising campaign product awareness increased from 0 to 23.8 per cent and in Table 14.4 company awareness increased from 4.8 per cent to 64.3 per cent.

Table 14.3 Product awareness

	Pre-ad mentions (%)	Post-ad mentions (%)
Lexan	85.6	88.1
Noryl	80.8	52.4
Cyclolac	77.9	81.0
Tenite	53.8	90.5
Sta-flow	0	23.8

Table 14.4   Company awareness

	Pre-ad mentions (%)	Post-ad mentions (%)
GE	79.8	85.7
Eastman	74.0	90.5
Borg-Warner	62.5	73.8
Mobay	53.8	76.2
Air Products	4.8	64.3

Attitude studies

A natural sequence is to determine the attitude of the buying public to a product. This may come from questionnaire research—'which is the most reliable voltmeter?', 'which is the least reliable?', 'which is the best value for money?'—and so on. A technique often used in the consumer field for motivation research is guided group discussion. This can be applied to industrial matters by getting together a group of buyers without disclosing the precise nature of the question to be answered, or indeed the name of the company concerned, and starting discussion of the subject in general with a group leader guiding the conversation towards the topics being researched.

Such a study was conducted to determine the attitude of packaging buyers to *solid* fibreboard cases and why it was they preferred to buy *corrugated* fibreboard cases. The fact emerged that the buyers did not know the difference between the two products and as far as they were concerned simply bought fibreboard cases. This led to a campaign to identify solid cases as a specific product with certain outstanding qualities. Research was undertaken before and after the campaign to measure the level of knowledge which buyers had of the benefits associated with solid cases.

Product–company association

The question of which supplier comes first to mind when a buyer is seeking a given product can be explored by postal research. A question such as 'which first three company names come to mind when considering the purchase of . . .' generally produces an answer. This kind of research is especially useful since not only does it enable a company to determine its own position in the market, but also shows up the relative position of its competitors.

Thus in a campaign to promote a new quality of raw material a company was able to see its product–name association creep up from 3 per cent to 18 per cent in a year, while its principal competitor dropped from 16 per cent to 8 per cent. Clearly the campaign was achieving a tangible effect.

A problem related to product–company association is brand-name–

company association. It is not uncommon in industrial marketing to come across a 'Hoover situation' in which a brand-name becomes generic, and applicable in a buyer's mind to any one of a number of suppliers. If this happens unknown to the company it will in the long run nullify the value of the brand-name.

Brand-name research

A campaign may be required to establish a new brand-name, or to reinforce an existing one. In the first instance, research techniques can be applied to the selection of a new brand-name.

If a brand-name is designed to conjure up a certain image a number of possible names can be put to a sample of respondents to comment on what connotation they would associate with each name.

It is useful to make such an investigation a personal one, and invite people to speak each name. This will produce another valuable indicator, whether or not each word is easily readable, and if so whether it is pronounced as intended.

The memorability of a brand-name is particularly important, and this again can be measured. An example was a new material for which a short-list of three names was produced. These were each printed on a card, and one hundred people interviewed. The procedure was to ask each person to look at each name in turn, while it was exposed for a standard time. No reason was given for the request. One week later each individual was re-interviewed and asked to write down the three names. The results were that one name had a much higher recall factor than the other two, and over one-third of the respondents could recall the name exactly as it was shown to them.

The next step with the brand-name adopted was to launch a campaign to establish it. At the outset, the level of knowledge in the potential market was zero, but research was conducted to discover which was the leading brand-name for that particular product group. After an extensive campaign of six months, further research showed that the new name had already secured top place in the ratings. It is significant that the sales of the new product, a basic raw material, were at that time not more than a few per cent of the market whereas the brand-name preference had a rating of several tens per cent. This is to be expected with such a product where long-term contracts inhibit a rapid change in the purchasing pattern. The campaign was in fact a success measured in communications terms: had sales in the short term been used as the criterion, it would have been regarded as a failure.

Image research

A less tangible objective is the establishment of the right image for a company or brand. It is doubtful whether many companies have defined formally and in exact terms the precise image they wish to project and yet they will have an image, whether they like it or not, and moreover will not infrequently spend a good deal of money to enhance what has been referred to as their prestige.

The fact that all organizations have an image is indicated by a panel research which asked buyers to discuss certain companies and how they viewed them in terms of price, quality, delivery and so on. The research company inserted a 'control' name, that is of a company which did not exist. Many of the discussion group were found to have decided views on its image, even though the majority registered that they had never heard of it.

An example of formal research into the public's attitude towards a company was exemplified by one very large manufacturing group which was number two in size in its particular industry. It was a public company and was beginning to realize that apart from the effect on sales, there were such matters as raising loans, and the value of shares to be considered in connection with the expense of promoting a company name. Initially research showed that it was hardly known at all to the publics the company considered to be important. The company agreed to spend a large sum of money on prestige advertising, but in order to obtain tangible value for money, it set the objective 'to be listed among the top three' in response to the question 'name the leading company in the industry'. Two years later the objective was achieved.

The test in any campaign is whether or not value was obtained for the money spent—whether the objectives were achieved, and if not why not. For an organization not to bother to measure the result of its expenditure on advertising and promotion is simply neglect of managerial responsibility.

Checklist

1. Does your promotional budget include a sum for campaign evaluation?
2. Has each of your campaigns a specific objective which is capable of being measured?
3. Has provision been made for continuous checks to be made to ensure that results are being obtained?
4. Is there a system for feedback of results to enable changes to be made to a campaign in sufficient time to achieve the final objective?

References

1. L. W. Rodger, *Marketing in a Competitive Economy* (Associated Business Programmes, London, 1974), p. 216.
2. R. W. Revans, *Science and the Manager* (MacDonald, London, 1965).

Part 4

PUBLIC RELATIONS

15

PUBLIC RELATIONS

The fundamental difference between public relations and press relations (or editorial publicity) is that editorial publicity is a medium just as much as press advertising and exhibitions, while public relations is an element of publicity dealing with all the many publics which can be involved in influencing the operation of a business from whatever point of view, sales or otherwise. It includes customers and prospects, but here the concern is not so much to be directly involved in selling, but rather to project the company image, and create a climate in which the selling operation can be conducted with greater efficiency.

In broad terms the public relations function is to establish and maintain a mutual understanding between an organization and its publics, to communicate a company's views, objectives and purposes, while at the same time monitoring, feeding back and correcting the publics' attitudes and reactions. The publics with which an organization may be concerned include the following:

1. Customers and prospects
2. Employees and trade unions
3. Shareholders and 'the City'
4. Suppliers
5. Local communities
6. Opinion formers
7. Specialized groups
8. Government departments
9. Local authorities
10. Educational bodies
11. People in general.

In developing a public relations programme the procedure follows the development of a marketing strategy, namely to produce an overall plan with written objectives broken down now under publics instead of products. The methods of achieving these objectives may utilize the same media and techniques as are used for marketing communications. Press advertising, direct mail, photographs, editorial publicity all have contributions to make to the public relations programme but there are a number of differences in detail and a number of techniques not dealt with under marketing communication.

Having widened the scope of public relations beyond its more common 'press officer' context, to be effective the executive responsible for it needs to be an experienced publicity person rather than the conventional ex-journalist. His place in the management structure needs to be examined in this new light, and this is dealt with under Publicity organizations, Chapters 16 and 18.

Public relations activities need creativity. Frequently, to secure the greatest impact, the techniques require novelty and need to be adapted to the particular audience, the subject and the existing climate of opinion. There will therefore only be general guidelines and examples here.

PR activities are broken down under the key publics to whom they most often refer, though any one activity may influence more than one public or indeed all of them.

Customers and prospects

In considering public relations activities aimed at influencing customers and prospects, it is inevitable that there will be an overlap into what may be considered the sales promotional area. For instance, is prestige advertising PR or marketing communication? This question also applies to editorial publicity about new appointments, technological advances, large contracts. Indeed the closeness of these facets of publicity would tend to indicate the need for some form of central control.

Overall, one may say that public relations is concerned with creating a favourable image, or, to use a less emotive word, a favourable reputation. Evidence of the value within a marketing context is provided by Dr Theodore Levitt in his study *Industrial Buying Behaviour* for the Harvard Graduate Business School:

> One of the venerable questions in marketing, and particularly the marketing of industrial products, is whether a company's generalised reputation affects its ability to sell its products. With the great flood of new products in recent years, the question has been focused more sharply around the extent to which a company's generalised reputation affects its ability to launch new products. While nobody claims that a good reputation is an adequate substitute for a good product supported by a good sales effort, the question remains as to what contribution a good reputation can make to a good selling effort. Thus, all other things being equal, does a relatively well-known company . . . have a real edge over a relatively obscure company? Would it pay for a relatively obscure company to spend more money to advertise and promote its name and general competence or to spend more on training its salesmen?

Following this question, the study goes on to identify sixteen areas in which a good reputation can be shown to have a positive benefit. It concludes: 'Having a good reputation is always better than being a less well-known or completely anonymous company.'

Some of the PR opportunities which can be used for public relations purposes with particular relevance to influencing customers and prospects are discussed below.

FACTORY OPENINGS

The building of a new factory or a major extension provides the opportunity to generate enthusiasm and goodwill as well as publicity in the press and on radio and television.

For any large-scale operation it is essential to produce comprehensive plans well in advance, and six months is not an over-estimate particularly if there is a VIP opener.

Arrangements in a large factory are complex and involve a great number of people whose co-operation is essential. It is important to include on the planning board of a factory opening, the most senior executives of the company. Personal responsibility is essential for the efficient running of the operation: key executives must be allocated to such matters as transport, security, catering, cleaning and painting, press, unveiling, public address system, signboards, first aid, publications, gifts or mementoes, special treatment for VIPs, protocol and precedence, trades union relations, technical explanations, tour parties and even lavatories!

The rehearsal is particularly important and must simulate as realistically as possible the conditions which will apply on the day. The results of factory openings are hard to measure but clearly the fact that a hundred or so of a company's most important customers and outside contacts should think and talk about a company for a whole day has very great value.

FACTORY TOURS

One does not need an 'opening' to justify taking a group of people around a factory. Quite apart from the opening of a factory, there are often valuable opportunities in organizing a regular programme of visits or tours.

If done they must be done well: planning and execution must be immaculate, and visits must not interfere with production.

Care is necessary to ensure that tours are not too much about the company and its processes but rather tailored to the interests of a particular group. People are impressed by a programme which avoids delays or too much walking: also an adequate number of guides are necessary to ensure personal attention.

For important groups a great deal of benefit can be obtained by arranging for some unusual feature, such as a special train or chartered aircraft. People visiting a factory must be made to feel they are really important, which of course they are.

An opportunity sometimes occurs during a trade exhibition for a member of staff to contribute at an accompanying conference on aspects of a company's activities. Even if there is not an official conference it may be useful, while customers are concentrated in one place, to stage a conference either concerned solely with company interests, or perhaps sponsored by the company. A variation on a conference is a seminar which can deal in depth with some aspect of a company's activities, maybe from a more academic point of view.

Again if a number of customers and prospects are known to be spending some time, maybe overnight in London, this is an opportunity to offer some completely social function, the contacts from which will pay off handsomely in terms of strengthening personal relationships.

The cost of such functions may seem high but this is often apparently so of other public relations operations as well as exhibitions and advertising, but if an investment is needed in order to develop a business then the investment should be made. Investment in PR may be intangible, but so is the investment in machinery which will stand idle if the orders are not forthcoming. It must be clearly understood that PR is not free or cheap publicity: it can be very expensive: it can also be very worth while.

Employees and trade unions

While the task of dealing with employees falls to line management, public relations executives should occupy a primary role in the means of communicating with workers and staff and also in anticipating and interpreting their reactions.

INFORMATION

Notice boards are the traditional medium for communicating with employees. They are often poorly designed, badly sited, inadequately lit, and frequently contain a hotchpotch of out-of-date, poorly duplicated notices in language which is difficult to understand.

It is surprising that since so much industrial unrest is due to misunderstanding, greater attention has not been given to communicating information accurately, effectively and speedily. One reason is that line managers regard themselves as the proper channel for communications and are sceptical of the value of PR here. Certainly they must not be short-circuited, but their efforts can benefit substantially from support from other channels of communication.

Notice boards have a part to play, but responsibility for their presentation and maintenance should rest with the publicity department.

Other methods of communicating with employees do not differ fundamentally from those used to influence customers. Direct mail can be used, literature suitably written and designed, stuffers in wage packets, posters, display units and exhibitions, open days, receptions and lunches. The formula is similar since the objective is the same: to influence people and to inform them with impact of the facts. The difference is often that customer publicity tends to be handled by professionals, and employee publicity by people whose skills lie in other parts of the business.

A particularly interesting comment on employee communications came from a UK survey by *International Management* magazine. This concluded that: 'Audio visual aids are an effective way for a company to communicate with its employees. Yet this is the method least used.' The survey measured the cost-effectiveness of different methods of communications. It found that although slide presentations, overhead projectors, films, and video tapes are all highly effective ways of passing information to workers, these methods are rarely used. Notice boards are widely used, it said, but are generally ineffective.

More than half of the companies surveyed communicate corporate policy and objectives to employees through the annual report or a popular version of it. These methods scored low in effectiveness.

The survey also found that employment policies and procedures seldom are passed along to workers during induction programmes.

The report suggested that companies publish more frequent and relevant news sheets for individual plants or units, rather than company-wide magazines.

HOUSE MAGAZINES

These are essentially part of the process of feeding information to employees, though in fact they can achieve much more by building up a corporate spirit and a feeling of unity.

A firm employing one or two hundred people does not need a house magazine, though an occasional news sheet from the chairman is often appreciated. With larger organizations a magazine of some sort is a useful vehicle for providing information and building up goodwill amongst employees. No doubt there are publications which are welcomed, and secure a fairly high readership rating. The editing of these publications is not the job for a part-time amateur nor should it result in a highly polished magazine which sets out to compete with professional glossy monthlies. It should have written objectives, a carefully planned editorial and a presentation which is compatible with the audience it is addressing. Readership research can be applied here with considerable effectiveness.

PRODUCTIVITY AND SAFETY

Effective communications are necessary to get across to employees ideas on safety, productivity, cleanliness, tidiness, good attendance, personnel lateness, and indeed many aspects of management. Line or staff specialists, maybe the safety officer or the company doctor, will provide the ammunition, but the firing of the bullets can only properly be the function of the publicity department who will call upon conventional publicity media to achieve the result. A works or a shop seminar on safety, or a specially designed campaign incorporating leaflets, films, posters and displays, are as valid on the shop floor as the market-place.

INDUSTRIAL DISPUTES

There are occasions in a company when an industrial dispute arises, and when there is a need for swift and decisive action not only in negotiations, but in communications.

It is all too common that the press is able to get hold of a story from the employee's side so much more easily and quickly than from the management. This is understandable, since an employee has to refer to no one in expressing a point of view whereas a company official has to exercise great care to ensure that he or she is putting across company policy and is doing it in a way that cannot be misinterpreted.

Though situations are diverse it is possible to lay down general procedures which provide machinery for handling the press during a dispute.

The press officer must be fully informed of a dispute as soon as it arises, or even if it is anticipated, so that he or she has the opportunity to gather the necessary facts and to advise on a plan of action. Whether to say nothing, a little or a lot; whether to be conciliatory or vigorous—these are matters which cannot be left to develop at random during a press interview.

If the press and the public (including shareholders, customers and employees) are to get a balanced view, it follows that an authoritative statement by the management is necessary. Such a statement can be prepared in advance and issued to the press, preferably in writing. Where supplementary questions are asked, these should be noted, and answers written down, considered, and then read back to the press. In practice an experienced press officer can write out likely questions and produce in advance answers which are unambiguous and in accordance with company policy.

The use of a public relations executive in this way calls for a person of ability and seniority coupled with a close involvement in top management thinking.

Shareholders and 'the City'

Public companies need to pay high regard to the way in which any story about their activities is likely to cause repercussions on the stock market.

Financial PR is not random action to keep bad news from the press and inflate good news. It calls for careful planning and involves a range of activities, including press advertising, literature, financial and policy statements, shareholders' meetings and the annual report. Advance planning will ensure that each opportunity is exploited to the full.

The overlap with other key publics should not be forgotten. Employees read annual reports, and take pride in the company they work for. Customers and suppliers have an interest in such information.

Share values and the response to an issue depend largely on financial criteria, but a company's reputation can have a significant bearing on the matter. Press releases dealing, for example, with winning important contracts will be designed initially to influence potential customers, but they also contribute to the building up of a firm's image with investors, stockbrokers and bankers.

Economic and industrial journalists probably have most influence in interpreting a company and its policies to the public, and relationships of mutual understanding must be cultivated. Journalists can, after all, only report on events in the light of their own personal knowledge and experience. A very useful operation in this respect is to arrange for groups of journalists to meet informally from time to time with members of a company's top management. Such functions should not be centred around a particular news item, but be planned deliberately to exchange views and impart information of a general nature. It does no harm, either, for top management to understand and respect the requirements of journalists.

Suppliers

Suppliers make up one of a company's key publics. The building of a good business relationship depends in part on an understanding of one another, and the respect of suppliers for their customers can be valuable. Suppliers, after all, have preferences among their customers and these can well lead to benefits in terms of service, delivery and even price.

A further factor is that suppliers have many contacts within their trade and their views often reach a wide variety of influential people. Their recommendations count in building up a company's reputation.

Local communities

Much of the strength of a company lies in the quality and attitudes of the people it employs. Local communities are a major source of recruitment at all levels, and local public relations activities can be a source of encouragement to potential employees. Existing employees, too, like to feel that the firm they work for has a favourable reputation in the locality, is known to have enlightened management policies, and is providing a useful service to the community.

A company also depends a great deal on the local authority, on councillors and permanent officials, especially when acquiring new premises or expanding its operations. It needs good relations with public utilities, with the police, educationalists, local organizations, and other businesses in the area whose co-operation is sometimes of considerable value in matters of common interest whether rateable values, rates of pay or the sharing of a common bus service.

A firm which sets out to play a part in the life of a local community has much to gain for little investment, though its obligations cannot be satisfied simply by sponsoring a football match or contributing to a charity or two. Senior people from the company must take a genuine interest in local affairs and be seen to be doing so.

Opinion formers

This is one of the 'jargon terms' of public relations practitioners. The thought behind the term is that within a community there are certain people who by reason of their function or position are likely to be able to exert a special influence on public opinion. The contention is that general opinions are formed or changed by people whose views are respected. A teacher or a youth leader for example may have a specially high influence on young people, while other typical opinion formers include members of parliament, academics, top business men, clergymen, local community leaders and lawyers.

Having defined what amounts in selling terms to the potential market, it remains to plan the action necessary to direct an adequate level of persuasive communications at them in order to achieve the desired effect.

It is true that such an operation can be expensive and also that the results are difficult to measure. More than usual judgement must be exercised in order to equate the investment to the likely return in terms of impact upon sales, finance, recruitment and all the many activities which contribute to a company's profitable existence.

Specialized groups

In most organizations a situation arises which requires a special group of people to be informed or persuaded in order to understand fully a company's point of view.

This was the case when radioactive isotopes were first introduced into industry for measurement and control. There was concern about radiation hazards among safety officers, trade unionists, government departments and members of parliament. In particular there was the suspicion that material passing in front of an isotope could itself become radioactive. This was scientifically unfounded but nonetheless had to be treated as a serious potential point of sales resistance. A good deal of scientific publicity and official backing was required at a number of levels in order to overcome what were quite genuine and serious fears.

Another interesting problem confronted a certain manufacturer who relied on large quantities of waste paper as a basic raw material. One major source of supply, the housewife via refuse collection, began to decline. There were a number of specialized groups to be informed of the importance of saving paper, and of its value to the economy. The housewife was the primary source, but her co-operation was of no avail unless the dustman kept paper separate from other refuse. Here it was necessary to influence the public cleansing officer who controlled the dustmen, the local authority committee and even the mayor. Other sources of supply were youth organizations, who could raise funds by collecting waste paper, and industrial concerns like printers who as a matter of course were large producers of waste.

A solution to the shortage of waste paper could have been to increase the price paid for it until supply caught up with demand, but the cost would have been very great and in turn would have been passed on to the consumer. In the event a major public relations campaign was mounted to reach all the interested groups. For housewives, conventional consumer media were used such as television, radio, posters, door-to-door circulars and talks to women's groups. The annual conference of public cleansing officers included in their programme a visit to a factory to see waste paper being used. The Lord Mayor of London held a reception, which every London mayor attended, and heard of the national need for waste paper. A novel feature which caught the imagination of journalists was an exhibition of waste paper which involved dumping several tons of it in the middle of the Savoy Hotel. A pop song was written and recorded, a film made, schoolchildren were informed, and the network of publicity spread to the key publics likely to affect the situation.

When a company decides to move from one location to another, a very well-planned public relations campaign is required not just to employees, but more important to their families. In setting up a new factory there are often local community interests that must be considered. Largely it is a matter of informing people well in advance and of giving them an opportunity to express their views. They will want to know how it will affect them personally, for instance will there be opportunities for employment? Will there be undue smell or noise, or an increase in traffic? Will it disturb a local bird sanctuary? And so on.

A feature of public relations in connection with specialized groups is the tendency to wait for a situation to arise before taking action. This is sometimes inevitable, but a plan to maintain good relations and provide an adequate flow of information to such people on a continuous basis can function even if at a relatively low intensity. Indeed, such a procedure will do much to avoid crises arising which require crash action, usually expensive, and sometimes too late.

People in general

'How do we want people to see us?' This is a question that a company should ask itself periodically, and work out an answer in some detail and in writing. This will then become the foundation of public relations policy.

Consider how an impression of an organization is formed. Is it through a salesperson, or a buyer? Perhaps it is through the receptionist or a van driver? Maybe it is the letter heading or the exterior of a building: perhaps what appears in the press as editorial or advertising. Whatever the medium and whatever its primary purpose, it also has a public relations connotation.

An important factor is 'house styling'. The process begins with the name of the company and its subsidiaries. The name should be simple, appropriate, easy to pronounce, memorable and, of course, registerable. Is a trade mark or symbol necessary? If there is a house colour, is it useful and is it the most effective colour?

If a 'style' is to be established to what should it apply? A designer must know this before starting work, and the items may include letter headings, invoices, order forms, visiting cards, vehicles, notice boards, advertising, products, company ties and even security police cap badges. There can be many complications and arguments for deviation from the standard specification, and much expense in implementation, but in practice the introduction of a new house style can lead to considerable economies. Standardization of paper sizes and of forms can save hundreds of pounds. A change from embossed letterheads to litho printing, a reduction in the number of colours on vehicles, the elimination of copperplate visiting cards, provide opportunities for savings, especially where a company has grown up over a number of years and each element of the business has been developed on an individual basis.

Corporate relations

The need for a planned programme of corporate relations stems not from some new management concept but from the fact that organizations are finding, somewhat to their dismay, the need for a formalized corporate strategy. This need is being interpreted in a number of ways, but simply stated is that it is no longer good enough to take random actions for long-term effect: rather it is necessary to give mature consideration to future objectives and the means of achieving them. Such objectives will incorporate financial investment, labour force and staffing, marketing aspects, production, research and development, and of course profit. This is no more than a move from past practices in which future events were just allowed to take their natural course, to a position in which a company sets out deliberately to move to a predetermined position. The weakness of any attempt at corporate planning is that unforeseeable events are bound to cause the objectives to be changed, but this is no reason for not taking action to influence the course of events so as to hit the desired target as closely as possible. Corporate relations are but one of the management functions which can be used to help achieve this goal.

The need for corporate goals and for a strategy to achieve them stems from a growing number of influences, external and internal, which if ignored may well undermine the profitable development of a company and indeed threaten its very existence. The increasing tendency by governments to impose controls is a major factor as are international regulations at one extreme and a vigorous consumerist movement at the other. Thus trade barriers and constraints, scarcity of raw materials, inflation, high taxation, are factors which play a larger part in the development of business. Equally the growing interest by employees and trade unions with their sometimes massive influence must be taken into consideration in any future planning.

In this section an examination is made of corporate relations from the point of view of *what* they are, *why* they are necessary, to *whom* they should be addressed, *when*, and *how*. Finally, the all important question of the results that might reasonably be expected of such an activity.

First *what*. Corporate relations is a term used to signify the deliberate attempts by an organization to maintain the best possible relations with each and every identifiable group of people whose interests and activities may be supposed to have an effect, for good or ill, on the prosperity and progress of the business. Such an operation is intrinsically linked with communications in both directions since without communications of some kind it is difficult to see how any change or impact can be obtained. It is important at the outset to realize two things. First that no matter how efficient any corporate communications system may be, it will be of no avail unless the object of the communication is sound. In just the same way no amount of advertising will ever sell an unsatisfactory product. The second point to be made is that every single means of communication must be considered for possible use, not just the classical PR media such as press releases, factory visits, booklets and special events. Corporate relations then are the building up of a good *reputation* with a company's many and varied publics. An old-fashioned term sums it up very well—*goodwill*.

Clearly the kind of activity being described is going to cost money. Hence the need to ask *why?* The plain fact is that all companies have an image whether they like it or not, or even if they are totally unaware of it. That is to say that a company is perceived by people in a variety of ways, depending upon the messages, conscious or unconscious, they have received about it. And the perception varies from one public to another. Customers may view a supplier as a thoroughly reliable and trustworthy organization with which to do business, whereas its employees may take the very opposite view.

The reason *why* corporate relations are important is that it is only when relationships are positive and sound that the most effective and efficient business can be conducted. For example is it reasonable to expect the best possible applicants for a job with a company which has a very poor reputation as an employer? It may be argued that in such a case the simple solution is in changing the conditions of employment so that they are really attractive, but this is overlooking the essential ingredient of corporate communications for if people are unaware of a situation they cannot react to it. And if, as often happens, they are misinformed about it the opposite result to what was intended may be the outcome. The reason why corporate communications are important is that in one direction a company is receiving messages about itself from all the interested publics, and on the other hand it is sending out messages to those same people to ensure that they are fully informed, that they understand and that they are convinced. The reason *why* thus is in order to establish and maintain a series of relationships in which business can be conducted most efficiently.

The *when* of corporate relations can be dealt with simply. A reputation is with a company all its life. It's no use having a corporate relations function, and a corporate communication programme for a couple of years and then closing it down. People's memories and attitudes are dynamic and will change over time. A company must decide whether or not it is really serious in the matter of building its reputation, and if it is, and it wishes to maintain it, this can be achieved in one way only, and that is by a continuous programme of activities. It should also be borne in mind that the time-scale to achieve any major change is likely to be of the order of years rather than months, so advance planning is required as well as continuity.

Turning now to *how* corporate relations are to be achieved, this of course is where the difficulties arise and where the answers tend to become diffuse, uncertain and even contradictory. In outline it can be said that the starting point is to draw up plans, both strategic and tactical, to set objectives, to measure results, to co-ordinate all related and parallel activities, and to ensure that an adequate administrative and professional facility exists to guarantee proper execution.

STRATEGIC PLANNING

The key to successful strategic planning for good corporate relations is in the setting of comprehensive objectives. Two examples have been chosen to illustrate this point. First a major multinational corporation which listed five aims:

1. To increase the share of people's minds available to the company.
2. To engender favourable attention and acceptability from its diverse publics.
3. To explain the realities of the company's social and economic contributions to the countries where it did business.
4. To state the case for business in general and MNCs in particular.
5. To correct some of the myths and refute irresponsible allegations.

The programme which evolved consisted of a package of five interdependent activities, each mutually supporting, making its own unique contribution, but working to the same plan and objectives. The elements of the package were an advertising campaign, a public information brochure, an external house magazine, a press relations programme and the establishment of a speakers' panel, and the complete programme was based on a publicly stated philosophy of openness, frankness and fact.

The second example is for a well-known company in the high technology business. The programme had five objectives:

1. To extend the company's corporate identity and to enhance/improve attitudes held towards the company among the defined target audiences.
2. To establish and promote the company as a leader and innovator in advanced technology.
3. To promote the company's capabilities and achievements in selected areas of advanced technology.
4. To create a high level of awareness and knowledge among target groups in prospective market areas for the technological excellence of its products.
5. To create a favourable attitude among target groups so that divisional marketing activities for particular products or systems could be carried out more effectively.

The main thrust of the campaign to achieve these aims was a most adventurous press campaign of very large advertisements in the colour supplements, backed by supportive advertising in 'management newspapers' and the specialist press.

TACTICAL PLANNING

It is not sufficient to produce one major homogeneous campaign and leave it at that. It is vital to examine each and every other sector of communications with its own specialized objectives, audiences, messages and media in order to ensure that these contribute also to the common objective of the company's reputation. In this way marketing communications, employee communications, a safety campaign, city and financial news, and all the rest add together to make up a synergistic whole. It can be seen that organizationally there is a need for the provision of top management direction to ensure the proper orchestration of all the many parts which are being conducted on a day-to-day basis.

The second part of tactical operations relates to what might be termed 'reactive activities'. This is where over and above the carefully constructed ongoing campaign there arise events which, if not handled properly, can work against the corporate objectives or alternatively fail to give the potential support that may otherwise be achieved. Examples may be in an industrial dispute where bad handling can undo much of the goodwill which might have been built up over a period of years. It is necessary then to develop a programme for crisis management in which plans are laid down for handling any particular contingency that may arise. Equally, but in the opposite direction, failure to exploit fully the securing of a major overseas contract is a loss in terms of the very favourable light in which such an achievement can be shown to the target groups that together make up the corporate public.

Such contingencies cannot by their very nature be incorporated in any plan, but the organization must be sufficiently flexible to be able to react fast to each of these as they occur and to have in mind not just the event itself and how to solve or exploit it, but also the overall objectives.

The most important factor here is to be pro-active rather than reactive.

CORPORATE RESEARCH

Early in the growth of the marketing concept and of corporate planning, communications activities were characterized by 'prestige advertising' and by a narrow form of public relations which relied mainly on what was loosely termed 'press relations'. It was unusual to have specific goals, and large sums of money were invested to put out almost self-congratulatory messages about oneself without much regard to the interest of the audiences or indeed what the effect on them might be. Companies indulging in these activities became sceptical of their value and as economic conditions became tougher any attempt to buy prestige declined.

The growth of corporate affairs as a function, and corporate relations as an activity, has been accompanied by the precise setting of objectives in quantified form, and by a programme of research to ensure that any investment will achieve tangible results. Business people have begun to demand that expenditure in this area should be accountable and the effects measurable.

The starting point of any properly constructed programme of corporate communications is to make bench-mark measurements against which progress can be compared as the campaign proceeds. It is no use making such measurements at the end of a campaign as by that time it is too late to take any corrective action. A company may decide that it wishes to increase the level of awareness among certain discrete publics and at the same time gain an improved attitude towards itself and its products. Sample groups from each segment must be chosen and an assessment made of their current level of awareness and the nature of their attitudes. Only with this information can an effective plan be drawn up. From this a budget is set with the task to move from a current level A to a targeted level B in a given period of time. Using the same audience segments, methods of sampling and questioning techniques, research must be planned at intermediate stages in order to find out whether the results are on schedule, in advance of it or behind it. Variations can be made at this stage in order to bring the campaign back on to course and the changes may be simply in the direction of the campaign, or it may be necessary to increase expenditure, or for that matter cut it back. So the operation breaks down into four stages—set objectives, quantify, research, verify.

BENEFITS

A well-constructed and properly funded corporate relations programme can lead to many benefits of which the following are but a few of the more obvious examples.

1. Increased market reputation and market share
2. Happier and more satisfied employees
3. Rise in share prices
4. Greater productivity
5. Favourable government support
6. Better quality applicants for jobs
7. Improved treatment from suppliers
8. Better understanding by, and less criticism from outside pressure groups

While benefits will accrue to any company the chances are that the larger the organization, the greater the need for a formalized corporate communication policy. This applies with even greater effect where the products concerned fall into the category known as 'undifferentiated'. With little to choose between one brand and another—for example with petrol, oil, banks, cigarettes, detergents, what are the real determinants of a purchasing decision? There is a good deal of evidence to suggest that the customer will go for the brand or name he or she knows best and for which he or she has the greatest regard. Where products are intrinsically the same, the most important factor must become that indefinable property which lies behind the product—its reputation. And this applies with equal force to industrial products and services as to consumer ones.

At the end of a chapter on public relations, it is relevant to stress that the greatest single factor in a business is the people who work for it. It is true that sophisticated communications techniques must be used to make the company's operations clear to the world. But paramount in relations with the public is the chief executive and an enthusiastic staff and workforce. The public relations practitioner will only succeed in projecting what exists. If a company deserves a bad reputation, no amount of public relations expenditure will eliminate it. The only remedy is to concentrate on the source of the trouble.

Checklist

1. Has the difference between public relations and press relations been established? Do top management understand this?
2. Has a plan of action been drawn up to influence the following audiences?
   (a) Customers and prospects
   (b) Employees and trade unions
   (c) Shareholders and investors
   (d) Suppliers
   (e) Local communities
   (f) Opinion formers
   (g) Government departments
   (h) Local authorities
   (i) Educational bodies
   (j) Specialized groups
3. In drawing up such a forward plan, has each medium been considered, i.e. in addition to editorial publicity—press advertising, direct mail, exhibitions, literature, films and so on?
4. In addition to conventional media have opportunities under the following headings been examined?

(a) Factory openings and tours
(b) Conferences and seminars
(c) Speakers panel
(d) Notice boards
(e) Closed-circuit television
(f) House magazine
(g) Factory signs
(h) Employees' clothing, overalls, uniforms, badges
(i) Meetings between journalists and top management
(j) Sponsored events—local, national and international
(k) Involvement in local community activities
(l) Demonstrations
(m) House styling

Part 5

PUBLICITY ORGANIZATIONS

16.

MARKETING SERVICES

There has been considerable change in the past decade in the position of the publicity function in relation to the top management structure of a company. The most significant development was that publicity in the industrial field achieved recognition as a serious and valuable operation, albeit as a part of the selling activity. A typical company organization chart (Figure 16.1) in the classic tradition was:

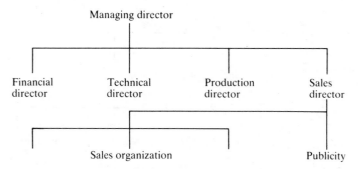

Figure 16.1 Company organization chart 1 (sales orientation)

This scheme was usual whether the company was large or small, and would range from large publicity departments with managers responsible to sales directors, to small operations in which the chief sales executives handled the publicity themselves.

In changing from a sales- to a marketing-orientated organization there have been, and still are, a number of interim stages in which for instance the publicity manager reports to the managing director who (unknowingly) thus assumes the function of part-time marketing director. Sometimes a marketing director was appointed, but placed alongside a sales director, with the inevitable clash of interests. This is not to say that a company cannot operate efficiently and effectively without conforming to some theoretical ideal structure. Each situation requires its own solution having regard to variables such as the size of the company, the nature of its products and market, and inevitably the capabilities and personalities of the people it employs.

Figures 16.2, 16.3 and 16.4 represent typical organizational structures for industrial companies which are marketing oriented, have 'own products' but vary considerably in size. Such a company, as in Figure 16.2 may employ a few hundred people and have a turnover of a million pounds. Here the sales manager is very much out in the field with accounts of his or her own. The publicity manager would in some cases have no more than a good secretary as an assistant, and would not only handle sales promotion and public relations, but also arrange whatever marketing research was required. Marketing planning would be the job of the marketing director who, as the company developed in size, might add a marketing executive as an assistant but in a staff rather than line capacity. Much of the publicity work would be bought in, and in a small company this is far better than employing a number of specialists with a corresponding increase in semi-fixed overheads.

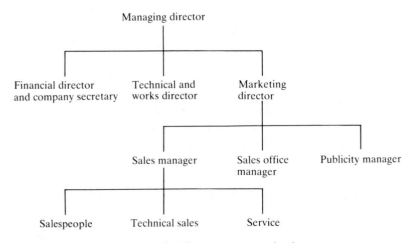

Figure 16.2   Small company organization

Figure 16.3 represents a company with a turnover of several millions and employing a thousand or more people. A new title has been introduced, 'marketing services manager', a function designed to supply every service required by the marketing operation. There is still no separate marketing planning function, but this takes place within the marketing services department under the direction of the marketing director. No independent provision is made for product development, but depending on the nature of the business the function is shared between the technical department and the marketing services department.

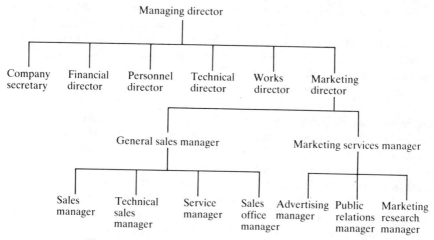

Figure 16.3 Medium sized company organization

The three functions under the marketing services manager then break down as follows:

1. *Advertising*
   (a) Press advertising
   (b) Exhibitions
   (c) Direct mail
   (d) Literature
2. *Public Relations*
   (a) Public relations
   (b) Press relations
   (c) House magazines
   (d) Films
   (e) Photography
3. *Marketing Research*
   (a) Market research
   (b) Product research
   (c) Product testing
   (d) Attitude research
   (e) Campaign evaluation

Whether to put films under public relations is simply a matter of which category films most often tend to fit in a particular company. As the company develops within this structure, the number of specialists can be increased so that there will be an exhibitions manager, a press officer or a photographer under public relations, and a statistician or economist under marketing research.

Where there is a wide variety of products in a company of this size, an alternative is to break down the marketing services department into product or brand specialists. This has the merit of getting greater knowledge of products and markets amongst the individuals handling the promotions, but these same people now need to have a very broad experience of every aspect of persuasive communications.

In Figure 16.4 the overall company structure has been omitted to look in more detail at the marketing function. This scheme is more appropriate for a company with a turnover of tens of millions of pounds. Here the strength of a centralized structure can be seen in that it is possible to deploy a number of specialists who concentrate exclusively on one aspect only of marketing. One person or even a department will be concerned specifically with the search for new products: similarly with the planning of marketing operations and the development of marketing strategies. Research and economics have been taken outside the marketing services function, which is now concerned principally with making a direct contribution to short- and medium-term marketing operations. The 'brand manager' concept is introduced in the form of product group executives and they, in turn, can call upon specialists in particular media to contribute to their operations.

Figure 16.4   Large company organization

It is arguable whether public relations should be allowed to go so far down the line as shown in this structure. An alternative is to make this directly responsible to the marketing director, but with a connecting link to the managing director.

It may be necessary to have a number of sales managers reporting to the marketing director. When the span of control begins to become too great a marketing manager can be introduced to administer the other marketing functions. No provision has been made in any of the structures described for the 'creative' function. It has been assumed that outside agencies will be used and that the need for visualizers and copywriters will not arise. This will be discussed in the next part of the chapter.

A matter of continual debate in larger companies is whether to centralize publicity or to split it up amongst the operating divisions, each with its own publicity department. It is probably not important, providing those operating the business believe strongly and enthusiastically in the system they are using. This is often borne out by the changes recommended by management consultants. Frequently if publicity is centralized, consultants recommend decentralization and vice versa. Both systems work. If anything the balance must be slightly in favour of central control since the increasing use of sophisticated marketing techniques calls for specialists who cannot be justified, or indeed fully utilized, by a small organization.

A final point to be made emerges from research by the author and that is the significant replacement of sales directors by marketing directors. It is also noticeable that increasingly advertising and PR functions are being merged under the umbrella of someone at board level with a title like Corporate Affairs Director. Where this happens the responsibility and authority for advertising and related functions rests with just this one person—which is a good reason for having him or her. In the majority of cases however the advertising manager, or equivalent, has the responsibility but not the authority. Research has shown that only 37 per cent of publicity managers can approve an advertisement and only 12 per cent a campaign. In 75 per cent of the cases authority for approving an advertisement had to come from at least one director.

In-house services

It is now necessary to consider briefly each of the publicity functions and how, if at all, a publicity department should set itself up to handle them. An examination of such departments shows a wide diversity of views, with some industrial companies making do with a very modest staff, and others employing tens and sometimes hundreds of people.

A good basic rule for the creation and development of a publicity department is to keep it as small as possible. The reason for this is twofold. Specialist services are almost always available from outside agencies and they are often of better quality than an internal department can provide. Secondly, if a company goes through a difficult financial period it is sometimes forced to make drastic cutbacks in current expenditure, and such economies are inevitably made in activities which will have the least deleterious effect *in the short term*. These are generally publicity and R&D,

often with results which are later regretted. The comments which follow are of a general nature and it is to be expected that there will be exceptions which work extremely well.

PRESS ADVERTISING

Few firms produce their own press advertising, and thus there is rarely a case for a company to employ its own advertisement visualizers, typographers and artists. Far better ones are available outside, and certainly no top-grade creative person will stay for long with an industrial company. Even if that person is brilliant to start with, this will soon wear off without the variety, challenge and stimulus of an agency or studio atmosphere.

With technical copywriting there is a strong body of opinion that an agency cannot produce adequate copy, and that it takes longer to produce the brief than to write the copy oneself. This is not only untrue: it is nonsense. Writing is a highly skilled and creative function, which requires a top-rate craftsman. Few advertising managers (or sales managers) would claim to have this facility. It is true that most advertising agencies find technical copywriting difficult, and that many are incapable of doing it. The solution is not to do it oneself, but to change the agency.

The production side of press advertising, voucher checking and so on is usually handled well by an agency, and there can be little justification for a publicity department being involved in this.

MEDIA PLANNING

Agencies are in a difficult position on press media planning. They cannot obtain adequate data from publishers, and clients as a rule are unwilling or unable to allocate adequate funds for a thorough investigation to be undertaken. Some agencies are breaking new ground in this respect and much progress will be made over the next ten years but, in the mean time, the solution seems to be to encourage the agency media department in every possible way, but for the publicity department to retain a strong measure of control and scrutiny.

As regards the media mix outside press advertising, most of the 750 or so agencies in the United Kingdom have good experience of press media, and some of literature and exhibitions, but for other media few have strong enough all-round experience to compete with a company's own publicity department, particularly in the specialized industry and product groups in which a firm is operating.

DIRECT MAIL

This is usually most efficiently directed and executed within the publicity department. Partly the reason is that many agencies are not set up to process this medium: partly because the maintenance of lists can usually best be handled at the client end: partly because action is usually required at a moment's notice: partly because this is very much a personal means of contact from supplier to customer.

A sales letter, for instance, is usually something which a sales manager or an advertising manager can do better than a copywriter. This is not to contradict the argument in favour of professional writers for press advertising: it is a matter of horses for courses, and the professional in sales letters is, or should be, a sales manager.

Direct mail is, of course, not confined to writing a letter, and there is a good deal of outside creative expertise from advertising agencies, art studios, freelancers or direct mail houses, which can be used with considerable advantage.

The lead and initiative should, however, rest with the publicity department.

EXHIBITIONS

These must be a co-operative effort. Only rarely can an outside consultant or agency know enough about a company to be able to handle the whole process from the initial briefing to the final opening. This is particularly true in view of the company changes in policy and personnel which may take place over the period of planning an exhibition. Moreover a stand is a highly complex publicity medium and should be produced as an environment where company personnel will be required to sell actively and efficiently.

It is equally rare that a company employs people on its staff who have adequate knowledge of design, writing, architecture, décor and construction to be able to do the job independently.

The answer is to organize a joint effort, but to do this formally with each element of the job analysed, isolated and planned so that the appropriate specialist is used for the appropriate job, and then integrated into the whole. Figure 16.5 is a simple diagram that can be used as a starting point for a more detailed network which will incorporate a time-scale.

LITERATURE

Organizing literature usually involves another compromise. Few publicity departments can carry out the visualizing, and few agencies or outside consultants are capable of writing the text. The final difficulty is that very few publicity departments are able to write the text either, unless they are large enough to justify the employment of specialist writers.

There are agencies who employ writers able to do the complete assignment, and there are freelance writers who can sometimes be used. Technical

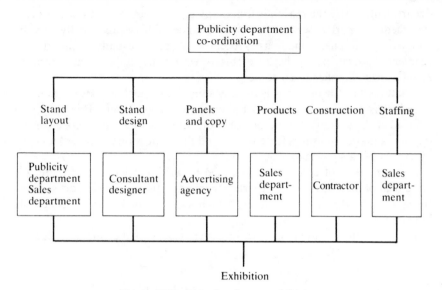

Exhibition

Figure 16.5   Planning for an exhibition

journalists can be hired on a freelance basis and generally produce good work. Alternatively, someone inside the company may write the basic text to be passed on to a professional writer for finishing.

On the production side there is not much to choose between using an agency or having a specialist on the staff of the publicity department. If the workload is steady and sufficiently great, it pays to employ a full-time executive: if not, an agency will probably do a first-class job, but will charge anything between 15 per cent and 25 per cent of the total print bill for the service. For the smaller company, many printers have their own designers, or maintain a close contact with a design unit. This can be satisfactory, especially if the work is not too detailed or specialized but the disadvantage is that it lengthens the chain of communication.

For house magazines, the solution is to appoint a professional editor. Whether that editor should be on the company's staff is immaterial provided he or she is capable and is given a wide degree of freedom to implement editorial policy within the budget.

PHOTOGRAPHY

To have a staff photographer is a decided advantage providing this does not mean that every photographic job must be handled by him. Some photographers specialize in creative work, others in industrial work, portraiture, news, landscape, advertising, and it is too much to expect to find all these skills in one person employed as a member of staff. Alternatively, much company photography required quickly, or for record purposes, or at little expense can best be done by a staff photographer.

PRINTING

No matter how many, or how sophisticated, the offset litho machines a company installs, they cannot replace outside printers. With a larger firm, a print department can make great savings on forms and routine internal jobs. Even some external work is acceptable for certain purposes— a news-sheet, manuals or an exhibition handout for example. Outside this, however, for sales literature, it is unusual for a company to be able to produce work of acceptable quality or even at competitive cost.

FILMS AND VIDEOS

Hardly a firm in the country is equipped with its own film unit. A video-camera has some use for sales and the management training, and perhaps for other internal communications, but not much else. If films or videos form a large part of a company's publicity programme it is essential to have an executive on the staff with specialist experience or alternatively to take counsel with experts at the advertising agency.

The essential function for the company is to make active provision for the promotion and distribution of films. This cannot be farmed out, notwithstanding the existence of one or two distribution libraries. These provide a good physical distribution service, but films are made to be shown actively to specific audiences, and this will not happen unless a company plans for it and sets up the necessary organization.

With the emergence of video recording there has been a swing back to using in-house facilities which with care can result in very competently produced programmes. This however is more in a technical sense than creative where the services of an outside specialist are vital.

EDITORIAL PUBLICITY

It is difficult to justify employing an agency for editorial publicity as distinct from public relations. The preparation of press releases and of press conferences calls for a professional executive, but the degree of in-company knowledge, contacts and accessibility required favours the employment of a staff person. Furthermore, the press tend to prefer to deal direct with a company since they need answers with both speed and authority. An agency or a consultant is at an inherent disadvantage in this respect.

An outside PR organization has contacts as part of its stock in trade of course, but these can be matched in time by most companies themselves and with greater effect.

PUBLIC RELATIONS

Even the best of public relations practitioners, after immersion in a company environment for a few years begin to acquire a biased point of view. They are, after all, subordinate to the management they are advising and must exercise a certain caution in giving advice which in turn is not always regarded as highly as that from an outside source.

There is much to be said for retaining a public relations consultancy to give top-level advice, to work in conjunction with a company's own PR staff and to be available to provide assistance for special events which are outside the scope, capacity or experience of staff executives.

The staff person has an important function, and as already indicated, should have direct access to the chief executive. The range of public relations activities, however, is so broad that an agency can usually bring to bear a good deal more experience on a problem than a staff executive who, as time goes on, becomes more and more specialized, and operates within a restricted environment.

MISCELLANEOUS PUBLICITY ACTIVITIES

All manner of miscellaneous activities fall to a publicity department, and rightly. The publicity staff are the company's experts in communications whether internal or external, and should be used as such. Sales conferences, gifts, Christmas cards, samples, factory signs, notice boards—all these and more fall to the publicity department to organize. Some limits may be necessary, particularly as when the department is asked to produce raffle tickets for the sports club dinner, and the procedure here is to require that some estimate should be produced of how much it costs to use an in-house service for some of the smaller items which could just as easily and effectively be produced elsewhere.

PLANNING AND BUDGETING

This task cannot be delegated. It is in fact the single most important job of a publicity department, and the only one which emphatically cannot be 'put out'.

The one key function of a company's publicity department is to operate within the framework of the marketing strategy, to plan, budget, administer, monitor and to assess the overall range of publicity activities.

17.

PUBLISHERS

Publishers of periodicals merit special attention since they play such a significant role in industrial publicity. The United Kingdom is unique in this respect, both in the number of publications (2000 trade and technical), and in the share of publicity budgets allocated to press advertising (about 40 per cent). Even if the average circulation for a journal is taken at a modest 5000, with 2000 publications, this would amount to 10 million copies per month (or whatever period) and multiplied by the 'pass-on' circulation, perhaps five per copy, this results in a total potential readership of 50 million. Clearly there is much duplication in the figure of 50 million.

Quantity, however, is not necessarily a sign of strength: indeed the number of periodicals currently being circulated is likely to prove to be the weakness of the publishing industry, in that there is a limit to the amount of reading time that any one person has. Nevertheless, considerable sums of money are invested in press advertising; one estimate puts it at well in excess of £1000 m a year, and this is adequate justification for a detailed examination of publishing.

Development of the press

There have been three distinct phases of development that have taken place over the past decade or so, and these are very akin to the changes that were earlier outlined for products in relation to marketing development, i.e. product orientation followed by sales orientation and marketing orientation. In the publishing world it is possible to restate these developments as journal orientation, circulation orientation and audience (or readership) orientation. It is necessary to look into each of these phases since many publishers are still heavily entrenched in the first two stages.

Each stage of development tends to be characterized by the nature or function of the person at the head of a publication. In the first phase it is the editor who is primarily responsible for laying down policy. In the second phase the advertisement manager emerges as the principal executive. Finally, and some companies have moved well into this position, the senior executive is a general manager or publisher who can call upon all the modern marketing services to assist in the promotion of his or her product. This leads to an alternative method of identifying the phase of development reached, by asking 'what is the product that a publisher is marketing?'. In the first phase the answer is a journal: in the second, it is circulation that is being sold. In the third phase the product being marketed is an audience or a readership—vastly different from circulation. Apply the classical question 'what business are we in?'. The answer is surely not writing (phase 1), or publishing (phase 2) but communications. It is only by accepting this concept that periodicals can maintain their predominant position in the publicity mix.

Publishing organizations

A good deal of change has taken place, not only in the emergence of a marketing concept, but in rationalizations and amalgamations which have facilitated the implementation of a marketing approach. The three organization charts (Figs 17.1, 17.2 and 17.3) represent the three phases of development, and while it may appear that they cover respectively small, medium and large operations, there are examples of the smallest of publishers being completely marketing-orientated and the largest still operating around the journal-production concept.

Many publications exist today which fit into the pattern outlined in Figure 17.1. Some are extremely successful in financial terms: others may even be satisfactory communicators. The basis of operation is that the editor produces an editorial mix intuitively which he or she has found over a period of time to be successful in terms of paid-for circulation. Advertisers, if they have liked the appearance and contents of a publication, have been welcome to participate providing they did not get in the way of the editorial. It was commonplace, and is still not unknown for publishers in phase one of development to be unwilling to disclose even their total circulation let alone other data. The product is the journal.

Figure 17.1   Publishing organization—phase 1

The editorial department here decides on editorial content regardless of any other considerations. It will usually control layout and presentation, production and sometimes circulation and distribution. The advertisement department is concerned with selling space, and indeed in the absence of adequate information to reinforce a sales argument, many space representatives are, through no fault of their own, little more than collectors of orders for space. At best they are salesmen of the old school whose success depends upon their personality and their ability to capture the confidence of a prospect—but in themselves rather than their product.

This over-simplification does not imply that a given management structure automatically places a publisher among the has-beens, nor that a managing editor is incapable of comprehending and implementing the marketing concept. There are exceptions as always with general rules and procedures.

The organization in Figure 17.2 may not appear much different from that of phase 1, but there is a higher degree of specialization, and the addition of some central services.

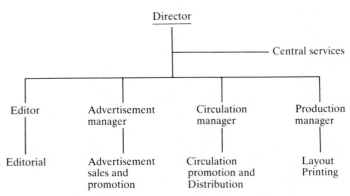

Figure 17.2   Publishing orgnization—phase 2

The differences lie not so much in the organization chart as in the significance of each of the functions in the business operation. A director at the head is to signify that it is an all-round business executive who lays down policy and makes decisions, and that these are on a commercial basis. The editor is rated level with the other departmental heads, and the advertisement manager, for instance, can expect to have as much influence on the make-up and presentation as the editor. Significantly, circulation is treated as a separate and important function with paid-for circulation giving way to free distribution if this is considered necessary to secure business.

Central services are an indication of the growth of publishers into larger units which can provide specialized facilities such as an art department and publicity. Further developments of central services take over responsibility for printing, sometimes distribution and even production and circulation.

Adopting the phase 3 concept of the 'product' being an audience and the 'benefit' exposure or access to that audience, it follows that the product development function in publishing is concerned with maintaining the right readership to meet the advertisers' needs (see Fig. 17.3). While many products in industry remain static, at least for a short period of time, and therefore may not require development, in publishing, the audience is in a continual state of change. As new readers register, and people move jobs, the audience mix will become unbalanced and therefore in effect a different product which may not be wanted by advertisers.

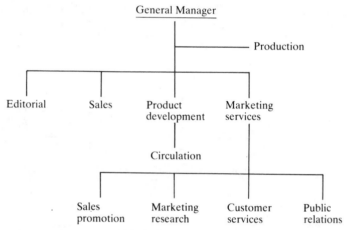

Figure 17.3   Publishing organization—phase 3

The 'market' is of course the potential advertisers, and so the starting point in the development of a product in publishing is to assess the market's needs i.e. what audience does it wish to reach. This requires to be broken down into segments which will relate to, for example, industrial classification, job category, geographical location and size of firm. From this point it is necessary for the editorial team to devise an editorial mix that will appeal to the audience which emerges, and for a method of circulation to be set up which will reach it.

In marketing services, the research people will be monitoring the success of circulation, and the interest of readers in the editorial. They will study the impact of advertisements, the number of 'pass-on' readers and various other factors of importance to advertisers such as the value of different positions in a journal, the influence of colour, bleed and so on. This data will provide the ammunition which will be fired first by the sales promotion department and then by the sales force. Public relations will take as its task the building of good relations and a good understanding with all the publics of a journal including readers, advertisers, distributors, contributors, trade associations, suppliers and shareholders.

Customer services is a function which is not yet fully established in publishing. Each journal has certain strengths which derive from being in its particular business. Some of these strengths can be marketed in one form or another to existing and prospective customers. For example, a journal's circulation list can be hired out as the basis of a direct mail operation. The editorial team have technical knowledge which can be applied to the staging of seminars and conferences. The editors are writers, and some of this talent can be expanded into writing house magazines, leaflets for clients or film scripts. Publishers are also in a good position to sponsor exhibitions. 'Customer services' will also include carrying out specific assignments for customers, such as working with them to measure the total effectiveness of a campaign. Split runs for instance are easy to arrange, but few technical publishers offer this facility, let alone promote it as a sales feature.

Production is shown as a central service. So probably should be marketing services unless the idea of product groups is adopted. In this case, a number of complementary journals are marketed within one product group. The editorial teams need to be separate, but the sales force and all the other functions can be operated to serve all the publications in a group. This method of operation is particularly suited to larger organizations: indeed with large numbers of publications, it becomes necessary in order to maintain a workable span of management control.

Departmental functions

EDITORIAL

It has been said earlier that press advertising is 'too cheap'. This is evidenced throughout all departments in a publishing organization, but no more so than in the editorial department. Considering the national importance of technical journals in disseminating information on new developments in industry and commerce, it is disconcerting to find the conditions under which the editorial side is often forced to work because of the limited finance available to it. An editorial team often consists of little more than an editor and an assistant, and sometimes works under conditions of employment which are not attractive to specialists of stature and calibre. A comparison with the situation in the United States where there are relatively fewer publications, shows that an editorial team may be made up of a dozen or so specialists, each a respected authority in his or her own right.

Inadequate staffing leads to a high proportion of technical journals which are produced largely from press releases selected almost at random and mixed in with contributed articles from sources that may or may not be authoritative, dealing with subject matter that tends to be determined by the contributors rather than defined as part of a planned editorial programme.

There is also a lack of research data to assist editors who therefore do not acurately know for whom they are writing: nor are they accustomed to having a feedback on which items are of interest to readers and which are not. Editors of most journals have to operate largely on the basis of experience and intuition.

ADVERTISING

Many publications function with only an advertisement manager and a secretary to sell their advertising space. Others have one or two space representatives. A commission system is usually built into the salary structure so that when a journal does well (often a matter of chance) high incomes can be obtained, and when it does badly the advertisement staff are underpaid. Opportunities for promotion have tended to be few, though this is changing as publishing groups grow and encourage interchanges between publications.

Publishers have difficulty in recruiting sales staff of high quality, and it is argued by many space buyers that representatives have little or no influence on the choice of media in an advertising schedule. The lack of media data is obviously a contributory factor here.

CIRCULATION

The traditional circulation manager on a subscription magazine may be little more than a senior clerk, sending out occasional mailing shots to prospective subscribers, attending trade exhibitions and dealing with renewals and the paper work involved in handling thousands of low value accounts. It is not generally realized that the cost of securing renewals is usually as high as the total net income from subscriptions; that is to say, it makes no difference financially to a publisher whether it sells a publication or gives it away.

Circulation departments are changing and some of the more advanced publishers are utilizing the most sophisticated equipment and techniques to secure at least the right circulation mixture, if not the right readership.

PROMOTIONS

In general, little effort is put into the promotion of either advertisement sales or circulation. This is rather strange when it is considered that the publishing industry represents the largest single item of promotional expenditure among its clients. Very few magazines use any form of advertising themselves, neither for that matter do they invest in any of the other channels of persuasion to any marked degree.

Lack of promotional activity is often an indicator of lack of anything to promote. Where this is not the case, an increase in sales promotion would help the publishers by making their marketing operations more efficient, and it would help the advertisers by providing them with more information.

PRODUCTION

Few publishers are themselves involved in the business of printing. Their production side then comprises one or two people concerned with bringing manuscripts to the galley stage, and pasting these up with illustrations according to a laid down design formula for the make-up of the journal including the disposition of the advertisements.

Methods of circulation

There are a number of basic methods of circulation, each with variations and each having advantages and disadvantages. Broadly it can be said that methods fall into two categories, paid-for and free.

PAID-FOR CIRCULATION

It may then be supposed that a paid-for readership is by definition an interested one, and indeed this is still arguable. There are two factors which operate against it from an advertiser's point of view. Firstly, many readers receive their publications from within their company, and therefore to them they are free. Secondly, a company tends to have an internal distribution list which often means that some readers receive a magazine weeks or months after publication, by which time it may not be of any great interest. Publishers of subscription journals will argue that the in-company distribution of their publications represents a strength in that it results in a readership many times greater than circulation. It could, however, be a weakness.

A special category of paid-for circulation is when a subscriber receives a copy of a publication as a result of being a member of an institute or association. Here there is often no pass-on readership: indeed it is not unknown for real readership to be somewhat lower than total circulation.

The problem with subscription journals is that since anyone can buy them, the publisher cannot, or does not, control who receives them, and therefore is not able to direct the circulation into those areas which are wanted by the advertisers. The circulation therefore is random, often highly fragmented and as a result sometimes not commercial. There are also real difficulties about determining where copies go, particularly if they are obtained through newsagents or bookstalls.

FREE CIRCULATION

The first journal to receive popular acclaim in the field of free circulation was *Industrial Equipment News*. Nowadays a good proportion of trade and technical publications are distributed free of charge either in part or in entirety.

The term 'controlled circulation' needs to be examined since the degree of control is entirely at the discretion of a publisher. The result is that in some instances it is applied only in a very loose sense and is often under the jurisdiction of a relatively junior employee. The fault lies as much with the advertisers, as with publishers, for not taking a stronger line and applying a greater degree of scrutiny.

At the lowest level there are journals which are simply sent out to a mailing list, with no requirement for readers to register or to qualify. Publishers may argue that such circulation is controlled since they control who they send it to. For instance, they may take the published list of members of an association and mail personal copies to each member. A refinement could be to eliminate people working for companies employing less than 100. Mailing lists can be purchased from specialist sources—some advertisers are willing to make their lists accessible, for instance, but it is important to realize that such mailing lists for a free circulation journal are never likely to be as good as those which a firm can produce for itself. Special caution should be applied to journals which overnight increase their circulation by a significant number, for instance, from 5000 to 7000. This can be, and is, done quite simply by finding some additional source of names and adding it to the existing list. Alternatively, by sending to the same companies on the lists, but instead of addressing one copy to the buyer, to address two copies one for the buyer, one for the works manager. There is maybe a case for doing this, but the advertiser is well advised to scrutinize the details of the circulation methods adopted.

A number of free circulation journals require a reader to register and to be in one of a number of defined categories, for example to exercise a purchasing influence. Such registration ensures a measure of interest in a journal but if copies are sent only to those taking the trouble to register, the coverage of any one market is no longer 100 per cent. A further problem with registered readers is that they seldom cancel or transfer their application when they change jobs or retire. This leads to publishers inadvertently sending sizeable proportions of their circulation to dead-end addresses or recipients who no longer have any interest or importance. Moreover, there is no practical way in which an applicant's form can be authenticated by a publisher, and so the validity of a circulation even of 'applied-for' journals depends upon the validity of the data supplied by the readers, who tend to inflate the importance of their position as a means of obtaining a personal and free copy of a journal.

A method known as rotating circulation is a lesser used practice but poorly regarded. The technique is to build up a list of, for example, 50 000 firms, then send each consecutive issue to a different 10 000 until after five monthly issues all the mailing list has been covered. This tends to bring high enquiry response rates initially and enable a publisher to make claims about his circulation which may be misleading.

In general the concept of free circulation publications is based upon the sound marketing philosophy of defining a market then going all out to achieve a maximum share of it. Many magazines in this category have achieved outstanding success and are firmly entrenched as valuable advertising media. Readership researches confirm that they are hitting the target. While they do not get the same pass-on readership as subscription journals, they have the merit of going directly to the person most concerned who is able to give his immediate attention to it.

The editorial format which has become associated with free-circulation journals is perhaps unfortunate in that the concentration on new products, sometimes to the exclusion of features, confuses the issue and has led to the assumption that maximum reader response comes from free journals and that serious articles in depth are published only in subscription journals. This is not inevitably so: either editorial treatment or a mixture is suitable for either type of circulation.

HYBRIDS

Almost all circulations are hybrid in the sense that there are a proportion of copies which are free and a proportion which are charged at a lower rate than usual. Perhaps what is not realized is that many formerly paid-for journals have been forced by competition to inflate their circulation, and that this has been done by giving away copies. It is not unknown for a journal to have as many free copies as paid-for, but to trade under the heading of a subscription publication.

Authentic data

Publishing has been described as 'the last refuge for a gentleman', but this is not always true. Advertisers have been misled deliberately by some publishers who have blatantly said one thing and done another. This situation is changing fast under the influence of various organizations, notably the Audit Bureau of Circulation, but there are still many publications which are not prepared to submit their circulations to the independent audit which an industrial advertiser requires.

The Media Data Form represents a valuable step forward and its continued development will do much to increase the efficiency of media selection and thus advertising efficiency. In the mean time the growing demand from advertisers for data has led to a variety of publishers' information being supplied, and experience has shown that some of this is irrelevant, inaccurate or misleading. Circulations are known to have been quoted well in excess of the total market, and in excess of the print order. Circulation breakdowns by category have been known to be closer to wishful thinking than the actual facts of the case.

As always, the buyer would do well to exercise considerable caution, and adopt a tough line with suppliers who will not supply the service that is required.

18.

ADVERTISING AGENCIES

Advertising agencies still suffer from their origin as agents for publications, selling advertising space to 'clients' in consideration of a commission from the media owners. From that point the situation developed to where agencies competed with each other by offering free services, primarily the creation of advertisements for their clients who not unnaturally accepted the services and asked for more. Gradually agencies identified themselves with clients rather than the media they represented until they cut adrift completely from individual publications and set up exclusive relationships with their clients, the advertisers. It was, and still is, difficult for them to be completely independent and objective in their relations with the media since the press (and TV) continued to pay a commission whereas certain other media, for example exhibitions, did not. Thus many supplementary services were provided for clients but were paid for out of commission from press advertising. The merits or demerits of this situation are examined later, but it explains why many agencies are still oriented around 'above the line' advertising, while their clients are often heavily involved in other forms of persuasive communications.

Agency organization

There are over 700 advertising agencies in the United Kingdom split in numbers about evenly between London and the provinces. Since the larger agencies are almost exclusively in London this is where the greater majority of advertising agency activity is concentrated.

Agencies vary from those consisting of one or two people, with a turnover of a few tens of thousands of pounds, to very large businesses employing hundreds and sometimes a thousand or more people and having turnovers of many millions. In comparing such turnovers with other businesses it should be remembered that profit margins are of a relatively low order, usually little over 1 per cent. It is true of any business that its strength lies first in the calibre of the people it employs, and this is especially so in agencies since that is all they have to offer—there is no plant and equipment to make good the deficiencies of human beings and relatively little in the way of scientific research, quality control and inspection to safeguard the quality of their output.

The organization of agencies is extremely varied in detail. There are some structural characteristics which can be isolated, and these are indicated in the following examples which are examined from the point of view of handling industrial accounts.

SMALL AGENCY

The organization shown in Figure 18.1 might be typical of an agency employing up to around twenty-five people and having a turnover of up to and over five million pounds. It is more than likely that the managing director will handle one or two accounts himself or herself, as indeed may the creative and production directors. This would leave each account executive with maybe £200 000 of billing. The primary business of this kind of agency is likely to be heavily directed to trade press advertising but it often possesses special skills in the particular requirements of its clients, perhaps in sales literature or direct mail. It will be necessary to utilize outside services even for creative work, and the amount of effort available for media planning, at least in the media department, will be small. There is no built-in provision for press relations, exhibitions or research. The span of control is already approaching a maximum especially if the managing director is handling accounts personally as well as running the business.

The number of clients, product groups and campaigns will probably be small, and most people in the agency will know and care about most of the clients. The staff will therefore be sensitive about the needs of clients and the organization will centre around these needs rather than expecting clients to fit into a rigid procedural pattern. The following are some of the advantages and disadvantages which may apply from a client's point of view.

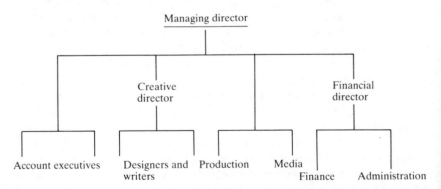

Figure 18.1   Small agency organization

1. Advantages:
   (a) Attention from top management
   (b) Quick response to needs
   (c) Short chain of command
   (d) Attention to personal details
   (e) Ease of identifying with clients' business
   (f) Often locally situated

2. Disadvantages:
   (a) Lack of specialists
   (b) Difficulty in getting top calibre people to work in a small agency
   (c) Tendency to 'sameness' in creativity
   (d) Over-dependence on a single person in the handling of an account
   (e) Lack of breadth of knowledge resulting from small number of accounts

MEDIUM AGENCY

Such an agency may well be set up primarily with a view to handling industrial accounts and will employ people with appropriate talents and interests. The total number of employees may be a hundred or more with a billing of several tens of million pounds.

The organizational chart (Figure 18.2), shows a logical progression from Figure 18.1, with client service breaking into groups under the overall control of a director. Each group will contain three or four executives and be self-contained except for central services which may or may not include produc-

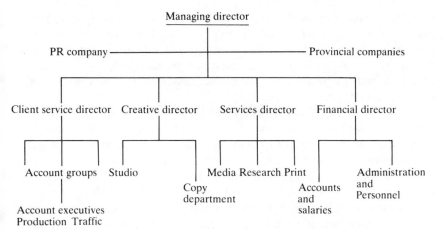

Figure 18.2   Medium agency organization

tion and traffic. It is a matter of opinion whether there is benefit in the creative unit being centralized or integrated within each group. Whichever way it goes, however, it is important to have a creative director who can not only supply ideas and creative stimulus, but also ensure the maintenance of creative standards.

A feature in this size of agency is that it can justify the employment of specialists in media, research and print, as well as having associated companies to handle press relations and perhaps exhibitions, artwork, photography and so on.

1. Advantages:
   (a) Stable business of substance
   (b) Top people are likely to be able and experienced
   (c) Large number of account executives with a wide range of industrial experience
   (d) Availability of specialists
   (e) Access to associated services

2. Disadvantages:
   (a) Lack of personal attention from the top
   (b) Longer chain of command
   (c) Difficulty in getting instant response and attention
   (d) Extended and diffused internal communications

LARGE AGENCY

The kind of structure which may exist in a very large agency which, in addition to handling major consumer accounts, will also make provision for industrial advertising, is shown in Figure 18.3. It is most likely that one or more account groups will set out to become a small industrial agency within the parent company. There will be a group head with a number of account executives (usually with some assistants) and probably a number of creative people as well as production and traffic assistants, and in the case of a technical group a media specialist.

To this extent, the technical group may look similar to the small industrial agency: it is probably even treated as a 'profit centre'. The differences will come largely in the variety of specialists and services that can be called upon. Furthermore there will be all the benefits of a large company—a good reference library, a management and staff development plan, a cinema or projection room, and maybe a computer. Most agencies of this size have not just overseas connections, but overseas companies with good communications, and the means of producing campaigns that can be readily projected on an international basis.

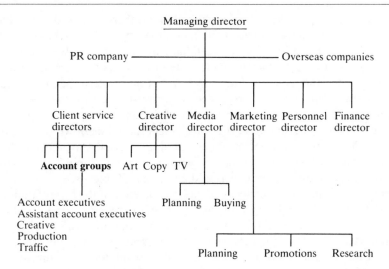

Figure 18.3   Large agency organization

1. Advantages:
   (a)   High calibre people at the top
   (b)   Sophisticated consumer techniques which can be adapted for industrial advertising
   (c)   Capacity to think big
   (d)   Can provide virtually every service from within the company
   (e)   Creative excellence

2. Disadvantages:
   (a)   The industrial side may be regarded as the poor relation
   (b)   Service is usually expensive
   (c)   Work takes longer to produce, due to lengthy communications and internal procedures and disciplines
   (d)   Staff are usually not so technical and have difficulty in interpreting a brief, particularly as regards copywriting
   (e)   Smaller clients have to fit into agency organization rather than the agency changing to suit a client

Agency procedures

It is useful to examine the stages through which a typical job is likely to pass. It will be seen that, except in a small agency, there are a large number of people likely to be involved in the processing of a single advertisement. The question of effective communication becomes vital to ensure that the initial message and purpose is not lost or blunted, but rather sharpened and refined. It is not always appreciated by the client how important the brief is to the agency. This, after all, is the raw material from which the advertisement or campaign is to be constructed. Inadequate briefing may be compensated by the persistence and tenacity of agency staff, but this is often the cause of high charges and jobs which are regarded as unsatisfactory by the client. The client must put as much into preparing the brief for the agency as the agency will subsequently put into its proposals. Briefs should be in writing in order to exclude the possibility of misunderstanding. A good starting point is to ensure that everyone in the agency who is involved should have had a thorough background brief covering the points in Table 18.1.

Figure 18.4 shows the likely steps within an agency in the formulation of a campaign plan. Though appearing as a series of discrete steps, there is always a good deal of intercommunication throughout the preparation of a campaign. Media is very much influenced by research: the account group will have strong ideas of its own, and creative ideas will interact on almost every aspect of the campaign.

Table 18.1   Points to be covered in agency brief

Strategic and corporate objectives	Where does the business wish to be in 5/10 years?
Marketing objectives	Market share, market/product segmentation, product portfolio, sales targets, territory/product
Communications objectives	Company/product awareness, perception/positioning, sales leads, reassurance, information
The market	Size, location, trends, decision-makers
The market need	Customer requirements, buying motives, changes in demand
The product	Specification, assessment of benefits in relation to customers' known needs
Competition	Market shares, product specifications, prices, promotions and expenditure, company images, nature and magnitude of selling activities, strengths and weaknesses
Price	Pricing strategy in relation to competition, special incentives and discounts
Selling platform	Unique selling propositions, outlines of features to be stressed in all selling activities—the differential advantage
Distribution channels	Retail outlets, wholesalers, agents, delivery times
Pre- and post-sales service	Consultancy and advisory services, customer reassurance, technical advice

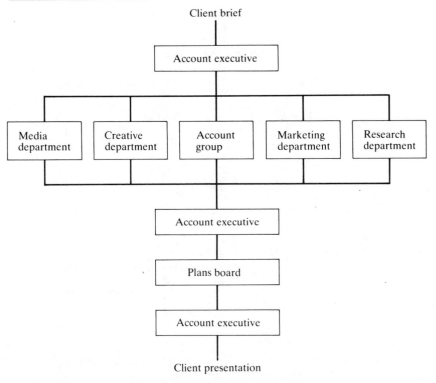

Figure 18.4 Agency procedural chart

First there is the brief from the client giving the objectives and requirements. The account executive is responsible for interpreting these to the various agency departments that are likely to be involved. The account group is shown as a separate function in this operation since while the account executive will bear the main load, there will usually be executives both junior and senior to him or her who will contribute to the plan. Research may be necessary to assist media planning and to provide intelligence for the marketing department. Creative personnel will not begin designing advertisements at this stage, but they should have the opportunity to express an opinion on whether press advertising is an appropriate vehicle from their point of view, or whether for example, three dimensions are required: if press advertising then does the nature of the objective indicate a need for double-page spreads, half pages or inserts? This will interact with media planning who may be concentrating on national dailies while creative want four-colour reproductions on art paper. The marketing department will examine the brief in a rather broader context and may be questioning the client's advertising brief in relation to its own marketing plan. There may be a call

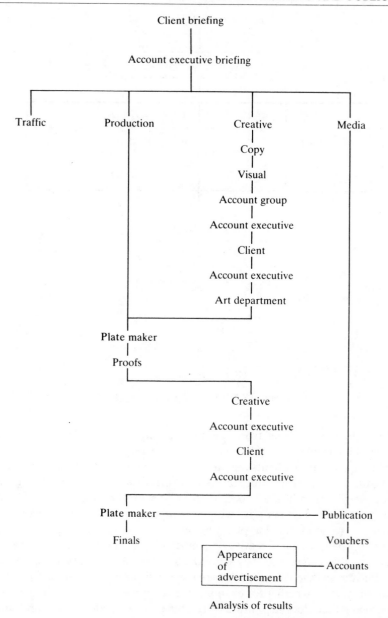

Figure 18.5 Advertising progress chart

for a higher concentration on certain market segments—a proposition which if accepted will invalidate much of the media planning and perhaps throw the whole job back into the melting pot.

The planning of a campaign within an agency can be looked upon as a very intensive 'think' workshop: almost a long-drawn-out brainstorming session.

After the plan is agreed, it has to be implemented, and Figure 18.5 shows the stages through which a press advertisement is likely to pass.

This somewhat complex chart is an outline of what is probably a minimum of activity for an advertisement which develops without complication. At any stage there is likely to be a 'rejection' which can put the whole project back to an earlier stage, or even back to the starting point. The visual may be rejected by the creative head or by the group head or account executive. At the client end there may be two or three, or more, people who need to express an opinion. The artwork and sometimes the type mark-up may go through the same process, and the proofs may be subject to a number of revisions before everyone is satisfied. In the process of creating an advertisement there may well be two dozen or more points of decision-making before it is finally 'passed for press'. It will be seen that there is an uncomfortable similarity between this operation and a game of snakes and ladders!

Departments and functions

The functions and departments within an agency have been outlined, and their interrelationships examined. The roles of the principal ones are now considered in more detail.

ACCOUNT GROUP

Since there may or may not be an account group as such, it is the account executive who is considered principally under this head.

There are unquestionably some account executives (or supervisors, or associate directors) who are little more than message carriers between the agency and the client. At best such people might be regarded as liaison men or women. In industrial advertising, this is an unacceptable situation. The executive is the key person in the whole operation. He or she must understand fully the client's needs and interpret them with precision to the supporting staff at the agency. Thereafter the account executive must maintain a close watch on every stage of development, exercising direction and control where necessary, while retaining the respect and confidence both of the client and the agency personnel: he or she must mediate, persuade and enthuse colleagues, be a combination of diplomat, wet nurse, salesperson and dictator, and above and beyond all that must be a first-rate all-round industrial marketing executive.

MEDIA DEPARTMENT

Apart from routine functions such as collecting rate cards, specimen and voucher copies, and checking invoices, the media department has two main operations, planning and buying. Both of these are important and call for a good deal of expertise.

The lack of adequate data on industrial media (by which is usually meant only press and, where applicable, television) is such that media planning is often highly superficial. General experience of industrial media is not enough in view of the large number of publications, and the large number of different products and markets which are all part of determining the media mix. A fully effective media planning operation is therefore likely to involve a good deal of investigation and research by very able specialists.

Media buying is not such an intangible business, but it is one in which significant sums of clients' money can be saved by careful planning and investigation coupled with ruthless negotiation and bargaining.

CREATIVE DEPARTMENT

This will usually comprise a mixture of writers, designers and typographers whose collective creative talents need to be welded into a cohesive team which will interpret product benefits into a visual selling proposition having impact upon potential customers. It is from this department largely that the spark of genius is needed to lift an advertisement out of the ordinary and into the outstanding.

It is basically 'ideas' which emanate from a creative department, not words and pictures. Its work therefore must be judged in terms of creative expression of a client's goods rather than by the graphic excellence of a final proof.

RESEARCH DEPARTMENT

Too little research is put into industrial publicity, due often to the reluctance of clients to invest money in what at first sight seems a non-productive activity. Nevertheless agencies are developing their research facilities which are being concentrated into media, advertisement and campaign evaluation.

Research departments are also able to carry out desk research themselves into markets both to supplement clients' own activities, and to provide data for the planning of campaigns within the agency.

MARKETING DEPARTMENT

Such a department usually exists only in the medium to large agencies, though some marketing expertise is usually available from other staff within an agency. There is also a trend to combine research and marketing into one 'planning' group.

Any agency marketing function can operate where the client has only a limited operation himself, or it can supplement it, or operate it as a second opinion. Furthermore it can work in conjunction with other agency departments during the preparation of an advertising plan. This will help to ensure that the advertising fits into the overall marketing strategy.

Often a marketing department will be a strategic point in an agency where the communications mix can be formulated, and it is not uncommon for this department to be responsible for 'below the line' activities, that is those that do not bring a direct media commission.

PRODUCTION AND TRAFFIC

This is usually a central agency service but is sometimes carried out within an account group. The function, however, is to translate the 'creative' specification into printing plates. That is to take the design, artwork, copy and type mark-up; order plates and setting, obtain proofs, see to their progressing and eventual distribution.

Coupled with the production is the overall progressing of a job which begins when space is booked and goes on continuously, monitoring every stage until the advertisement appears and the invoices are cleared.

These are important services and are usually carried out very well by agencies: far better than a client could hope to do.

PRINT DEPARTMENT

A number of agencies providing a service for industrial accounts have found that there is a demand for sales and technical literature which can best be handled by a separate print department. This will usually include posters, showcards and sometimes direct mail.

The writing and design work for literature will often be carried out by the main creative department, or perhaps by freelance people. The print department is then a specialized production unit which includes the function of print buying. Though the cost incurred may seem to be high, the result will usually show a good standard of professional workmanship.

PUBLIC RELATIONS

Most agencies do not have a public relations department, but rather an associated company which is thus enabled to take on business from companies not necessarily clients of the parent agency.

Editorial publicity in support of an integrated campaign will, in these circumstances, go through the separate company. Indeed, even where an agency has an integral PR department, it is more than usual to find that a separate executive has to be briefed on editorial publicity. Where this happens it is time wasted for a client, since the basic information is the same regardless of the medium. The selling platform, the product benefits, the creative expression, must be the same if a campaign is to have overall cohesion and impact.

EXHIBITIONS AND DISPLAY

As with public relations, it is not uncommon for exhibitions to be handled by an associated company. The same comments therefore apply as those on public relations.

One agency has a philosophy that an exhibition is only an advertisement with a third dimension. There is much to commend this attitude since many of the criteria for a good advertisement apply also to a good exhibition stand, for example stopping power, easy to read headline, punchy copy, and so on.

Methods of remuneration

As distinct from consumer accounts, which usually obtain their agency's services entirely out of the 15 per cent media commission, industrial advertising is usually undertaken only on the basis of an added fee. This may be to 'plus-up' all media commission to an agreed level, or it may be a flat rate per annum with or without media commission rebated. In between there are almost infinite variations, adjustments and understandings which enable an agency to recoup its expenses, though it is sometimes not realized how unnecessarily expensive the more complex payment systems are.

It is necessary to be clear about the method of remuneration for an agency. While, in the past, an agency was a representative for journals and newspapers, it was logical that it should be remunerated by a commission from the publishers.

If, however, an agency is operating on behalf of advertisers there can be no logical justification for payment other than from the clients it serves. The amount of space booked is quite irrelevant to the amount of work that is done by an agency either in terms of publicity as a whole or even press advertising alone. The creative time, the media planning time, the space booking time, the production, are the same whether for a 25 × 20 cm space in a plastics magazine or in a national daily. They are still the same if there is one appearance, or ten, and they are not much different whether they appear in one publication or a hundred. Furthermore, how can an account executive justify taking a briefing for a piece of direct mail when he or she is being paid out of commission from a magazine, for example?

Publications will continue to offer commission since in doing so there is a built-in attraction to agencies to place their business with them as opposed to other media. Agencies for their part are content to leave matters as they are since they can argue that only by using a 'recognized' agency can a client recoup the commission.

This is unsound practice from every business point of view and encourages inefficient operations and biased recommendations. The only basis upon which agency services can be justified is to pay for work done which, if not satisfactory, can soon be rectified by finding another supplier. It is difficult to see how the ending of the commission system could do other than benefit advertisers.

Client–agency relationships

This is a problem which is written and talked about whenever advertising people meet.

It may be that the method of agency remuneration leads to clients being apathetic towards the quality of service derived from an agency, and this apathy encourages unwillingness to provide the material necessary for an agency to do a good job. The view often expressed by clients that an agency cannot produce good technical or industrial material is matched only by the view from the other side that clients seem incapable of providing a thorough and comprehensive brief. This is a failure in communications, and the failure is allowed to continue because neither side considers the real cost involved. The only other possible explanation for this communications gap is that the people concerned are inadequate, and if this is so, the solution is to employ people who are capable of doing the job properly.

If clients can obtain several designs and copy platforms 'free' they will not feel under pressure to ensure that they are precise in their briefing, nor will they put themselves out to spend time gathering background material which will enable agencies to hit the mark first time. Similarly there is no great pressure on account executives to put undue effort into projects since, if clients do not approve the first attempt, they can always have another. If, on the other hand, every advertisement design and copy was charged at market price, perhaps £300 or so, and similarly every redesign, the whole procedure would necessarily tighten up considerably.

Over and above any considerations of the method of payment, most agencies can and will provide almost any service for which clients reasonably ask, providing there is a margin of profit. It rests then with the clients, who after all are the buyers, to demand the best standard of professional service, but to be prepared to pay for it. The mutual respect and confidence which must exist to obtain the best results will follow automatically.

Choosing an agency

The first question to be answered is why an agency should be necessary at all. The fact that almost all industrial advertisers use an agency does not necessarily prove that they are right.

The worst reason, but probably a common one, is that it is to obtain the benefit of the publishers' commission. The right reason has been summed up in an IPA publication.[1]

> The agency's most valuable asset is it objective and professional viewpoint. The analysis and assessment of a client's problems together with the unbiased, unemotional appraisal of specific market conditions, make a real contribution to efficient marketing and effective advertising.

An objective assessment of the need for an advertising agency leads to consideration of precisely which activities require servicing. This can then become the basis on which a choice is made. In other words a 'services specification' is required that will act as a coarse screen to filter out those companies that do not match requirements. Then their level of performance can be examined.

The objective assessment must come before involvement with the personalities concerned. Next comes the cost of the service, and the best value for money.

Finally, but in the end most important, are the personalities involved. The finest brains and the most businesslike organization are of little avail unless it is possible for the principals on both sides to establish an easy rapport which will enable them to work together as a team. The key figure here is the account executive who will ensure that the client receives the service he or she needs and demands. A weakness in creativity within the agency, for example, can be overcome by an effective account executive who will possibly insist on freelance services being used. As against this an excellent creative team will find it difficult to produce effective advertising if the account executive is inadequate.

Perhaps it is appropriate at this stage to refer again to the role of the publicity manager. To obtain effective publicity, the manager must not only be professionally capable, but must be given real responsibility and authority. It follows that the appointment of an advertising agency is the responsibility of the publicity manager. The marketing manager will certainly be involved, and is right to express his views, but the decision to hire and fire should rest with the chief publicity executive. The results, good or bad, become his or her personal responsibility with all the advantages this brings.

Checklist

In evaluating your present agency, or in making an assessment of a new one, have the following criteria been examined?

1. Agency management structure
2. Internal procedures
3. Basis of remuneration
4. Internal method of costing, plussing-up and charging: allocation of overheads
5. Legal and financial status: major shareholders: issued capital: turnover
6. Clients—names, industry groups, billings, number of years, with named contacts for references
7. Experience in relevant industries and markets
8. Quality of advertisements in relation to brief of
   (a) Copywriting
   (b) Headline
   (c) Sign-off or action
   (d) Visual
   (e) Campaign continuity
   (f) Measurement of results
9. Campaign assessment in relation to brief of
   (a) Campaign plan
   (b) Copy platform
   (c) Media mix
   (d) Visual continuity
   (e) Measurement of results
10. Media services and expertise in
   (a) Press
   (b) TV
   (c) Direct mail
   (d) Merchandising
   (e) Packaging
   (f) Point of sale
   (g) Sales literature
   (h) Technical publications
   (i) Exhibitions
   (j) Photography
   (k) Press relations
   (l) Public relations
11. Research
   (a) Advertising
   (b) Media

    (c)   Campaign
    (d)   Market
    (e)   Product
    (f)   Other

12. Overseas connections
13. Provincial branches
14. Personal compatibility with and professional capability of

    (a)   Account executive
    (b)   Account director
    (c)   Creative head
    (d)   Media manager
    (e)   Research and/or market head
    (f)   Managing director

Reference

1. *Industrial Marketing and the Advertising Agency.*

GLOSSARY

ABC   Audit Bureau of Circulation.

Account executive   An executive in an advertising agency, or other such organization, responsible for the overall managing of a client's requirements. Sometimes known as account supervisor, account manager or account director.

Advertising   The use of paid-for space in a publication, or time on television or cinema, usually as a means of persuading people to take a particular course of action, or to reach a point of view.

Advertising schedule   Schedule of advertisement insertions showing details of costs, timing, and nature of the media and the bookings in them.

Artwork   The pictorial or illustrative part of an advertisement, or publication, in its finished form ready for production, e.g. a retouched and masked photograph.

Attention value   The extent to which an advertisement can secure the initial attention of a reader.

Attitude research   An investigation, often by personal interview or group discussion, of the attitude of people towards an organization or its products.

Base line   The wording or typesetting at the bottom of an advertisement, including the company's name and address often in a standard form or house style.

Below-the-line   A term frequently used to define non-commission-paying promotional media.

Bleed   An advertisement or printed page which utilizes the entire page area, i.e. extends into the margin.

Block   A plate of metal (or rubber or plastic), engraved, moulded or cast for printing.

Blow-up   A very considerable enlargement, say, of a photograph or illustration.

Brand name   A distinctive name by which a product or group of products is identified.

Brief   Summary of facts, objectives and instructions relating to the creation of a campaign, an advertisement, or any other element of a marketing mix.

Brochure   A stitched booklet, usually having eight or more pages, often with a prestige connotation.

Caption   Short description relating to an illustration or diagram.

Catalogue   Publication containing descriptions or details of a number or range of products.

CC   Controlled circulation.

Circulation   The total number of copies distributed of a periodical or publication.

Clippings   See 'Press cuttings'.

Column centimetres   Measurement of area derived from the width of a column of type, in a publication, multiplied by its depth.

Controlled circulation   In which the method of circulation is controlled by some specific criterion relating to the status of the reader, and for which no charge is made.

Copy   Text or written matter for reproduction.

Copy date   Date by which advertising or editorial material should reach a publisher for inclusion in a particular issue. (See also 'press date'.)

Copy platform   The main copy theme of an advertisement.

Creative   Relating to copy and/or visual content of an advertisement or similar promotional material, or to a department in an advertising agency in which copywriting and design are carried out.

Cut-out half tone   Printing block or area of a plate in which the background to an illustration has been cut out or eliminated.

Data sheet   Leaflet containing factual information and data about a product and its performance.

Decision-making unit   Group of people who together contribute to a decision on whether or not, and what, to purchase (DMU).

Distribution The means by which goods are moved from the place of manufacture to the point of purchase.

Double-page spread Two facing pages in a publication, combined into one integral advertisement; strictly speaking should incorporate the gutter.

DPS Double-page spread.

DRM Direct-response marketing—selling by means of press advertising or direct mail which invites a direct placement of orders without further negotiations or intermediate channels of distribution, e.g. retail outlet.

Dummy A made-up or faked version of a proposed publication.

Electro A duplicate of an original block: produced by electro-chemical deposition of metal on to a matrix.

Embargo In relation to press release, a time or date before which a particular items of news must not be published.

Facia In exhibitions, the headboard above a stand, usually giving the identity of the exhibitor.

Facing matter An advertisement which appears opposite editorial matter in a publication (abbreviation FM). In newspapers, a more common term is 'among matter'.

Final (proof) A print taken from the plate or forme of an advertisement as it finally appears.

Fine grain Descriptive of a photographic emulsion or the developer used to process it: results in a negative which can be enlarged to a high degree without showing excessive grain.

Forme Frame in which type matter and blocks are assembled for letterpress work.

Four-colour set Set of plates, one for each of the four colours (red, yellow, blue, black) used to produce a 'full' colour print. Term sometimes refers to set of colour proofs.

Full plate Photographic print 8 in × 6 in, sometimes known as 'whole plate': similarly 'half plate' is 6 in × 4 in.

Galleys Rough proofs of typesetting taken prior to the make-up of pages.

Give-away A cheap promotional piece, often a leaflet, which can be handed out to all and sundry. Sometimes known as a 'throw-away'.

Gutter The margin of a page adjacent to the fold in a publication, the vertical centre of a double-page spread.

Half plate   Photographic print or negative, 6 in × 4 in.

Half tone   Describes a printing block or plate of a tonal illustration, the reproduction of which is facilitated by breaking up the continuous tones to leave a series of dots which pick up the ink.

Handout   A cheap leaflet for handing out at an exhibition, for example.

House magazine   A periodical published by a company. Usually in one of two forms, external for customer readership, or internal for employees.

House style   A characteristic and standardized graphic form which is applied throughout a company to such items as letterheadings, publications, advertisements, vehicles and even packaging and product design.

Image   The mental impression which a person has of an organization or its products.

Impact   The force with which a selling message registers in a person's mind.

Insert   A piece of sales promotional material placed into the pages of a publication. Can be either loose or bound in.

Keyed advertisement   An advertisement designed to cause an enquirer to indicate the source of his enquiry by quoting a code number, or a particular 'department'.

Layout   Accurate position guide of an advertisement or piece of literature.

Leaflet   Printed sheet of paper: maybe folded to make into four pages, or stitched with another sheet to make into eight. Term usually applies to publication with fewer than twelve pages. See also brochure.

Letterpress   Form of commercial printing in declining use. Consists of raised printing surfaces upon which ink is deposited, and subsequently transferred to paper.

Line block   Printing block for reproducing line illustrations (letterpress). Face of metal is solid without any half tone or screen.

Litho   Short for lithography, a form of printing from a flat as opposed to a raised surface. Ink impression is obtained by chemical treatment of surface such that certain areas retain ink while others reject it.

Local press   Local newspapers, usually covering a borough or rural district. Published once or twice a week. See also provincial press.

Logotype   Commonly used to describe a company symbol, badge or name style.

Mailing list   Classified list of names and addresses suitable for sending mailing shots.

Mailing piece   Letter, leaflet or other article sent through the post on a widespread basis.

Mailing shot   A single mailing operation. Two mailings to the same list would be referred to as a two-shot campaign.

Manual   Printed document of any number of pages, usually containing specific instructions, e.g. sales manual, operating or servicing manual.

Market   A collective term embracing all the people or points of purchase for a particular product both actual and potential.

Market penetration   The extent to which market potential has been realized. Market share.

Market research   Investigation into the characteristics of a given market, e.g. location, size, growth, attitudes. See also marketing research.

Market segmentation   The breakdown of a market into discrete and identifiable segments, e.g. types of company, industries, geographical location; also types of product requirements.

Marketing   The complete series of operations which ensure a compatibility between customer demand and product performance, and which results in customer satisfaction coupled with an adequate level of profit. The operations which may be encompassed by the term marketing include product development, marketing research, advertising, promotion, sales and service.

Marketing mix   A planned mixture of all the elements of marketing in such a way as to achieve the greatest effect at minimum cost.

Marketing research   Any research activity that provides information relating to the marketing operation. While embracing market research, it also includes media research, motivation studies, advertisement attention value, packaging effectiveness.

Marketing services   All those activities which are required to service a marketing operation, other than those which are concerned directly with the sales force and the sales office.

Marketing strategy   A written plan, usually comprehensive, of all the activities involved in achieving a particular marketing objective, and their relationship to one another in both time and magnitude. Will include short- and long-term sales, production and profit targets, pricing policy, selling strategy, staffing requirements, as well as the whole marketing mix and expense budgets.

Matrix   Paper or plastic mould from which duplicate printing blocks are produced. See 'Electro' and 'Stereo'.

Mechanicals/mechanical production   The processes required to achieve the desired reproduction of an advertising message.

Media commission   Commission allowed by publishers, poster, radio and television companies to recognized advertising agencies in consideration of the space or time they book on behalf of their clients.

Media Data Form   An established format for presenting audited data regarding a publication so as to facilitate comparison.

Medium   A channel of communication, e.g. a magazine, a television station, an exhibition, direct mail. Plural media, often used to refer specifically to periodicals.

Merchandising   The techniques for promoting sales at the point of sale.

Motivation research   Investigation of motives behind purchasing decisions. Often linked with the technique of small group discussions.

National press   Newspapers, daily or Sunday, having a mass circulation throughout the country.

News release   See 'Press release'.

Offset litho   See 'Litho'. Offsetting is merely part of the process by which the image on the plate is transferred to a rubber sheet which then prints on to the paper, thus avoiding a mirror or reverse reproduction.

Opinion formers   Groups or categories of people who because of their status or position are considered to exert more than usual influence on the views of others.

Overlay   Transparent or translucent sheet of paper laid over one piece of artwork carrying further artwork which is to be reproduced in a different colour; or for protection or to facilitate instruction on how it should be used or modified for production.

Page proofs   Proofs of a leaflet, brochure, booklet, magazine or similar publication taken at the stage when pages have been made up.

Page traffic   Number of readers of a particular page in a periodical, expressed as a percentage of the total readership.

Paper setting   The setting of an advertisement by the printer of a periodical, usually free of charge. See 'Trade setting'.

Pass for press   Final approval of a publication before printing.

Persuasive communications   Any form of communication which is intended to persuade, e.g. advertising, editorial publicity, speeches, films.

Plate Printing block or litho plate.

Point of sale (point of purchase) The place at which a sale is made, also refers to publicity material used there, e.g. posters, showcards, display units, leaflets (POS and POP).

PR 'Public relations' or 'Press relations', see below.

PRO Public relations officer—an executive responsible for planning and implementing the public relations policy of an organization.

Presentation A meeting in which proposals are put to an audience in a planned and usually formal manner.

Press All periodicals whether national, local, trade or technical.

Press cuttings Excerpts on a particular subject cut out from any kind of periodical. Used as a monitoring device to indicate the extent to which a subject is receiving publicity.

Press date The date on which a publication or a section of a publication is due to be passed for press.

Press reception A meeting to which press representatives—editors, journalists, reporters—are invited in order to be informed of an event, and to have the opportunity of questioning or commenting.

Press relations That part of public relations activity aimed at establishing and maintaining a favourable relationship both with and via the press. Also referred to as media relations.

Press release Written statement describing an event which is considered to be of sufficient interest to readers for an editor to publish some reference to it. Sometimes referred to as a news release.

Press visit Visit by members of the press to a place of interest to them usually coupled with a special event such as an official opening of a factory.

Production Putting into film form illustrations or words with a view to printing, e.g. plate making, filmsetting. Also the management of all mechanical processes required to achieve the reproduction of an advertising message.

Proof Preliminary printing by any process to facilitate checking and approval prior to final printing.

Provincial press Newspapers, usually daily, circulating in a restricted geographical region, e.g. a city or county.

Public relations The conscious effort to improve an organization's communications, relationships and reputation with such publics as employees, customers and shareholders.

Public relations consultant An individual or consultancy employed by an organization to advise and/or act on its behalf in the field of public relations.

Publicity The process of securing people's attention and imparting a message. See also 'Advertising', 'Public relations' and 'Sales promotion'—all of which fall to some extent within this term.

Quantify To express in measurable terms relating to quantity.

Rate card Document issued by publishers or advertising contractors showing the charges made for various types and sizes of advertisement.

Readership The number of people who read a publication as opposed to the number of people who receive it, or the number of copies printed or distributed.

Repros Good quality proofs of typesetting usually for use in making up artwork, or in enlarging for display purposes. Also known as repro-pulls.

Rough An illustration or design in rough form.

Run of paper The positioning of an advertisement in any part of a periodical, as against a specified or premium position (ROP).

Sales forecast A projection of likely sales, given certain defined criteria and making certain defined assumptions. Often based upon historical data. Not the same as sales target.

Sales promotion Any non face-to-face activity concerned with the promotion of sales, but often taken to refer to 'below the line' activities.

Sales target A set sales objective—a positive statement of intent, as against a sales forecast which arises out of a passive acceptance of anticipated criteria.

Same size Relating to a piece of artwork which is the same size as the reproduction for which it is to be used (SS).

Sample In research that specified subdivision of the universe (see below) deemed to be adequately representative of the whole and therefore to be interviewed or questioned.

Scamp See 'Rough'.

Service fee Charge made, usually on a predetermined annual basis, by an advertising or public relations agency for the service it is required to provide.

Shell scheme   Standard design of booth provided by the organizer at an exhibition.

Sign-off   Slogan at the end of an advertisement or piece of sales promotional material.

Silk screening   Method of printing by which ink is forced through a fine silk mesh on which have been superimposed opaque areas representing the reverse of the design and through which ink will not pass.

Single column centimetre   Standard measurement in newspapers and magazines based upon the depth of type matter contained in a single column (SCC).

Split run   In which a publication is printed and distributed in two parts, facilitating the comparison of two advertisements.

Squared-up half tone   Half-tone plate in which printing area is in the form of a rectangle. See 'Cut-out half tone'.

Standard industrial classification   Comprehensive listing of industries and services, published by Her Majesty's Stationery Office (SIC).

Stereo   Duplicate printing plate cast in metal from a paper or flong matrix.

Sticker   Label, poster, or other printed sheet intended for sticking on window, letter, envelope or other medium for display purposes.

Stuffer   Piece of publicity matter intended for general distribution with other material such as outgoing mail or goods, e.g 'envelope stuffer'.

Symbol   Distinctive sign or graphic design denoting a company or a product. Often a pictorial representation of a company or product name. See 'Logotype'.

Task method   A means of establishing a campaign and a budget by relating it to the objective to be achieved rather than for instance the amount of money arbitrarily available to be spent.

Technical press   Periodicals dealing with technical subjects. Usually grouped together as 'trade and technical', or business—referring in effect to all non-consumer publications.

Test-marketing   A method of testing out a marketing plan on a limited scale, but simulating as nearly as possible all the factors involved in the full campaign: usually carried out in a restricted but representative geographical location.

Trade press Strictly, referring to periodicals dealing with particular trades. See also technical press.

Trade setting Typesetting by a trade house directly for a client or agency, as against setting facilities by a publisher. See also 'Paper setting'.

Traffic Relating to the operation in an advertising agency of scheduling and controlling all stages in the preparation of a project. Relates commonly to production.

Two-colour The number of colours used in an advertisement or publication. Usually black plus one other.

Type area The space which is available on a page in a publication for printing.

Unique selling proposition A customer satisfaction or a product benefit which is unique as a selling argument (USP).

Universe In research, the total market—or other unit to be investigated.

Visual Artist's impression of an advertisement or other piece of publicity material. See also 'Layout'.

Voucher Free copy of periodical sent to advertiser or organization as evidence of an advertisement having been published.

Web offset A method of offset-litho printing in which the paper is fed into the press from the reel as opposed to sheets.

READING LIST

Marketing

Crouch, S., *Marketing Research* (Heinemann, London, 1985).
Davidson, J. Hugh, *Offensive Marketing* (Gower Publishing Company, Aldershot, 1987).
Delozier, M. Wayne, *The Marketing Communications Process* (McGraw-Hill, Maidenhead, 1976).
Hart, N. A., *The Marketing of Industrial Products* (McGraw-Hill, Maidenhead, 1984).
Hart, N. A. and Stapleton, J., *Glossary of Marketing Terms* (Heinemann, London, 1987).
Kotler, T., *Marketing Management* (Prentice-Hall, Hemel Hempstead, 1976).

Advertising

Broadbent, S., *Spending Advertising Money* (Business Books, London, 1984).
Broadbent, S., *Twenty Advertising Case Histories* (Holt, Rinehart & Winston, Eastbourne, 1984).
Director's Guide, *Choosing and Using an Advertising Agency* (Director Publications Limited, London, 1985).
Farbey, A. D., *The Business of Advertising* (Associated Business Press, London, 1979).

Public relations

Bernstein, D., *Company Image and Reality* (Holt, Rinehart & Winston, Eastbourne, 1984).
Hart, N. A., *Effective Corporate Relations* (McGraw-Hill, Maidenhead, 1987).
Haywood, R., *All about PR* (McGraw-Hill, Maidenhead, 1983).
Howard, W., *The Practice of Public Relations* (IM/Heinemann, London, 1982).